Reprinted courtesy *Survival in a Nuclear Attack: Plans for Protection from Radioactive Fallout* (State of New York, 1960).

SURVIVAL CITY: Adventures among the Ruins of Atomic America

SURVIVAL CITY:
Adventures among the Ruins of Atomic America

TOM VANDERBILT

Princeton Architectural Press

Published by
Princeton Architectural Press
37 East Seventh Street
New York, New York 10003

For a free catalog of books, call 1.800.722.6657.
Visit our web site at www.papress.com.

© 2002 Princeton Architectural Press
All rights reserved
Printed and bound in the United States
05 04 03 02 5 4 3 2 1 First edition

Project Editor: Nancy Eklund Later
Copy Editor: Bruce Murphy
Designer: Josh Hooten

Special thanks to: Nettie Aljian, Ann Alter, Nicola Bednarek, Janet Behning, Megan Carey,
Penny Chu, Jan Cigliano, Clare Jacobson, Mark Lamster, Linda Lee, Evan Schoninger,
Jane Sheinman, Lottchen Shivers, Katharine Smalley, Scott Tennent, Jennifer Thompson,
and Deb Wood, and of Princeton Architectural Press
—Kevin C. Lippert, publisher

Library of Congress Cataloging-in-Publication Data

Vanderbilt, Tom.
  Survival City : adventures among the ruins of atomic America / Tom
Vanderbilt.—1st ed.
    p. cm.
  ISBN 1-56898-305-0 (alk. paper)
  1. West (U.S.)—Description and travel. 2. West (U.S.)—History,
Local. 3. Vanderbilt, Tom—Journeys—West (U.S.) 4. West
(U.S.)—Social conditions—20th century. 5. Cold War—Social
aspects—West (U.S.) 6. Nuclear weapons—West
(U.S.)—Testing—History—20th century. 7. Landscape—Social
aspects—West (U.S.) 8. Cold War—Social aspects—United States. 9.
United States—Social conditions—1945– 10. National characteristics,
American. I. Title.
  F595.3 .V36 2001
  355.02'17'097309045—dc21

2001007800

TABLE OF CONTENTS:

Introduction
LOOKING FOR DR. STRANGELOVE:
The Cold War as Archaeology

> *But the closer I came to these ruins, the more any notion of a myste-*
> *rious isle of the dead receded, and the more I imagined myself among*
> *the remains of our own civilization after its extinction in some*
> *future catastrophe.*
>
> W. G. Sebald, *The Rings of Saturn*

I want to get to where the Cold War is still ending in America, so I set out after sunrise one early July morning from Grand Forks, North Dakota, bearing west on U.S. 2. After some 45 miles, I turn left on N.D. 1, then drive another 45 miles down a road of typical Dakotan sparseness, so empty that passing drivers wave with old-fashioned courtesy at the sheer novelty of human company, or on the fair assumption they probably know you anyway. I eventually reach Cooperstown, North Dakota, billed on a sign as "Tree City U.S.A.," a neatly arranged farming town that scrupulously adheres to its slogan. I catch a glimpse of lawn that turns out to be the town's municipal park, barely visible beneath a thick canopy of oaks and elms.

Turning left on Main Street, I park in front of an unmarked, nearly empty storefront, nestled between a theater showing *Mission Impossible 2* and a quaint apothecary. On the storefront window is a single ten-by-twelve color photograph depicting what appears to be a tornado, brown and angry and heaving with dirt and debris, boring into one of the state's endless green horizons. What it actually shows, if one steps inside and takes a closer look, is the implosion of one of the state's 150 Minuteman missile silos, the invisible fortresses of the atomic age. For decades, they stood silent sentinel beneath the whistling prairies, scattered across some 7,500 square miles—from Valley City, North Dakota clear through to the Canadian border. Only their three-phase power poles and some small brown signs (attached to nearby "Stop" signs or sometimes standing independently) bearing designations like "C-28" and "D-15" gave evidence they were there. Like those inscrutable markings

B-52 Stratofortress tail at Muroc Dry Lake, California

found in cities, the "Siamese attachment only" sign and surveyor's chalk marks on streets, these signs were codings useful only to members of a secret initiate, providing directions to a Minuteman launch facility to those who could decipher them.

The unnamed storefront is the temporary quarters of Veit Demolition, a Minnesota-based firm that in September, 1999, was awarded the $12.1-million contract to demolish the state's 150 silos, in accordance with the 1991 START treaty. Over the course of the next year, the Veit crew began removing the last vestiges of the Cold War from the North Dakotan fields, generally at the rate of two per week. This is a harvest of sorts: Its reapers rise with the dawn, study the weather, wind, and soil conditions, and, having completed their task, move on to the next bit of acreage.

Today an implosion is scheduled for 10:00 A.M., and my guide is Donald Speulda, a Nebraskan who is the point man on the project for the U.S. Army Corps of Engineers, Omaha District. We climb into his white Jeep Cherokee, our destination site M-22. Like all North Dakota drives, this one involves a series of endless stretches of road and exclusively right-angled turns—no state adheres to the original land ordnance survey grid like this one. The length of the drive seems compounded by the repetitive scenery, the unending vistas of wheat fields punctuated by prim, evenly distributed white farmhouses ringed with trees for windbreak. It is a landscape where sublime moments come like comets. "Won't be too long before the combines are up here," Speulda says in the stoic register of the Plains states, his gaze drifting over a sea of wheat.

North Dakota is a Cold War landscape, however, which means that one should not necessarily trust the emptiness. Every grain silo above invokes its subterranean opposite. "Running through the land here are cables," Speulda says. "You'll see 6-foot posts with three silver strips—although the Air Force has come down and removed a lot of them. Beneath those posts is a junction box with cables that run to the missile sites." Those cables were the conduits by which a missileer, sitting in the hardened underground command capsule of a Minuteman launch control facility, could send signals to launch any of the single missiles contained in each of the ten unmanned launch facilities, which were separated from each other and the control facility by 7 miles. "They are happy to be rid of them," Speulda says of the farmers whose land was veined with the infrastructure of nuclear weapons command-and-control systems.

We pass through a town called Hope, a quietly barren coda to pioneer optimism, and then arrive at the site, where a group of men stand milling around pickup trucks. As with all of North Dakota's missile silos, there is little to see on the surface, just a fenced parcel of land in the middle of a bean field, out of which sprouts a handful of power poles and a scattering of vents, like the kind one would see on the roof of a mall. It is as if there *was* a building

Demolition of Minuteman silo D-36, north of Lakota, North Dakota

here but it has sunk into the land, its poles rising out like the masts of a sub-merged ship. Speulda confers with the men, then returns with a hardhat and small box connected to a wire. His instructions are simple: On the count of five, press the button. I am expecting more of a ceremony, but for these men, removing the silo is as world-historical a task as extracting rocks from fields is for a Dakota farmer.

Five, four, three, two, one . . . The words summon rich technicolor visions of Ian Fleming heroes racing to defuse doomsday devices planted by organiza-tions with complex acronyms. The countdown brings images of shimmering Cape Canaveral rockets trembling in their gantries; the detonator button becomes the symbol of that push-button age (never mind that missiles were launched by turning keys). I have never held a detonator before, but it feels warm, intuitive. I press the button.

A football field away, a geyser erupts. A funnel of rocks and dirt showers upwards, and a low, flat *whump* shakes the soft grass. A handful of spectators clap as the dust settles. The explosion is satisfying in its immediacy, but it, too, seems strangely anticlimactic; then I remember that the curtain went down on the drama the minute the treaty-signing u.s. and Soviet pens were laid down. This is compliance, mere housekeeping.

I walk toward the wreckage with a Veit employee named Pat Hockett, a recent graduate of North Dakota State University who is excited to explain to me the process of dismantling the nation's former line of defense. "First we have our salvage company come in and strip all the salvageable material," he says. "The computers, the compressors, the brine chillers." The first smell of ammonium nitrate stings my nostrils. "Then we come out and drill sixty-nine holes, anywhere from 3 to 22 feet. It's about two days' work. Once the holes are drilled, we'll come in and fill them with dynamite and anfo [ammonium nitrate fuel oil]—it takes about 200 pounds of dynamite, and 600 pounds of anfo."

M-22 is now a fracture in the land, an open mouth smashed by a fist. Smoke seethes through jagged slabs of teeth and tangled spines of no. 18 rebar snaking out like ruined dental work. Standing at the precipice above the former silo, I ask Veit's demolition expert, Roger Livesy, to explain what 800 pounds of TNT *means*. "We would use 200 pounds of TNT to take down a ten-story building. Here, we use 800 pounds to go down 20 feet," he says, as in the background a piece of metal groans as it collapses into the hole. Given that the silos were presumably meant to withstand a near-miss from an incoming intercontinental ballistic missile (ICBM), the arithmetic seems comforting. Soon another crew will come along and begin to extract the tangled webs of rebar; then a concrete cap will be placed 6 meters down to prevent further sinking, followed by a "geomembrane" (a fabric used to line asphalt roads) to prevent seepage. A separate observation hole is dug to allow compliance monitoring by Russian satellite for ninety days. The hole will then be covered, the land returned to the farmers, whose plots already creep up to the very fence line, and this segment of North Dakota's massive nuclear arsenal—the old saw went that North Dakota, after the United States and the Soviet Union, was the world's third-largest nuclear power—will again turn into just another plot of agricultural landscape. No plaques or markers will commemorate a site that once, as preposterous as it seems, was deemed of strategic importance.

This is not the end of North Dakota's nuclear power, of course. Near Minot, traveling down Route 83, one can see an active launch control center for the still-active squadron of Minuteman III missiles. Located 100 yards from the road, the otherwise unremarkable ranch house has several Humvees parked in the front yard, a massive American flag flying overhead, and an array of antenna far more exotic than the satellite TV variety. Beneath, in a capsule hardened to withstand the effects of a nuclear explosion, a two-man squad will be going through the motions of what all American missileers have done for the past four decades: watching and waiting. If military architecture, with its ramparts and bulwarks and turrets, was once meant to project a visible show of force, to connote civic order with architectural majesty, here the house has been specifically chosen to be as prosaic as possible, to blend in seamlessly with the surroundings.

The next morning another contractor, Dem-Tech, has assembled at site D-36 with Speulda, along with a delegation of former missileers from Grand Forks

Air Force Base. A lieutenant (who's now in "intel," he explains) is given the blasting honors. This time, a fragment of concrete whizzes over the group of spectators. "If it works out right, you shouldn't see any debris," explains a Dem-Tech employee. Again, we approach the simmering fissure. I point to a small white cylinder, housing a radio antenna, that has survived the blast. "Usually the top of it just pops out, like a nice little cone," Ronnie Goodman, a former U.S. Air Force missile engineer, tells me. "Because of the different mixture of the concrete, or depending on who built it, no two silos are alike." As the crew scrambles over the overturned plates of concrete armed with video cameras, they pour over the upended shards of metal and rebar, pointing out idiosyncrasies of the blast with the precision and passion of connoisseurs. "Are you saying this concrete was soft?" one jokes to another as they peer into the wreckage. A section of concrete groans and falls into the depths below. "I got one like that when it was caving in on film and you should see, it's beautiful," Goodman says, standing on a pie-wedge slice of concrete. As the ammonium nitrate clears, another smell seeps into the clear morning air, a dank and ominous mixture of steel, concrete, and years of mildew. It is a peculiar odor, heavy with age and pregnant with meaning, which I have come to associate with the underground structures of the missile age. The former missileer has pushed his button, but not *the* button, and the crew is already making plans for next week's demolition of silos in the "O" (they call it "Oscar") flight of Minutemen. Sometime in the next ninety days, somewhere overhead, a Russian satellite will take note.

With the morning radio announcing news of an upcoming launch from California's Vandenberg Air Force Base of an exostatic anti-ballistic-missile "kill vehicle," the putative standard-bearer of the National Missile Defense Program, I embark on an expedition to the site of the former Stanley R. Mickelsen "Safeguard" anti-ballistic missile system, erected in North Dakota in 1974 and closed shortly thereafter by congressional order. I dial up a number for the site, which is mothballed and under caretaker status by the U.S. Army. "Wheeler's," comes a gruff answer; Wheeler's, I later learn, is the name of the contracting company hired to maintain the site. A man named Neil informs me I will have to get permission "from Huntsville," i.e., the U.S. Army's Space and Missile Defense Command, before visiting. Calling Alabama, I get a Spacecom official with a molasses drawl who sounds, appropriately, like Slim Pickins in *Dr. Strangelove*. Viewing the exterior of the site's main structure will not be a problem, he tells me, but then drops his voice a notch and informs me I will not be able to see inside. "We had an individual who died there," he says. "He was walking around the inside of the complex when he fell 30 feet through a hole." I assure him that the inside—which in any case has been gutted—is of no interest to me.

With that, I am off on another set of horizontal and vertical North Dakota byways; down Highway 2, past the Grand Forks Air Force Base and the ambitiously titled Grand Forks International Airport, to Lakota, after which I head right on N.D. 1. The road is a scalpel cutting through endless wheat fields and the ultramarine waters of cattail-clotted marshlands that creep right up next to the road. I pass the odd farmstead with metal silos and whitewashed house. The setting seems African in its vastness, but Northern European in its careful ordering and aesthetic sobriety. The car scatters flurries of blackbirds (a recent, and vexing, plague upon the state). The sky is stretched like a Mercator projection, so vast it seems to contain dozens of varying and seemingly unrelated weather events.

After forty minutes, I spy the blunt, gray top of a sheared-off pyramid jutting above the low line of trees to the north. Even from here, the Missile Site Radar (MSR), called "Nixon's Pyramid" by some after the president whose administration installed it, is a commanding presence in the landscape, like a Mayan temple dominating the jungles of the Lacandón. On each of its four faces a large Cyclopean eye stares out like the dollar bill's "Great Seal." Of all the things the American eye is used to seeing, pyramids, those symbols of death, are not among them, and especially not in North Dakota, where grain silos and rural Lutheran churches are about the most elevated features in the otherwise unending agricultural panorama. Taking the turnoff for Lakota, I pass a sign advertising the centennial of the local Lutheran church and then a small, neat cemetery. To the left lies the Safeguard complex, a series of cinder block buildings, maintenance sheds, and barbed wire. I drive through a gate marked "Military Installation" and park at what I assume to be the site's headquarters. A diorama features two scale-model missiles and a row of color photos of the site's former commanders.

Neil Holmen, a grizzled middle-aged man sporting a Harley-Davidson tee-shirt, a ruffled handlebar mustache, and a healthy Dakotan paunch, hails me and asks me to sign the visitor's register, a few pieces of paper on a clipboard that show me to be the first guest in months. We climb into his pickup truck and drive the 200 yards to the pyramid. "We used to watch them building it," says Holmen, who was in high school at the time. "It was really something," he adds with characteristic understatement. For a time, in the late 1960s, Nekoma, whose population is now around forty, was a boomtown. Construction teams were encamped nearby, bars opened to serve them, and the town was expecting the arrival of more than one thousand army personnel. It looked as if this nondescript farming outpost would be one of the two bulwarks of the anti-ballistic missile system (another site, in Ledger, Montana, today is a slab of graffiti-covered concrete in the middle of eastern Montana wilderness). But history was moving faster than events in Nekoma.

Nixon's Pyramid perimeter acquisition radar at the Safeguard site, Nekoma, North Dakota

Ruins of Safeguard missile defense system, Nekoma, North Dakota

Like the pioneer towns that sprang up on railroad lines in the nineteenth century, Nekoma was a boomtown of the missile age gone bust. Nearby farmers dislike the site, Holmen says, not for its one-time nuclear arsenal but as the latest in a series of failed government promises.

Silently looming out of the freshly cut fields of hay, there is a brute honesty to the pyramid, whose 4-foot-thick walls are angled 35 degrees to deflect the pressure of a nuclear blast wave. Its "eyes," a series of four phased-array radars, could acquire targets from 300 miles in any direction. When Holmen first went inside the pyramid, the military had removed the radar components, and contractors had hauled away every last scrap of metal. "It was almost eerie," he says. Off to one side is a forest of rusting white pipes, elements of the former battery of Sprint and Spartan missiles, nuclear-tipped solid-propellant rockets that were designed—there was disagreement whether they actually worked—to combat an incoming "threat cloud" at two separate altitudes. If the pyramid seems like the ceremonial seat of power, then this field of Sprint and Spartan missiles seems like an ancient garden, with its rows of pillars that may once have been covered in ivy. "I can't believe that after thirty years we still don't have a nuclear defense," Holmen says, as rain begins to fall. As I leave the site, the MSR glowers in the rearview mirror over fields of sunflowers—the machine in the garden, a mechanism of the nuclear age sown in the ground like a dormant crop.

I eat at Gracie's in Langdon, reading small-town obituaries and ads for used grain implements, then drive half an hour to the Cavalier Air Force Base, where the looming, trapezoidal Perimeter Acquisition Radar leased to the U.S. Air Force is still active, part of the Spacetrack missile warning system. Unlike the pyramid, this eye looks only to the north, where it would pick up incoming missiles as they crossed the North Pole, some 1,800 miles away (at which time there would be six minutes to deploy an ABM counterattack). I do not have permission to visit this site, so I watch it from across a field, as somewhere deep inside someone looks at a picture they cannot really see, only interpret. We both stare, entranced by the void.

The Cold War nuclear weapons development program, according to the Brookings Institution, cost the United States more than $5.5 trillion.[1] This not only makes it the most expensive military undertaking ever, it also makes it the most expensive war that was never fought. There were battles, there were wars that were not called wars; but the Cold War, as an epic conflagration toward which massive armaments were positioned, was an "imaginary war," without ticker-tape parades, without statues in small-town parks, without movie stars returning from tours of duty, without medals (only many years after men had returned from Arctic postings on the Distant Early Warning (DEW) Line did the Department of Defense finally issue a citation for Cold War service). As Klara Sax, the artist whose medium is the junked B-52 bomber, says in Don DeLillo's novel *Underworld*, "But the bombs were not released . . . The missiles remained in their underwing carriages, unfired. The men came back and the targets were not destroyed."[2]

It was a war of light and shadow, illusion and reality, truth and counter-truth. War was not declared, nor was peace assumed, but the country remained in what was termed a "Defense Condition" (DEFCON), like a patient relying on the reports from strange machines to know his condition. Battlefields were everywhere and nowhere, an abstract space on wall-size screens in situation rooms, prophesied in emanating-ripple damage estimates on aerial photographs of cities, filtered down to backyards where homeowners studied government-supplied plans for bomb shelters. Attack was instantaneous, with no spatial component: The command to "Duck, and Cover!" turned a school desk or a roadside curb into a portable shelter, while government pamphlets such as *Four Wheels to Survival* hinted at the need for constant protection from an invisible threat: "Shelter is an unexpected bonus you get from your car. More importantly, the car provides a small moveable house."[3]

The country was on a war footing and simultaneously awash in peacetime prosperity. Both conditions were dependent upon each other, a contradictory

Spacetrack missile warning system perimeter acquisition radar, Cavalier Air Force Base, North Dakota

existence that played itself out in everyday life. The Cold War landscape, too, had these contradictions. The Cold War is defined by obvious architectural metaphors, clear demarcations of form: the Berlin Wall, in John Le Carré's phrase "a dirty ugly thing of breeze blocks and strands of barbed wire, lit with cheap yellow light, like the backdrop for a concentration camp,"[4] a barrier designed to keep people not out, but in; the Iron Curtain, a metaphor Winston Churchill adapted from the stage (a ferrous wall that would protect the audience from a fire); and the DEW Line, that solid-state Maginot Line stretched across the Canadian Arctic, an electronic trip-wire signaled by encroaching Soviet planes. The Pentagon is another Cold War architectural "monument," a five-sided icon of power whose labyrinthine interior mirrored the cryptic codes and chains of command that marked the institutionalized military after World War II (Marshall McLuhan dubbed it the "world's largest filing cabinet"). And there was the Demilitarized Zone, which paradoxically was at times the most heavily militarized region in the world; meanwhile, the celebrated fallout shelter, amid the technological utopianism of the postwar period, symbolized a return to one of man's most primitive habitats, the cave.

At the same time, the Cold War landscape was defined by what could *not* be seen. The realms of public and private knowledge were bifurcated, and so too was space: A secret landscape was installed from Greenwich, Connecticut to Greenland, an invisible terrain replete with underground command facilities and emergency relocation centers. Unseen communications networks—ranging from CONELRAD to AT&T's AUTOVON to the Defense Advance Research Projects Agency's skeletal forerunner of the Internet—promised post-attack, off-the-grid command-and-control networks, while tracts of land that rivaled or exceeded Eastern states in size were appropriated to test the various instruments of a war that never came. In the same way that the air-raid drones and piercing television tone of the Emergency Broadcast Network (designed to allow the president to broadcast over 8,000 radio and television networks within five minutes) were both comforting and alarmist—"This is only a test," the voice reassured, while raising the specter of what would happen if it were *not* a test—the Cold War landscape promised security from an invisible threat with a range of deterrent forces that also could not be seen.

The phrase "Cold War architecture" is a rather common one; however, it has nothing to do with buildings. It refers to the security arrangements—e.g., the NATO alliance—nations constructed during the period. This, too, is symbolic, a web of relationships formed to maintain order (or, as Chicago's Mayor Daley once said, "to preserve the existing disorder"), but embodied in no actual structure. The architecturally Delphic United Nations headquarters, as Lewis Mumford observed, typified the problem of trying to visualize what he called the "New World Order."[5] To imagine a Cold War architecture in the usual sense of architecture is to conjure a world from dim historical memory, from conjecture, from the fantasies of films. As historian Stephen Whitfield notes of the set design for Stanley Kubrick's *Dr. Strangelove*, "since officialdom had never admitted that an underground crisis center in the Pentagon even existed (much less released a photo of it) [Kubrick] designed the war room out of his own and his art director's imagination."[6] "Cold War" evokes images of poured-concrete bunkers, steely gray doors, red phones on desks, enormous tables around which are gathered nervous men, sentries standing under cones of light, a wall of mainframe computers with whirring tape-spools and blinking lights, radiation symbols, the ghostly green clock-hand sweep of a radar.

But what does it mean really to speak of Cold War "architecture"? To begin with, one must look beyond accepted architectural typologies or the signature names of the period, for the architecture of the Cold War does not appear in standard histories, nor does it have a unitary style. Some of this is architectural bias: It took a Le Corbusier to champion the American grain silo as an eminent form, but there has been no Le Corbusier of the missile silo—the deadly connotations may be too grim. Nevertheless, the missile silo represents one of the country's largest public works programs in history, one that had a profound impact on the landscape. Yet any single building by Mies van der Rohe has occasioned more architectural consideration than all these structures combined, though silos and installations are in a sense the highest expression of the modernist dictum "form follows function." To understand the decisions that went into the design and construction of a missile silo or an underground command post—to know why this form or material was chosen over that one—is central to understanding the brilliant and terrible science occasioned by the Cold War, the architectural logic that underlay the policy described by John Foster Dulles: "How should collective defense be organized by the free world for maximum protection at minimum cost?"[7] The Cold War persisted for decades as a mindset, a state of being, a condition. To think of a Cold War architecture is not only to think of those structures expressly built for the Cold War—mute memorials, nodes of nuclear stalemate, vast spaces like the "Manhattan Engineer District," not found on any map—but to look again, through the prism of Cold War thought, at landscapes normally associated with the more benign themes of progress and rationality.

The scale and scope of structures built for the Cold War is impressive. They include: Oak Ridge, Tennessee, a.k.a. "Site x," the "atomic city" that helped bring Skidmore, Owings and Merrill (SOM) to prominence as one of the country's largest architectural firms; "Cheyenne Mountain," the hardened, self-contained core of the North American Aerospace Command Center, designed to survive nearly a month after a nuclear blast; and NASA's

"Vehicular Assembly Building," designed by Max O. Urbahn, which for a time possessed the largest interior volume in the world. Other structures were built for civilian use but contained some implicit defensive function: an underground school built in Artesia, New Mexico; the countless office buildings, hospitals, and government buildings with purpose-built shelter areas; and the thousands of unseen and forgotten basement and backyard home shelters. There are the myriad laboratories and research complexes, the Hanfords, the Pantexes, "Tech Area II" at Sandia, and "Building 20" at M.I.T. As physicist Niels Bohr told Edward Teller, the father of the H-bomb, "I told you it couldn't be done without turning the whole country into a factory. You have just done that."[8] And there are simply those buildings built during the Cold War period, which, like all architecture, reflect the cultural ambitions and technology of their time, as well as current architectural styles. One could argue that the International Style, with its machine aesthetic, was representative of the Cold War, or that modernism's distrust of monumentality and impulse toward democracy were reflected in Cold War architecture. Was a building such as SOM's Lever House a celebration of American wealth and technological mastery, or did its sheets of glass—a material that was anathema to civil defense planners—represent a revolt against Cold War realities? Mumford wrote that, "Fragile, exquisite, undaunted by the threat of being melted into a puddle by an atomic bomb, this building is a laughing refuta-

Atomic weapons production storage bunker, Wendover Air Force Base, Utah

tion of 'imperialist warmongering,' and so it becomes an implicit symbol of hope for a peaceful world."[9] Or, as the architectural historian John Burchard wrote, "Historians trying to generalize from our buildings may develop elaborate hypotheses to explain the metal and glass cages as an expression of the feeling of a society with a sense of death, 'ephemera, ephemera, all is ephemera,' in which building for permanence was obviously futile and for which there was something symbolic in using fragile and transitory materials; or as the desire of the same society to catch all the physical light since so much of the spiritual world was dark."[10]

The Cold War was—and is—everywhere in America, if one knows where to look for it. Underground, behind closed doors, classified, off the map, already crumbling beyond recognition, or right in plain view, it has left an imprint as widespread yet discreet as the tracings of radioactive particles that blew out of the Nevada Test Site in the 1950s. In search of its peculiar legacy, wanting to know what the Cold War *looked* like, I got in a car and drove, aided by that fabled creation of the Cold War itself, the Interstate Highway and Defense System.

The first ruins of the atomic age I ever saw were on the outskirts of Wendover, Utah. I had seen them before in the photographs of Richard Misrach, but nothing quite prepared me for the strange feeling of pathos and chilling solemnity that came from seeing them in person. Past the former Wendover Air Force Base and the rusting hangar that once housed the *Enola Gay*, they are best approached by foot. As one walks across the occasionally active runways of what is now Wendover Airport (what seems to be a vintage C-130 is actually a non-working movie prop for the film *Con Air*) and into the soft areas where the mud is bleeding up into the salt, the remains gradually emerge: a settlement of sloping, earthen structures that seem to rise out of the ground, looking like miniature versions of the mountains behind them. These bunkers are the last remaining physical evidence of Project W-47, a top-secret operation launched in 1944 to assemble and test the atomic bomb. Under the direction of Air Force Col. Paul Tibbets, some 1800 men of the mysterious-sounding 509th Composite Group were brought to Wendover. Civilian scientists worked at W-47 on the final assembly of three bombs: the "Little Boy" dropped on Hiroshima and the "Fat Man" bomb dropped on Nagasaki. Pilots flying the *Enola Gay* executed practice runs in the nearby desert, using pumpkins as ammunition. As Tibbets wrote in his memoirs, he chose Wendover for its isolation. "There was no place nearby for fun-loving men with six-hour passes to get into trouble and leak information."[11] Apart from the Air Base, the town had just one casino and a hundred residents.

More than half a century later, the atomic bunkers are now used as storage facilities by the local casinos, which have blossomed to become the economic mainstay of Wendover, Nevada, the municipal alter ego that exists just over the border. I had come to Wendover to visit a friend who was making a film about the nearby Bonneville Salt Flats and living in the hot and dusty former barracks of w-47. As we explored the area around the bunkers, a collection of wood structures overseen by a rickety observation tower, we would occasionally find scraps of wreckage jutting out of the pale white sand. It seemed a trove of modern archaeological history, and as we climbed the tower we imagined ourselves gazing on the site the way some sentry must have once done. As I was to find out later, however, both the aged military surplus sitting in the sand and the observation tower were traces not of Cold War history but, once again, of the film *Con Air*. We could still find scatterings of weathered Hollywood paperwork in the various buildings (the tower was later moved for *another* film).

The afternoon's wanderings were to remain poignantly with me. Here was a landscape as central to the nation's history and identity as any restored Civil War battlefield or presidential home, and yet it was languishing unseen, its meanings obscured, grafted onto the imaginary terrain of Hollywood. It was also on that trip that the military presence in the American West, which during the Cold War had evolved into a kind of checkerboard archipelago of autonomous states, became apparent to me in myriad small ways. One morning, my friend and I were breakfasting outside a dented Airstream trailer, facing the atomic ruins hundreds of yards in the distance, when suddenly, out of the southern sky a half mile or so away, a military jet came roaring into view. It descended quickly, its engines searing the cool morning sky, and it seemed intent on landing. It glided to within what seemed feet of the runway and then lifted upward, thrusting off over the nearby town and out of view. "Touch and go," military pilots call it, and it is one of the many military exercises one sees routinely undertaken here, minor dramas written into the margins of everyday life.

From the ruins of the past, we had seen a startling herald of the present, a swept-wing messenger that suggested to me that only now with the Cold War ended, its installations entombed, could one begin to understand its presence in America. On that morning a question arose within me that was to remain for many months and many miles: What other sites, similar to w-47, existed elsewhere in the country? What sorts of places were created in the name of a Cold War military mobilization? Where did the military fit into the landscape, and how did the Cold War help determine that presence? What stories might these Cold War ruins have to tell, and, finally, what perspective might they offer to a later generation that seemed intent on replicating this ghost landscape, albeit in a technologically upgraded vein?

And so I became a Cold War tourist, visiting the places not listed in guidebooks (and some that now are), glimpsing places that seem in danger of vanishing even as we are just beginning to understand their history (as in the case of the North Dakota missile silos), seeing the raw spaces that may some-day be refurbished and outfitted with carefully selected curatorial text, but which now stand empty, eerie, and fascinating. These are the tombs of an unknown war, which was once incomprehensibly directed toward the obliter-ation of civilization. I necessarily became a tourist in history as well, through documents and stories. Much of the Cold War landscape is, of course, still quite secret, beyond the reach even of the Freedom of Information Act, which is in itself an admission that it has not entirely ended; this also turns history into a sort of voyeurism, a hopeful glimpse through curtains that rarely part for more than a moment.

Of course, I as a novice and someone used to going about things the stan-dard way (and seeing the strangeness in the mundane) relied on the fairly straightforward mechanisms of press credentials and official permission—only occasionally slipping through a fence—and in this regard I could not approach the exploits of Walter Cotten, the colleague and friend whose photographs are found in this book. For the last few decades, well before the current climate of

Sign at McGregor Range, Fort Bliss, Texas

openness found around many military reservations (one trip to Nevada's Fallon Naval Air Station resulted in an encounter with military police and handcuffing), Walter has traveled the back roads of the West on a kind of aesthetic reconnaissance mission, in search of the strange vistas found beyond the warning signs—the bits of exploded ordnance dotting an otherwise pristine ground, the lone instrument bunker wedged among the sagebrush, the traces of a history seen by few. Unlike my more recent obsessions, Walter's interest in the military landscape took root on childhood drives through the West, past places like "Rocket Ridge" at Edwards Air Force Base or the legendarily secret China Lake Naval Weapons Station. "Driving past you'd see all this stuff in the distance. My father [an Air Force officer] would explain, 'That's a radar reflector, that's a rocket test stand.' Sitting in the middle of a dry lake bed, the objects were without scale—they took on a monolithic, monumental quality," he explained to me as we sat one afternoon in his temporary summer studio in Roswell, New Mexico. After studying cultural anthropology in college and joining several archaeology expeditions to South America in the late 1960s (where he had, in 1969, the curious task of explaining the news—just acquired by short-wave radio—that the United States had just landed on the moon to a tribe of Indians in a place reached only by canoe; "they looked at me as if I had just told the best joke they had ever heard," he recalls), Walter returned to California to study art. There, on climbing trips in the Sierra Nevadas, he became reacquainted with the landscapes of his childhood, "driving past all kinds of strange stuff." But now, they registered as archaeology, aged but somehow new, "abandoned in place" when a particular military program was cut or its technology became outmoded. He compares the attraction the far-off objects had to being at sea. "If you're in the ocean and you see something strange floating, of course you'll approach." On his climbing trips, the night would bring an array of strange lights and the incandescent trails of parachute flares ("this was during the Vietnam War, so it was completely intriguing and horrifying," he says), while the day would yield unnatural apparitions on the desert horizon. "You'd see something shimmering in the heat of the desert. There's no scale, you can't tell what it is. It might be a square concrete cube belonging to the Geological Survey or a two-story test building."

On one occasion in the mid-1980s, Walter retrieved a cardboard box filled with photographic negatives from a parachute test tower on a piece of land that may or may not have belonged to California's El Centro Naval Air Station (the military has been known to casually annex thousands of acres of land rather surreptitiously). He made prints from the negatives (which dated from the 1960s), and the resulting images represent what might be called the "military panorama." The frame's periphery is marked by target sights, and the image itself is a grainy shot of a desert, with small checkered targets visi-

Photographs retrieved from an abandoned weapons targeting camera at El Centro Naval Air Station, California

ble in the distance. The purpose of the camera is to record the accuracy of bombing, and in the photographs the land behind becomes a blank space, a zone of collateral damage. Around the same time, Walter, with a fellow artist named Steven De Pinto, moved from merely documenting the military ruins of the Southwest to creating their own, fashioning simulated test bunkers and radars out of materials such as masonite and styrofoam. "There were odd shapes that looked as if they had been subjected to intense amounts of pressure. Lots of areas of scorched earth and twisted metal." The "installations"—a phrase that applies to artworks and military bases—were then photographed and presented as a series of "ambiguous landscapes." When I arrived in Roswell, Walter was busy incorporating a number of recent salvages, such as a wooden training mockup of a missile silo control panel, scavenged from the desert or New Mexico's strange junk shops, into his photographs of sculptural forms, "recontextualized" as objects in and of themselves. In Walter's work I saw a correlation to my own travels. What one might dismiss out of hand from an anti-militarist worldview turns out to be quite fascinating—traces of a civilization that was "abandoned in place," not unlike previous inhabitants of the desert such as the Anasazi, whose reasons for disappearing are still open to interpretation.

Cold War traces are everywhere, but it is no surprise that Wendover should have proven such a fertile ground zero in my imagination. This whole region—the vast stretch of sullenly barren Salt Desert between Wendover, Utah, and Salt Lake City—is what Wallace Stegner called "the land nobody wanted." In its nineteenth-century incarnation it was no more than a wasted obstacle to be crossed, a forbidding patch of Purgatory barricading the course of westward expansion. By 1942, however, Stegner was able to observe that "there is a kind of satisfaction in the thought that the desert is being put to use as a bombing range, as a race-track, as a highway... it is well to know that anything, even that, can be used for something."[12] The desert, in other words, had become *modern*, functional. Bonneville Salt Flats racers were vying for absolute speed records, bombers were honing techniques to be employed in war, and a shimmering strip of blacktop turned a once-arduous crossing into an air-conditioned abstraction (even though the 1930s-era *WPA Guide* noted that wagon tracks from the pioneer crossing were still visible in the sand). The desert was alive with the technological sublime, a proving ground for America's military superiority, technological prowess, and mastery over the limits of nature.

No enterprise required more—or larger—proving grounds than the Cold War, and in the decades following World War II enormous tracts of the deserts of the American Southwest were partitioned into sprawling test landscapes, outdoor laboratories sequestered behind jagged peaks where the Grable "shots" and Operation Teapots of atomic weapons displayed their infernal majesty. The country's most primitive terrain was suddenly host to its most sophisticated technology; the putative American frontier was literally being reconquered, even as the frontier myth, as historian Richard Slotkin has argued, was being re-enacted in America's neo-imperial sphere of influence and in the new reaches of space: "[W]e stand today on the edge of a new frontier," began Kennedy's speech at the 1960 Democratic convention, "the frontier of the 1960s, a frontier of unknown opportunities and paths, a frontier of unfulfilled hopes and threats." In a land where the technological advances of previous societies lay buried in the sand, the Cold War's presence has become another in a series of ruins, a fact that was made clear to me one spring morning in the California desert, on the grounds of the Fort Irwin National Training Center—another Rhode Island-sized patch in the continuum of western military terrain.

I had come to see the Pioneer Deep Space Station, now a derelict grouping of low-slung institutional buildings arranged around the site's centerpiece, a looming tower capped off by a 26-meter-diameter aluminum radar dish. To get to this remote natural bowl formation, I had driven with Dr. Mark Allen, an archaeologist employed by the army to monitor the rock art and other specimens of Native American history frequently discovered in Fort Irwin's capacious environs. As we drive past such ruggedly scenic vistas as the "Hand Grenade Familiarization Course," Allen tells me he is one of the few archaeologists in the u.s. to worry about unexploded ordinance (or "uxo," as it is dubbed in military parlance) when exhuming the remains of ancient civilizations.

Pioneer is the ancient ruin of an accelerated culture. Built in a blistering six months on the heels of the launch of Sputnik, it is the last remaining structure of the network of communications facilities built to track the Pioneer 3 space probe. Standing here, one can envision chain-smoking radar technicians watching screens on 24-hour shifts, wearing skinny ties and thick black glasses, charting the edges of outer space as the Earth itself hung in the shadow of annihilation. A tunnel running from the antenna to an underground bomb shelter would have ostensibly allowed the technicians to reach safety in the event of an incoming Soviet missile attack; as I peer in for a closer look, Allen warns of the dangers of the Hanta virus, spread by rodent fecal matter (which is abundantly on display). The fear that built Pioneer has today subsided, and ironically, just a few miles away, a scattering of active Jet Propulsion Lab arrays search in vain for signs of the vanished Martian probe—itself a peace dividend of sorts from the Cold War. As we sit staring at the defunct radar dish, a red-tailed hawk flaps out from within the dish's metal grid and off into the late afternoon sun. As dusk approaches and we return to the archaeological office, Allen admits that most of his time is spent unearthing Native American specimens; he fields few inquiries about Pioneer. Like many relics of the Cold War, it sits "abandoned in place," too old to be technologically useful but too new to be culturally venerated. Stuck in this limbo, many Cold War structures simply vanish.

The Cold War was a conflict projected toward the future: the race to see who would reach space first; whose air force would first reach 10,000 bombers; who would explode the first 25-megaton warhead. It also, despite its overwhelming aura of fatalism and apocalypse, contained a perverse undercurrent of optimism, a belief that the science and technology that was being funded by the so-called "imaginary war" would someday mean a better life for all—if it did not kill us first. That the same companies who created the bright technological wonders of the push-button age had other divisions working on weaponry capable of obliterating those same split-level ranch houses in which those appliances hummed revealed the dyadic nature of what Tom Englehardt called America's "victory culture": "The arms race and the race for the good life were now to be put on the same 'war' footing."[13] Rockets and refrigerators were equally weapons on the Cold War battlefield; one typical advertisement, for General Telephone & Electronics, is headlined "Massive voice for a missile base." Showing a red "hotline" phone among a sea of black rotary dials, it declared, "It is expressive of the way General Telephone & Electronics strives to serve the nation through advanced communications—not only for defense, but for homes and industries as well."

Abandoned Pioneer Deep Space Station, Fort Irwin National Training Center, California

The desert was the perfect home for the Cold War; not simply for its sheer size and ostensible emptiness, but because the desert has paradoxically come to signify the future in America. The desert is the last America, the last New Frontier, where dreams might be played out with a minimum of interference—if only, as in the scene in Joan Didion's 1970 *Play It as It Lays*, we can keep sweeping the drifting sand back to the perimeter of the yard. From the beginning, it has been perceived as a blank slate (though there is inevitably some prior resident, whose presence has been submerged, either forcefully or by neglect) where one's mark can be seen for miles—whether it be the earthworks of endowed artists or the pock-marked craters of an aerial bombing range. It is no surprise that the place where people often go to reinvent themselves in a country of reinvention is the desert city of Las Vegas; it has witnessed many futures—the Mormons, the Mafia, the Manhattan Project—and would not exist at the scale it does without the massive technological life-support systems upon which rests its confidence of unimpeded future growth. The desert has attracted all manner of dreamers, from millenarian cultists to visionary artists to the advanced weapons scientists of the United States Air Force. They have all made their mark, they have all tested something or other on America's proving ground. Like bleached bones these dreams lie in the desert sand, faded and chipped but intact; they have their own story to tell, as compelling as the accounts of written history or the stirring narratives of museums.

"I hope you didn't pay a lot for that vacation." The voice, megaphone-amplified and gently sardonic, crackled out across the sand and creosote from a high ridge a 100 yards away, where a white Jeep Cherokee—standard-issue for government security types—sat parked, its two occupants peering through binoculars at the group assembled below, who in turn looked back with their own binoculars.

Welcome to the "landscape of conjecture," a delicious phrase conceived by the Center for Land Use Interpretation, a Los Angeles-based group dedicated to, as the center puts it, the "increase and diffusion of knowledge of the nature and extent of human interaction with the earth's surface." The subject of conjecture is the Nellis Range Complex, some 5,000 square miles of land—the size of Connecticut—in the Southern Nevada desert that for five decades has served as proving ground for any number of hot and cold wars waged by the u.s. The place has its defined coordinates and physical features (it is, as the Air Force says, "almost a state of its own"), but it exists as much in the geography of the imagination as it does on any map, a secret landscape that compels those who view its perimeters to project their own fantasies on what might be occurring inside.

The gateway to Area 51, northern end of Nevada Test Site, near Rachel, Nevada

The guards have a point. There is a certain latent absurdity in the fact that a group of rational adults have paid to take a tour of a place that not only cannot be seen, but until recently was not even acknowledged to exist. The tour has culminated here, at the northern end of Nellis, on this dusty desert tract that borders Groom Lake, a.k.a. Area 51, Dreamland, or Paradise Ranch; the ground zero in the popular imagination about what governments can get up to behind closed doors—or, in this case, behind a cloak of rugged mountains, restricted airspace, and a variety of near-invisible security sensors. As the group shuffles legally about on Bureau of Land Management terrain, a few eventually summon the nerve to take photographs—mostly of the two prominent signs that read, "Photography Prohibited." The guards remain in the shade of their Jeep, in tacit recognition of the obvious: that in fact there is nothing to photograph here except the sign.

This small episode provides another window for understanding Cold War landscapes. The group of tourists squared off against the hostile forces stationed across what seems an arbitrary line; the former group suspicious of just what lay over that mountain range, the latter wary of our purpose here. What seems like uninhabited natural terrain turns out to be a landscape punctuated with surveillance and security measures. Radomes, those dimpled spheres that chart the new landscapes of the sky, bask silently on far mountaintops, seeming somehow part of the order of things, aesthetically incorporated, as were the smokestacks and factories in a certain strand of nineteenth-century landscape painting. Nestled among the desert brush, meanwhile, are a variety of motion detectors and other perimeter defenses. The place draws its power from what cannot be seen: invisible lines guarded by invisible means, protecting unknown "strategic assets" from unknown aggressors.

Ironically, with the Cold War concluded, the military is rather upfront when it comes to technology that is already acknowledged to exist. On one bright morning, a small group of CLUI's conjectural tourists drives to the southern end of Nellis's Range 63, past a small group of cinder-block buildings that bear labels like "Combat Arms School" and a sign that reads "Threat Condition Alpha." We are here for a "live fire" demonstration, which the Air Force conducts several times a year for the benefit of top brass and other dignitaries. The atmosphere lies somewhere between a country fair and a high school football game: a set of aluminum bleachers looking out over the desert, white-haired ladies carrying lemonade and cookies, rock music pumping out of amplifiers. Suddenly, a Jumbotron parked to the left fires into action with an Air Force promotional film.

And then, in the expansive sky ahead of us, a thin, silvery F-16 fighter comes flying in low from the right. As it passes the bleachers at perhaps half a mile away, a small cluster of white dots emerges from just below its tail. They drift through the air, falling further apart, hitting the ground with a flash of light and bushy brown smoke; seconds later, the bleachers are rattled by an enormous thump (the run is code-named "Bravo"). With a light speed-metal riff racing away on the amplifiers, instant replays beaming on the Jumbotron, the narrator continues in his military drone, blithely describing cataclysmic explosions as the delivery of "a strike package to sanitize the area." Watching the bulbous clouds of smoke rising from the ground, or seeing the white contrails of "Smoky Sams" sketched against the blue sky, I feel the narrator's voice taking on a sonorous, poetic cadence, as I let his terminology wash over me: "austere runways," "truly interactive battlespace picture," "precision engagement," "successful egress."

There is nothing secret in this—cars routinely pull off the road on highway 95 to watch the pyrotechnics. Even so, this is only the perimeter of the range, and most of what is inside remains open to speculation. This becomes clear when the CLUI bus enters the grounds of the Tonopah Electronic Combat Range, which it describes as a "purely electronic landscape of video tracking stations, radar facilities, electronic threat emitters, electronic countermeasure facilities, and control and communication sites, all wired together through fiber optic links and microwave relays." As the bus passes through the gate of the range, Mark Farmer (a.k.a. Agent x), an ex-military man turned defense journalist and onetime Area 51 voyeur, muses, "It's the spookiest thing—you can fight the battle without ever firing a shot. It's the greatest video game in the world." As the bus completes a turn just inside the gate, the driver bottoms out on a roadside gully, the bus cresting onto the sand like a beached whale. We are stranded inside of a restricted area.

As we leave the bus, the security guard, clearly unaccustomed to dealing with disoriented tourists, radios for help. Hours pass before a military truck arrives. We sit in the shade of vehicles, listening to Agent x spin stories of "Red Flag/Green Flag" air combat exercises and of the rich assortment of foreign military technology, either bought on the black market or captured, that lies over the blinding mountains. We watch a tarantula walk across the gravel. The guard tells one woman that while she is free to use the bathroom inside the guard's post, she cannot photograph the "Tonopah Electronic Combat Range" sign. Once again, photography is prohibited in this place where there is nothing to photograph.

Surveillance, however, is not limited to the visible in this stealth landscape. In Rachel, Nevada, home of the Little A'Le'Inn and the Area 51 Research Center, I found a mobile radiation monitoring installation tucked just behind a gas station; not surprisingly, the gas station pumps featured faded, cracked paintings of a small saucer over what could be Area 51. As people drive down the "Extraterrestrial Highway," their eyes drifting toward the dark sky for a glimpse of alien craft, the radiation station whirs, looking for the fallout of a war that cannot be seen.

The "new Area 51," according to a 1997 article in *Popular Mechanics*, was reputed to be in Green Valley, Utah, a small desert highway outpost overshadowed by its neighbor to the south, Moab. I stopped for the night, and waking early to get good light and avoid the expected security forces, I drove across Green Valley's highway exit overpass on a cracked road that quickly turns to dirt, with signs warning that "County Maintenance Ends." After a few minutes, I find the fenced-off remains of the Utah Launch Complex. I enter through a gap in the fence, examining the sprawling collection of metal sheds and concrete platforms connected by a snaking assembly-line track. Green River was built in 1961 to launch the Pershing truck-mounted missile and other armaments into the White Sands Missile Range; after complaints by those living in the flight path, the testing was shifted to Fort Wingate, Arizona. The launch complex has not been occupied for years and is strangely pristine, free of the traditional graffiti and smashed beer bottles found at atomic ruins. There are periodic discussions about reviving the site; in 1995, it was reported that the army had decided against new missile launches due to the "significant land-use problems" in dropping 1-ton missile boosters near

Spectators at "live fire" demonstration, Nellis Air Force Base, Nevada

Canyonlands National Park.[14] That such a decrepit place could have been the object of conjectures as the "new Area 51" speaks to the power of the psychic landscape: The *idea* of Green River was more necessary than the particulars of its existence. In the inherited worldview of the Cold War, the place that cannot be seen is all the more terrifyingly impressive than that which can be. On the edges of maps grow fables.

The largest all-wood structure in the world can be found on the grounds of Albuquerque's Kirtland Air Force Base. Constructed of more than six million board feet of lumber—enough to build some 4,000 three-bedroom homes—the Electromagnetic Pulse Trestle is, as its name indicates, similar to a nineteenth-century railroad trestle, a towering mass of wood pilings supporting a football field-sized platform. It looks like a bridge to nowhere, its twelve-story height belied by its siting on the barren desert floor—only when a vehicle is parked underneath does its scale become apparent. Despite its railway associations, the trestle is a highly representative piece of Cold War architecture: a limited-access, gargantuan, and tremendously expensive structure whose form is entirely dictated by a novel technological function.

To find out why the imperatives of the Cold War should require a piece of archaic railroad technology, I climb to the top with Rich Garcia, a public affairs officer with the Air Force Research Laboratory's Directed Energy Directorate. With the wind whipping and the incendiary roar of military jets constant, Garcia begins to explain the trestle's origins: "With nuclear detonation, you get blast, shock, heat, radiation, and EMP. EMP is an electromagnetic wave of energy that can travel hundreds of miles in an instant, and when it encounters electronics it tends to screw them up—if it's computers, it might reverse the polarity, ones become zeros." He points to the 1983 film *The Day After*, in which the explosion of Russian warheads is prefigured by a sudden mass short out in the electronic ignitions of cars. Of special concern to the Air Force Special Weapons Laboratory was the effects of EMP on the country's airborne retaliatory forces—whether ICBMs or B-52 bombers—as well as the E4-A Airborne Command Post (the plane that would spirit the president and top officials to friendlier skies in the event of nuclear confrontation). Military planners assumed a nuclear attack would begin with an exoatmospheric blast, high enough that the resulting EMP wave would cover most of the country with debilitating electronic interference—a giant remote-control unit opening all the wrong garage doors in America. As *Air Force* magazine observed, "Soviet military doctrine, which

Electromagnetic Pulse Test Trestle at Kirtland Air Force Base, Albuquerque, New Mexico

emphasizes creating confusion in the societal and military structure of opposing forces prior to surprise attack, is consonant with the use of EMP."[15]

Since the Air Force wanted to test planes in flight, and since it was unable to generate sufficient EMP airborne, it needed to build a ground structure that could simulate flight. Since metal and concrete create interference with EMP, the building material had to be wood. This proved more difficult than one might imagine. "The first two contractors defaulted on the project," notes Garcia. "The problem was the technology for building the trestles had pretty much disappeared—no one knew how to do it anymore." By the time a contractor was found who was able to compete the project, the budget had expanded to some $58 million. It took four years to build.

To create what they call a "threat-level electromagnetic pulse environment," the testers would tow a B-52 onto the test stand, lashing it down with ropes and putting wood blocks in front of the plane. "That's because when you're testing the airplane, you've got all engines running. You want it to behave as if it's in the air." To either side of the test stand are small white buildings, each with a round window. Inside the window is a 5,000,000 volt pulsar. When activated, the pulsars create an electromagnetic wave that comes down a v-shaped wedge, sweeps across the trestle, and then terminates at the end of the stand, where a tall cathedral-like outline of wood rises above the scene; attached to this is a grounded pole that absorbs the EMP. Wire mesh, which surrounds the test stand like the rigging of a massive ship, "catches" stray waves of EMP. The waves also travel down, hitting the ground and instantly bouncing back up at a speed of more than 200 million feet per second—which could throw off the experiment, but the fiber-optic instrumentation is able to record its finding in that split second. This is the future as prophesied decades earlier by the Italian futurist Marinetti in "Electrical War: A Futurist Vision Hypothesis": "These men live in high-tension rooms where a hundred thousand Volts palpitate between the plate-glass windows. They sit before switchboards, with dials to right and left, keyboards, regulators, and commutators, and everywhere the splendid flash of polished levers."[16]

Walking underneath the trestle, Garcia hands me a wooden bolt, one of the thousands that hold the structure together. Only here does he tell me that the trestle's distinction as the largest all-wood structure may not be earned. Inside each bolt, it turns out, is a small "o-ring" of metal, to prevent the shearing off that would otherwise occur when a many-tonned B-52 is resting on the platform. A crew performs regular checks of the integrity of the bolts—the inspections last a year. When I ask Garcia about the effects on humans of EMP testing (which has been banned in any number of other locations), he tells me, "I've been on the trestle when it's radiated, and you don't know it, you don't feel it. But if you're holding onto something that's metal, that metal acts as an antenna, and then you'll get it." As curious proof of the structure's safety, he points to a pair of Great Horned Owls who for years have made their nest amidst the timbers of the trestle. "They've laid eggs nearly every year," Garcia says. "We used to say as a joke, 'there's no damage to human tissue here—of course, those two owls started as parakeets.'" The owls are actually not the only tenants of the trestle these days; it is being leased by the White Sands Missile Range. Garcia says he cannot disclose its mission. As for Kirtland, he says, "we dropped our emphasis on nuclear weapons effects testing back in 1990, and started putting more effort into advanced weapons—lasers, particle beams, plasma projectiles, any kind of an energy force that might ruin the other guy's day."

The trestle is an archaic structure reincarnated as a type of architecture that emerged in the heyday of modernism: the test building. The test building could be, as it often was in its Cold War guise, a "shed" or a "shell," a mere covering for R&D—e.g., the gray blocks of the engine test cell at Wright Patterson Air Force Base, or the Cold Regions Test Center and Northern Warfare Training Center at Fort Greely, Alaska. In structures such as Eero Saarinen's Dynameter Building, however, at the General Motors Technical Center, the test building came into its own; the technical center was where, as William Curtis describes it, "abstract, mechanical processes of American management and industry were translated into a vocabulary combining reductivist volumes and a neutral, yet poetical handling of standardized steel and glass components."[17] As travel through the desert reveals, however, not all of these tests were strictly technological in nature; some originated in the dream scenarios of architects whose buildings were also laboratories for humans.

The metaphorical "machine for living" took literal form in Biosphere 2, which lies nestled in the mountains north of Tucson. What began as a fringe idea (i.e., Martian habitation) in the cultist confines of the 1960s Synergia Ranch (one of the numerous 1960s "Drop City"-like squatter settlements that found a home in the region) was transformed, with an infusion of oil money, into an extraterrestrial habitation simulation complex. It was a media spectacle in the 1980s, before the project collapsed due to problems ranging from the well-being of the "bionauts" to the integrity of the scientific research being conducted.

Appropriately, the Biosphere resembles some kind of alien landing craft, a massive hulled vessel of glass and concrete surrounded by an array of domes and service buildings. The site is now managed by Columbia University, which uses it to conduct research on global warming and other respectable topics. With a handful of other visitors, I register for an "Under

Inside the Biosphere, near Tuscon, Arizona

the Glass" tour, which means we don hardhats and pass through the airlock to view the former living and working quarters of the bionauts. While scientists still scuttle around the various passageways, it is clear, standing in one of the now-deflated dome-covered "lungs" that once served as the internal air source, that the Biosphere as originally envisioned is dead, replaced by a rather extravagant greenhouse. The interior is no longer self-sufficient, and the decontamination procedures that now occur at the airlock are intended to prevent bringing germs *outside*. As we sit on a concrete ledge watching the water of the "Ocean Biome" lap against the manufactured shore, the air warm and dank, we see hundreds of ants working their way along the concrete floors and walls. The proverbial cockroaches after a nuclear war, the ants are a symbol of the problems that plagued Biosphere: No one seems to know how they arrived, but once they began to proliferate no one knew exactly how to get rid of them, or the consequences upon the ecosystem if they did.

The Biosphere was designed by architect Philip Hawes, a former disciple of Frank Lloyd Wright's Taliesin West. Hawes cited Egyptian and Mayan influences and was concerned with creating environmentally sensitive architecture. But in its lavish funding, scientific trappings, and belief that humans could replicate their environment through technology, the Biosphere cannot be detached from Cold War thought. The airlocks and decontamination chambers, as well as the self-contained air and energy systems, are of a piece with the headquarters of the North American Aerospace Defense Command, that city within a mountain in Colorado Springs whose 10-ton blast doors and blast intake valves will, upon a nuclear explosion, "button up," allowing its residents to survive for thirty days with no outside exposure. The notion of extraterrestrial colonization was given its first major impetus by the military, with early Air Force studies noting that a "lunar base possesses strategic value . . . by providing a site where future military deterrent forces could be located."

I found deterrent forces of a more earthbound variety an hour south of Tucson, at former Air Force launch complex 571-7, once operated by the Strategic Air Command. It is the only place in the country where a tourist can view a fully preserved ICBM silo. With its coterie of polite elderly women volunteers, one might mistake the site—once the home of a 33,000 pound Titan II missile (the largest the u.s. ever built) with a range of 9,000 miles and able to carry a 9-megaton warhead—for a provincial historical society museum (*Dr. Strangelove slept here!*), were it not entirely underground.

The Titan site, with its echoing metal tunnels, banks of gray computers, and submarine-like vault doors, is a steely, chilly mausoleum of America's nuclear past, as well as a fantastic vision of an alternative future that proposed placing not only defense installations underground, but factories and housing. The strategist Herman Kahn envisioned a kind of evacuation nation, a permanent civil defense footing in which it was "perfectly conceivable . . . that the u.s. might have to evacuate two or three times every decade."[18] Yet in spite of its ominous atmosphere and connotation, the Titan is arguably of a piece with the technological optimism that characterizes not only the Biosphere but the factories and power stations so respected by Le Corbusier—a pure representation of function in poured concrete. The launch control centers buried underneath the site are domes, the favored form of Buckminster Fuller. The dome saw use both in Fuller's "Dymaxion" modern housing as well as in blast shelters built by the u.s. Army Corps of Engineers, who learned at places like the Aberdeen Proving Grounds that domes best withstood blast effects. There is nothing superfluous at the Titan

Titan II missile maintenance crew, south of Tucson, Arizona

Inside the Titan II missile silo, south of Tucson, Arizona

Titan II launch center, south of Tucson, Arizona

site—the "hard space" only covers those functions essential to launching the missile, with the "soft space" being everything outside of the 6,000-pound blast doors, reached via a series of catwalks and staircases. If forts were once constructed to house armaments, here there is no distinguishing between the weapon and the system constructed to house the weapon: the architecture is the gun, the missile the bullet.

Sitting in one of the jet-fighter chairs once reserved for the launch control officers, those flight-suited sentinels of America's underground Air Force, listening to the klaxon sound, watching the warning lights flash, staring ahead into the airspace charted on radar screens, the future as it was once imagined looks terrifying; its grandiose geopolitical rhetoric echoes in the cold array of the flickering console, the rotary-dial phones, and the safe containing the emergency war orders. If Biosphere 2 represented a form of folly, an outlandish vision of a better world, the Titan may be the maddest scheme of them all, a series of underground cities that actually got built, in places where no one was likely to pay much attention.

This book is an inquiry about space and how it exists during war. It is about how war defines space, and space defines war. It is about "black space," which cannot be seen, versus the visible "white space," and how the existence of one not only presupposes the other, but how they inevitably seep into each other, corrupting both in the process. It is about the spaces that are off the map and the spaces hidden in plain sight. It is about the dueling sciences of protection and destruction in an age when war went from a marked event to an underlying condition, when the city went from protective enclave to strategic target. It is about the quest to find safety in the modern world and to express it in physical terms.

One of the Cold War's largest "black spaces" is found at the White Sands Missile Range, an arid territory in New Mexico's Tularosa Basin equal to the land mass of Delaware and Rhode Island. For more than half a century, White Sands has witnessed the testing of prototype weaponry, ranging from the v-2 rocket to the atomic bomb to the Boeing 747-mounted airborne laser. Testing is part of the daily rhythms of life here; White Sands will throw

Abandoned rocket gantry, White Sands Missile Range, New Mexico

Launch Complex 33, White Sands Missile Range, New Mexico

500K Static Test Site, circa 1960s, White Sands Missile Range, New Mexico

Right: 500K Static Test Site today, White Sands Missile Range, New Mexico

up hours-long roadblocks during certain exercises. Rattling across its back roads (closed to the public), startling the occasional oryx—a Kalahari antelope introduced decades ago by the state's wildlife agency—in the mesquite brush, one sees squat dun-colored bunkers and shiny radar towers shimmering briefly on the horizon, only to vanish in a miragelike haze, as if jammed by the radar of the sun. Markers announce cryptic fields of activity: "Zurf Site," or "Phenomenology Test Bed."

White Sands bills itself as a "multi-service test range," which these days means the grounds are open to anything from automakers testing car paints to a solar furnace that can focus a 5,000-degree beam on objects. Its tenants include everyone from the U.S. Army Research Laboratory's (ARL) Information and Electronic Protection Division to NASA to the Directorate for Applied Technology, Test and Simulation, which boasts "the most complete assembly of nuclear weapons environment simulators in the Department of Defense." Another tenant, the ARL's Battlefield Environment Division, has the mission of "owning the weather," which includes the Biosphere-like task of recreating various global environments to test weapons systems. As my guide, public affairs officer Jim Eckles, and I drive past one of these "climatic chambers," he notes, "if we want it to be like Alaska in the middle of winter we can put a shroud over the launcher and cool it down to twenty below zero, or we can heat the item to recreate Middle East conditions—about the only thing we can't recreate is snow."

For every active facility, however, there seem to be three abandoned buildings. We pass a peaked concrete blockhouse with the logo "Army" stenciled on its side, which sits opposite a rocket gantry several hundred yards in the distance. "Launch Complex 33" is its formal name, and the humble building has the distinction of ushering in—in September of 1945—America's rocket age. Fogged window slits face the gantry, and as Eckles notes, "the walls are so thick it's like looking down a wrapping-paper tube." One story has Werner von Braun and a group of rocket scientists scrambling out of the bunker following a V-2 launch. "So they go out the door in the backside and they look up at this big empty sky," Eckles says. "[The V-2] only goes up 4 miles when they terminate the flight because it's erratic. So it starts back down and looks as if it's headed right toward them. They're all trying to get back into the blockhouse, while other people are still trying to get out." The rocket crashed a mile away.

Several miles away, jutting from the east side of the Organ Mountains, I see an even more strangely impressive site, the "500K Static Test Site," one of the last vestiges of the Cold War rocket program. A teeming array of blockhouses, gantries, catwalks, and domes, the site sits camouflaged on the side of the slope like a cliff-side Anasazi settlement. Here Von Braun and his associates tested Redstone rocket motors—they sat in observation bunkers (in front of which giant mirrors were angled to provide a safe view) as the giant engines burned through some 500,000 pounds of liquid fuel—the vehicle by which the United States sent up the first Jupiter satellite, some three months after Sputnik. "Most people think it's an old mine," Eckles observes. From the rusting top of the gantry, I glimpse a lone structure miles away in the late afternoon haze. "It's an atomic reactor," says Eckles, and he asks me not to take a picture.

White Sands was a place where the future itself was tested, where scientists and soldiers sent machine and man against the barriers of nature, confident that engineering would win the day. Here "bunker busters" were tested for their effectiveness at penetrating enemy fortifications; here Col. John Stapp, the "World's Fastest Man," rode a rocket sled to 632 miles per hour and then was stopped in 1.6 seconds, experiencing 42Gs of pressure; here operation "Minor Scale," a 4,800-ton conventional explosive simulating the aerial burst of an 8-kt nuclear weapon, produced in 1985 the largest planned nonnuclear explosion in history. White Sands was the imaginary battleground of the American Cold War psyche, with exotic weapons fighting unfought wars. Everywhere there are the ruins and relics of simulations and tests. On one playa rests what Eckles calls the "only landlocked ship in the u.s. Navy," a "desert ship" brought here to practice naval missile launching; in another area of White Sands is the "Large Blast Thermal Simulator," which, as Eckles notes, is the "world's largest shock tube." By transforming liquid nitrogen into a gas, the tube is able to create simulated "blast waves" of up to 1,250 psi. "You can have it flow down the tunnel of the shock tube and strike the item so you get a shock wave similar to the blast of a nuclear explosion," says Eckles. Built in the 1990s, the shock tube is now unused. "There's not much demand for that anymore," he says. The tube, along with the trestle at Kirtland, the wind tunnel at Wright-Patterson Air Force Base, the Vehicular Assembly Building at NASA—and so on—joins the Cold War list of superlative, "world's largest" structures, built not in relation to any human scale, but in proportion to the speed and space requirements of prototype technologies.

The final stop, appropriately, is the place where it all began: Ground Zero. A basalt obelisk marks the precise spot, while a nearby wooden structure covers what is one of the last intact sheets of trinitite, the glassy material that was formed on the desert floor in the heat of the first bomb's explosion. "A lot of people selling trinitite on eBay will advertise it as not radioactive," says Eckles. "Real trinitite *will* emit radiation. It's not hazardous—the only way it would pose any danger is if it were ground up and eaten." We have traveled to the realm of archaeology, the nuclear future entombed beneath the desert floor, the long-since bulldozed crater the ultimate sign of man's intent to make his mark on the desert.

Overleaf: Observation room of 500K Static Test Site today
(Note the remains of moveable mirrors to view rocket tests at an indirect angle.)

Ground Zero, White Sands Missile Range, New Mexico

Naval missile launch simulator, White Sands Missile Range, New Mexico

I am reminded of J. G. Ballard's *The Terminal Beach*, the story of a man marooned on a Bikini Atoll-like atomic test island. "The series of weapons tests had fused the sand in layers, and the pseudo-geological strata condensed the brief epochs, microseconds in duration, of thermonuclear time. Typically the island inverted the geologist's maxim, 'The key to the past lies in the present.' Here, the key to the present lay in the future. This island was a fossil of time future, its bunkers and blockhouses illustrating the principle that the fossil record of life was one of armour and the exoskeleton."[19] At White Sands and the other artifacts of the future found in the American desert, one sees in history a portent of how the future was going to be, and whether the visions were dystopic or Edenic, they summoned society's ultimate faith in technology, as well as the more primitive desire, reawakened by the Cold War, to find strength in the violence and promise of the conquering of yet another frontier.

1.
DEAD CITY:
The Metropolis Targeted

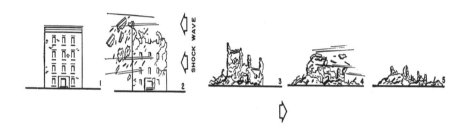

ook out the window the next time you are in an airplane. The comfortingly
legible baseball diamonds and DNA strands of mutating suburban subdivisions
change gradually from discernible units into an abstract grid, transistor buildings
fed by a circuitry of roads. This in turn gives way to a patchwork of varying colors and textures, more like a paint-by-numbers schematic of a landscape than an
actual landscape. This aerial view, at once familiar and otherworldly, has become
as routine as that from a passing car on the Interstate Highway System; yet if
asked to explain its nuances or fathom why it looks as it does, few among us
could reasonably hold forth for very long without digressing into simple ruminations on its scale. It is visual wallpaper, scrolling beneath us like a nineteenth-century panorama, even if eschewed in favor of in-flight videos.

In the history of sight, however, this view is a mere blink. A fantasy haunting the imaginations of artists for centuries, it was not until the balloon travel of
the nineteenth century that the world from the sky was first made visible, as a
sublime incarnation of nature's bounty and man's great works. And it was not
until the twentieth century that the wonder and novelty of the view was transformed into information—to be surveyed, pored over, processed, and stored
away. In the short course of this evolution, as the experience of the aerial view
and the meanings it held changed, so too did another aspect of airborne experience change: the capacity and will to inflict harm from above on those below.

A striking pattern emerged: As the ability to see and record aerial views
became ever more refined, ever more thorough, the altitudes higher and the

Target 103A at the El Centro Naval Auxiliary Air Station, California

horizons ever more distant, so too did the military aspect of the overhead perspective shift. It developed from the primal creation of airborne psychological chaos in the nineteenth century (the mere sight of the balloon was an occasion of terror); to aerial reconnaissance and limited, though spectacular, offensive maneuvers (limited mainly to the battlefield) in World War I; to comprehensive military aerial mapping and full-scale aerial bombing campaigns directed at the "areas" and "marshalling yards" of industrial infrastructure in cities in World War II; to the emergence of cities as targets themselves, with localized strategic objectives replaced by the abstract statistical categories of "megadeath" and "overkill." As the means of comprehending the city as a whole improved, so too did the means for wholly destroying it. It is perhaps no surprise that the ability to visualize the Earth in a single image coincided with the presumed ability to destroy the Earth with one massive unleashing of weapons, or that both accomplishments were byproducts of the same endeavor.

As mastery over the aerial view grew, so too did the presumption that landscapes and cities could be mastered, in two divergent enterprises. In the emerging field of urban planning, aerial imagery supported the assumption that cities and landscapes were scientific units of observation, aggregations of data that could be managed and fed into formulas. In the emerging field of strategic bombing, the same data provided by the aerial view helped transform cities and landscapes from places into targets. The Cold War was where the primacy of the aerial view and the targeting of the everyday environment intersected. The war was experienced almost entirely from an aerial perspective—the crime-scene photos of Cuban missile installations, the surveillance satellites, the overhead map projections of nuclear weapon damage, the airplane views of Bikini Atoll detonations—while there seemed no way more apt than the aerial view to capture the "exploding metropolis" (in demographic as well as strategic terms) as it stretched into new regions. As J. B. Jackson observed, at some point during the Cold War aerial photography went from a "photographic transcription of the eye" to "its own perspective, its own vision."[1] The Cold War was like one massive eye, a new way of looking at the world, including the city. This view has now become so familiar that we need to start from the beginning, to recreate the perspective and possibilities viewed in those first flights.

When the Prussian Prince Pückler-Muskau sailed over the city of Berlin in 1817, he reported being as astounded by the view as the means of ascension itself. Wrote the prince: "No imagination can paint anything more beautiful than the magnificent scene now disclosed to our enraptured senses: the multitude of human beings, the houses, the squares and streets, the high towers gradually diminishing, while the deafening tumult became a gentle murmur, and finally melted into a deathlike silence."[2] The aerial sublime had blossomed into view. In his 1836 tract *Aeronautica*, Thomas Monck Mason noted a similar sensation—a reverence toward some previously unimaginable whole as the familiar topography dwindled, and a simultaneous growth and reduction in the stature of the observer—aboard the *Royal Vauxhall* balloon with aeronaut Charles Green:

> Distances which he used to regard as important, contracted to a span; objects once imposing to him from their dimensions, dwindled into insignificance; localities which he never beheld or expected to behold at one and the same view, standing side by side in friendly juxtaposition; all the most striking productions of art, the most interesting varieties of nature, town and country, sea and land, mountains and plains, mixed up together in the one scene, appear before him as if suddenly called into existence by the magic virtue of some great enchanter's wand.[3]

The views that artists had constructed in their imagination for centuries had been made real, although it was unclear what reality signified in this vast new abstraction. Painters such as George Catlin rushed to document the new landscape in such works as "Topography of Niagara" (1827), but opinion divided as to the exact nature of the new perspective. The influential art critic Philip Gilbert Hamerton opined that "a landscape always presupposes the personal presence of a human observer," and that "views from the summits of lofty mountains or from a balloon may come under the term 'landscape,' but they are hardly landscapes, they are panoramas."[4] A true landscape, he wrote, would become clear were we to descend like the angel Gabriel:

> On a still nearer approach we should see the earth as from a balloon, and the land would seem to hollow itself beneath us like a great round dish, but the hills would be scarcely perceptible. We should still say, "It is not landscape yet." At length, after touching the solid earth, and looking round us, and seeing trees near us, we should say, "This, at last, is *landscape*. It is not the world as the angels may see it from the midst of space, but as men see it who dwell in it, and cultivate it, and love it.[5]

One could scarcely inhabit the air, but its temporary occupation seemed capable of affecting the relationship one felt to the ground. The art critic Robert Hughes, describing the 1889 unveiling of the Eiffel Tower, noted that ordinary Parisians, upon scaling the unprecedentedly vertiginous iron structure, experienced both a *frisson* at the sheer marvel of the view, as well as a more subtle, profound sensation: "As Paris turned its once invisible roofs and the now clear labyrinth of its alleys and streets toward the tourist's eye, becoming a map of itself, a new type of landscape began to seep into popular awareness. It was based on frontality and pattern, rather than on perspective recession and depth."[6]

As the nineteenth century progressed, the tone of the aerial view shifted from sacred reverence toward the sublime to a kind of mastery, which itself spawned two major technological impulses: the desire to photograph the terrain below, and the desire to use the overhead perspective for military advantage—for reconnaissance or bombing. The two strands quickly became interrelated, and thence proceeded at a complementary pace. In 1858, Gaspard Felix Tournachon (known as "Nadar"), sailing 258 feet above the valley of Bièvre, captured a daguerreotype of the Earth below, blurred by the vibrations of the balloon. "We have had bird's-eye views seen by mind's eye imperfectly," he wrote. "Now we will have nothing less than the tracings of nature herself, reflected on the plate."[7] Daguerre himself had propagated a similar view: "The DAGUERREOTYPE is not merely an instrument which serves to draw Nature; on the contrary it is a chemical and physical process which gives her the power to reproduce herself."[8] Nadar and Daguerre's comments betray what was soon to be a prominent current in aesthetic, as well as military, thinking: that photography contained truth, and that one could see things in a photograph that one would not necessarily see with one's own eyes.

A few years after Nadar's pioneering photograph, a Union officer in the American Civil War, Thaddeus S. C. Lowe, flying in the balloon *Intrepid*, employed the emerging science of "photogrammetry" in a flight over Virginia. Photographs depicted, on a single photo plate, the entire landscape between the westerly Richmond and Manchester to the easterly Chickahominy River. A map grid was overlaid on the resulting photographic print, and the aeronautical observer relayed—via telegraph wire strung to the ground— intelligence about Confederate activity to ground commanders, who themselves had a duplicate of the image.[9] With photogrammetry, observers could view the landscape *as it was*, rather than as it appeared in the often fanciful depictions of cartographers, even if photography, it would be shown, was not without its distortions.

Despite its infancy, photography seemed the ideal military science for airborne operations. J. C. G. Hayne, a nineteenth-century Prussian military engineer, predicted the balloon could be used to drop "grenades and other harmful things" on the enemy, who could retaliate by building houses with armored roofs.[10] Indeed, upon inventing the balloon, the French brothers Joseph Michel and Jacques Etienne Montgolfier immediately speculated on its use in warfare—specifically the proposed dropping of 14 tons of aerostatic explosives on the occupied city of Toulon in 1793—and as the Italian aerial warfare prophet Giulio Duohet pointed out in *The Command of the Air*, "long before the age of powered flight, men dreamed of employing aerial craft as weapons of war."[11] In June 1849, plotting an invasion of Venice, the Austrian army turned the dream into reality. An Austrian lieutenant of artillery, Franz Uchatius, had pioneered a "balloon bomb," essentially a floating explosive with a fuse timed to the corresponding air currents and target distance. Unleashing a series of balloons from the paddle steamer *Vulkan*, the Austrians detonated nearly 200 bombs over Venice. The bombing failed to produce the envisaged terror. In the words of one historian, "the Austrian press spoke of its 'frightful effects' and hinted that it would now be easy to reduce the Queen of the Adriatic to a pile of rubble. These reports were obviously quite far from the truth, for almost all the bombs seemed to have dropped harmlessly into the water."[12]

The balloon became a weapon of theoretical terror, whose appearance in the sky portended a more sinister outcome than it could actually deliver. In the 1880s, the British deployed the balloon in South Africa, where "its ascensions had a wonderful psychological effect on native populations."[13] But a military survey in 1886 downplayed the strategic capabilities of the balloon: "At best it could be used against a city under siege, where the charges it hurled down would undermine the morale of the inhabitants, for 'it undoubtedly produces a depressing effect to have things dropped on one from above.'"[14] The more lasting legacy of the balloon was the view it produced, a method for envisioning cities in their entirety rather than destroying them. When George R. Lawrence flew his "captive airship" kites over San Francisco, taking pictures of the scenes of urban destruction below, the images captured were not of a city destroyed by aerial means, but by an earthquake. In those ruins, however, one might divine a prophecy of cities whose destruction, and the visual record of destruction, were to be carried out from above.

A few minutes after noon on August 30, 1914, on the eve of the battle of the Marne, a German Taube Monoplane appeared in the Parisian sky, droning over the Gare de l'Est, and dropped a scattering of explosives at the railway station. A woman killed in that afternoon's bombing would be the first of some 500 Parisian victims of aerial attack, and the "five o'clock Taube" became inscribed in the narrative of urban life, as regular as the church bell, as unceremonious as the arriving Metro. Rather than an unhinged act of terrorism, the bombing was considered a plausible military action, as Paris was seen not as an "open city" but an enormous urban fortification, with even the

Eiffel Tower bristling with machine guns and searchlights. To be urban was now to be subjected to the industrialized instruments of destruction. Great cities had been sacked before, but usually with ample warning—the airplane could appear instantaneously, drop its charge, and depart, an anonymous anarchist bomber of the sky. The airplane was rewriting geography, extending the temporary contours of the battlefield into the tangled streets of the metropolis. There was still nothing comprehensive in the attacks; the technology had advanced little from the Italian aviator Giulio Gavotti's single-handed bombing of the Turkish position at Ain Zara ("Terrorized Turks Scatter Upon Unexpected Aerial Assault," noted one headline) in 1911. In Gavotti's day, aviators wore explosives around their necks. A 1916 German attack on London reads more like a police accident report than a chronicle of urban catastrophe. "[A] series of small explosions gently shook London's busy West End. Unannounced and unheard beyond a few streets, the feeble blasts inflicted some damage between the Brompton Road and Victoria Station. Quite suddenly, as if by lightning, a baker's shop lost its chimney. A stable was wrecked... 'One cobblestone was cracked in Eccleston Mews, opposite no. 23,' noted one meticulous report."[15]

At a 1907 conference in The Hague, article 25 of the Convention on Land Warfare had been changed, with looming air warfare in mind, to read: "It is forbidden to attack or bombard by any means whatsoever, towns, villages, dwellings or buildings that are not defended," a formula that left open the question of what it meant to "defend" a town. While air warfare had been long envisioned, as in Tennyson's 1842 line about "air navies grappling in the central blue" (Tennyson's recourse to a nautical metaphor hints at how alien the concept of aerial warfare actually was), the concept of bombing from above was mostly beyond the purview of military thought, whether in tacit recognition of bombing's chronic inaccuracy or in allegiance to some older code of battlefield ethics. Planes, the thinking went, were at best an ocular extension of the ground forces; one early British pilot declared that "no enemy would risk the odium such action would involve."[16] As the war progressed, however, and the technology improved, one German general observed that "the distinction between combatant and noncombatant began to blur."[17]

To undertake aerial bombing, the various burgeoning air forces first had to comprehend the new battlefield—not of the air, but of the ground below. The plane could fly faster and higher than the balloon, was less likely to be shot down by ground forces, and afforded the aviator greater control over the environment. Aviators seized immediately on the military advantage of flight. Flying a Wright BG model biplane in 1911, Lt. G. E. Keely of the u.s. Army observed that "flying a mile above earth, from which distance it would be easily possible, with proper equipment, to make photos which would betray every detail of the enemy's strength and equipment."[18] The airplane was the all-seeing eye, the camera the incorruptible recorder of truth. "It is fairly easy to hide from visual observation from an airplane if a few precautions are taken," wrote the author of an early treatise on aerial photography. "It is quite another thing to avoid detection on aerial photographs."[19] But what were those military personnel seeing? The bird's eye landscape was not a human landscape. An entire discipline, that of aerial photographic interpretation, needed to be invented. As an early document from the Royal Air Force describes it,

> The widening of the field of aerial operations makes the acquirement of an intimate knowledge of the ground very difficult and, with the object of enabling pilots and observers to know their ground before they see it, the following collection of photographs, illustrating the CHARACTERISTICS and LANDMARKS in the country behind the enemy's lines opposite the British front, has been prepared by the Branch Intelligence Section of the G.H.Q. Wing, R.A.F.[20]

Without clear precedents on how to describe the aerial landscape, the Royal Air Force analysts reached for the terms of art, labeling sections of the French countryside "futurist" or "cubist" country; with regard to the latter, they maintained, "South of Ghent and east of the Escaut the country combines the features of 'crystalline' and 'patchwork quilting' without hedges, but the fields are smaller than those in either of these types."[21] Just as the war on the ground, with its unprecedented scenes of mass carnage and mechanized horror, was reconfiguring the artistic relationship to the landscape, the war from above was inspiring the "aerial suprematism" of artists such as Kasimir Malevich, who "perceived flight's liberation of people from the earthly realm as analogous to his conception of Suprematism's freedom from the material and its representation of spiritual absolutes,"[22] as well as the *aeropittura* of the Italian futurists, for whom the aerial view was a literal representation of Modernity. Bruno Mauri and Alfredo G. Ambrosi fused a totemification of the airplane itself (one work showed an airplane morphed onto a woman's body) or landscapes of aerial impressionism, almost sculptural interpretations of the patchwork below. Wrote Marinetti: "From a plane the flying painter sees the essential features of a landscape flattened, artificial, shifting, as though recently fallen from the sky." The unreality of the aerial view was noted by aviators as well. As Charles Lindbergh would write in the next great conflict, "How can there be writhing, mangled bodies? How can this air around you be filled with unseen projectiles? It is like listening to a radio account of a battle on the other side of the Earth. It is too far away, too separated to hold reality."[23]

As the newly assembled photographic intelligence analysts hovered over the rush of incoming images, the formal guidelines of the discipline were established. In one respect, the truth-telling characteristic of the camera was justified. On snow-covered areas, for example, where the white background highlighted contrasting objects, it was discovered that paths would register as black lines. Peering into the grainy images, analysts discerned palimpsestic etchings on seemingly uninhabited terrain. "Untrenched machine-gun positions are invisible except on large-scale photographs," went one account. "They are detected by the signs of circulation: tracks made by the personnel establishing the position, and the paths used in bringing up ammunition and supplies. Only a small amount of circulation is required to leave evidences visible on a print."[24] Analysts learned to identify objects by context: "For example, a building may appear on a photograph as a small dot, and further identification seem impossible. However, a building is almost never without auxiliary features; if it is a farmhouse there are barns, stables, and the like surrounding it, and from these its true character is determined."[25] Likewise, types of human activity could be discerned from the below; whereas the paths of farmers in a field would be a pattern, deliberately demarcating cultivation areas, the paths of military movements in the same area would be a formless tangle of movement.[26]

Yet the truth of aerial observation was not always assured. The ground below was capable of shifting in appearance, whether from human effort, the angle of flight, or the intensity of light. As an R.A.F. manual described, "A good example of this is shewn on page 59, where ripe corn, which is of a golden colour, appears quite dark on the photograph before harvesting. The explanation is that the field of corn presents an absorbent surface, whence little light returns to the camera to affect the plate. When corn is cut the 'stooks' afford a solid reflecting surface and their high lights, therefore, appear white."[27] A battery of methods for camouflaging the landscape itself—including the city—emerged, ranging from "random disruptive patterns" painted on building roofs (or, in the case of Boeing's Seattle plant, the road grid itself) to the entire movement of a city center, through nets and camouflage painting, in Hamburg. One could not just make something disappear, for its disappearance was often as conspicuous as its absence. On the ground, such camouflaging looked ridiculous—painted patches on the pavement of Moscow's Red Square were "buildings" from the air— but the city as experienced from the aerial perspective was an entirely different creature. In camouflage, some saw a further vindication of the camera's objective eye. In one episode, a British commander covered 500 yards of trenches with "fishnets," to simulate barbed wire. Overhead, a German photographic plane captured images of the terrain. Since it normally took a day for engineers to install that quantity of barbed wire, photographic analysts were not only able to see the sudden blooming of wire below, but to discern that it was false. What the air-man would miss at a quick glance would emerge in the prolonged study of a photographic print his plane had captured; information, like invisible ink, would slowly grow from the static view.

Aerial photographic reconnaissance became professionalized, with the Eastman Kodak company establishing with the army, early in the conflict, a School of Aerial Photography at Cornell University. Bombing itself evolved from a sporadic novelty into a dedicated military program—of all the European capitals, only Rome, historian Michael Sherry notes, was spared from aerial bombing in World War I. Oddly enough, as the quality of aerial information improved—presumably distinguishing military from non-military targets—the discrimination in bombing runs seemed to lessen. As Germany's head of air service said of the first World War, "Our opponents knew as well as we did that in an aerial bomb attack it was not just military targets that would be hit."[28] While the editor of the London periodical *The Aeroplane* had hoped years before that the "London shopkeeper" would "realize that there is a serious chance of proper war being carried into the very heart of this sacred city,"[29] by war's end the city of London had come to view aerial attack as yet another trial of urban life. There was a surreal beauty ascribed to the incoming planes, and as the *Sunday Pictorial* described it, there was a kind of national redemption in the continuation of everyday life: "If the Germans could have only seen the streets of the City they would have been easily convinced that London has not been terrified, for all the streets were simply filled with people at the first sounds of firing and the roofs and windows of upper stories were framed with faces."[30]

The idea of the city, however, perhaps more than the actual condition of the city, was profoundly affected by the aerial bombardments unleashed during the war. The Italian theorist Duohet, whose proposal to bomb cities in World War I had been dismissed by his superiors, described a new geography of battle marked not by trenches or ramparts, but by the horizon: "No longer can areas exist in which life can be lived in safety and tranquility, nor can the battlefield be limited to actual combatants. On the contrary, the battlefield will be limited only by the boundaries of the nations at war, and all of their citizens will become combatants, since all of them will be exposed to the aerial offensives of the enemy."[31] Further limitations on urban aerial attack were drafted, but as one observer noted, "It is doubtful whether such rules for air bombardment as those drawn up by the jurists at the Hague in January-February, 1923, will save the world's great cities."[32] Prime Minister Stanley Baldwin, in a famous House of Commons address in 1932, darkly concluded: "I think it well...for the man in the street to realize there is no power on earth that can protect him from bombing, whatever people may tell him. The

bomber will always get through." The "man in the street," the very personage
of the modern, anonymous crowd, was soon to become a target, incinerated
in an atomic flash, the ghostly afterimage of a corporeal outline etched onto
the sidewalk, like police chalk around a vacant body.

On December 11, 1943, in the wake of British aerial attacks that destroyed more
than 70 percent of the urban area of Berlin, *The New Yorker* wrote: "Nobody
has pointed out that the destruction of Berlin established the fact that it is now
possible to destroy a city and that every city, but for the hairline distinction
between the potential and actual, is afire, its landmarks gone and its population homeless. From where we sit, the flames are clearly visible."[33]

As had been prophesied, total war effectively annihilated the boundaries
of military action. If modern war was waged with machines and material
produced in cities, then how could cities not be considered part of an
enemy's military forces? As in Britain's celebrated campaigns toward the
"wrecking of all housing," the bombing of residential areas was an interrup-
tion of the enemy supply chain, as efficacious as bombing railway lines.
"The cities themselves were the targets," wrote Royal Air Force Commander Arthur Harris. "They were to Germany what ganglia are to a living
body. If enough of them were destroyed, the body would succumb."[34]
Urban density proved an advantage in this respect, as Harris recalled: "The
targets chosen were in congested industrial areas and were carefully picked
so that bombs which overshot or undershot the actual railway centers under
attack should fall on these areas, thereby affecting morale." As in World
War I, as the war progressed the lines between acceptable and unacceptable
targets blurred, and phrases such as "precision bombing" typically entailed
something different in theory than in practice. As Michael Sherry points
out, "After years of bombing cities and the creation of rationalizations and
euphemisms to mask the terror, the distinction between 'military target'
and 'city' had totally collapsed."[35]

What had formerly been, in the target sights of bombers, places such as
Hamburg, Dresden, or Kassel, became dead cities. The reports of damage
recalled, in sheer apocalyptic fury, the millennial conflagrations of Thomas
Cole. "Kassel was a complete wreck," wrote one U.S. Air Force officer. "Until
you have seen one of these ruined cities you cannot really believe what they are
like. In all of the central part of Kassel there did not appear to be a single habitable dwelling or other building. The place is simply a mass of rubble."[36]
Dresden was described as "one great field of ruins," "a city with every street
etched in fire," and as the pilot in a British Lancaster bombing group remembered, "when we came to the target area at the end of the attack it was obvious

that the city was doomed."[37] According to one account of the Hamburg bombing, in which more than 12 square miles of urban land was burned, nearly three hundred thousand dwellings were destroyed, and tens of thousands of residents killed:

> In less than half an hour wide areas became a sea of flames. The houses not initially hit were soon involved by spread from burning adjacent buildings. The rising heat from this terrific concentration of burning buildings created a great draft. The inrushing air reached gale proportions. Sweeping down through the streets, it carried flame, burning timber and sparks to every combustible within the area. The enormous fire developed into a phenomenon known as a "fire storm."[38]

None of this was accidental. Writing in a 1946 book, *Fire and the Air War*, Horatio Bond, head of the National Fire Protection Association, noted, "This is a story about the destruction of cities. I must emphasize that it was not hit-or-miss. The amount of destruction to both cities and industries could be calculated in advance."[39] What was tested in Germany was perfected in Japan. Since the 1920s, Japan's vulnerability to incendiary attack had been noted by such seminal aerial strategists as Billy Mitchell: "These towns are built largely of wood and paper to resist the devastations of earthquakes and form the greatest aerial targets the world has ever seen. Incendiary projectiles would burn the cities to the ground in short order."[40] Beginning on March 9, 1945, Tokyo's stature as an "aerial target" was proven in the single greatest man-made calamity ever, greater even than the subsequent bombing of both Hiroshima and Nagasaki. The epic incendiary attack killed more than 80,000 people, destroyed nearly 16 square miles, and turned the city, as one journalist described it, into "an 'infernum,' like that which Dante...describes in his *Divina commedia*."[41]

The destruction of entire cities had progressed from a distant specter to a rational science. The aerial view was no longer a fleeting glimpse at an enemy, but a clinical crime-scene photograph of an urban corpse. The camera found the targets, and revealed the extent of their destruction. In a 1944 promotional booklet, the Fairchild Camera and Instrument Corporation trumpeted, "A quarter century ago we won a great world war—virtually without the aid of Aerial Photography. Yet in intervening years this new and exact science has become the single most widely-used weapon of military conflict!"[42] As depicted by the brochure, the camera was a kind of invisible exterminating angel. With medical accuracy (a metaphor that tidily overlooked the routine "malpractice" that bombing was actually performing) it

Hamburg fire storm damage, captured in U.S. Strategic Bombing Survey photographs

recorded the surgical removal of cancerous districts within enemy cities: "Equipped with these maps [produced from aerial photographs], our bombers reach the target and erase each specific objective with 'pin-point' bombing. Note that only military objectives have been bombed...adjacent homes untouched..." Another line continues the medical metaphor: "This photographic check-up of Huls after the raid reveals exactly which installations have been hit, the extent of the damage to each, and how much is left for a later attack. Such precision photography leaves nothing to the imagination."

Again, the camera was the perfect mirror of nature, the objective hanging judge of interpretation. Aerial photography did, however, leave plenty to the imagination. In the aerial view, bomb damage in cities was plotted in abstract shading, a statistical census of death and destruction. Allied military forces refused to release photographs of ground-level destruction, and it is only in then-classified documents such as the United States Strategic Bombing Survey's medical branch report on *The Effect of Bombing on Health and Medical Care in Germany* that the grain of the image is blown up, in horrific photos of what Germans called *Brandschrumpfleichen*—or "incendiary bomb-shrunken bodies." Looking like mummified remains found among the ruins of a once great city, the photos revealed the Dead City as it lived its last moment, bodies frozen in motion, reaching for the protective enclosure of architecture: "Every possibility of escaping the 'firestorm' behind rubble or remaining walls or corners was kept in mind. This was evident by the number of corpses found behind these ledges and corners. The same was true in open spaces where many sought safety behind tree stumps and parked cars."[43]

If the city was a corpse, then the forensic pathologist investigating the cause of death was the United States Strategic Bombing Survey. The survey, an empirically minded, social-science refinement of the methods explored in the Air Corps Tactical School and the later Target Information Section, was created in response to the fact that, as one historian puts it, "no system had been devised before the war to select the most vulnerable and productive targets."[44] The survey was, in effect, an urban planner, seeking to understand in a systematic way how a city worked—not to effect its improvement but to hasten its destruction. Aerial photographs of bomb damage were paired with statistical calculations of "mean area of effectiveness." "Industrial directors" were charged with analyzing economic sectors of a city, in order to estimate what loss of productivity could be attributed to bombing. Reading through the survey's reports, which are filled with tabular columns of data, maps, aerial photographs (often superimposed with target circles), and summaries of urban political economy, one is reminded of the documents generated by planners' charettes. In report no. 61, "Fire Raids in German Cities," produced by the survey's "Physical Damage Division," much time is spent discussing the urban character of Hamburg (here labeled "Description of the Target"—meaning the city itself): "The layout of a German city generally follows a set pattern. The 'old town' forms the center and is closely built up with narrow winding streets. The buildings are multi-story with several tiers of attics, strongly framed timber, and have roof ridges at right angles to the street. There is no separation other than a common party wall to prevent spread of fire."[45] The survey proceeded with scientific rigor, as in "Exhibit h-14," which noted that the city of Cologne had been entirely unprepared for the firestorms:

> Possibly due to the years of security from conflagration, which was taken care of in building design and building construction through-out cities and towns in Germany, conflagration experiences were not obtained, nor were they even visualized before the war, so therefore fire fighting techniques along those lines were not considered or developed. It is indicated in the constricted source of water supply from the small-size hydrant outlets and the small-size nozzles carried as equipment on apparatus.[46]

That the survey's methods resembled those of the emerging field of urban planning not only revealed a similarity in how one understood an industrial city and how one understood an industrial war; it also hinted darkly at the interconnectedness of the two enterprises. "It came as a surprise," wrote Martin Pawley, "to find that the link between planning and destruction (which can be traced from Nero's precipitate 'slum clearance' of A.D. 64 to Hausmann's 'strategic' replanning of Paris in the 1860s), became so very clear during the opening years of World War II."[47] Indeed, the smoke had not yet cleared on European cities when Eric L. Bird, editor of the *Journal of the Royal Institute of British Architects*, seemed obliged to note, "There could hardly be a less suitable time than the middle of this war to discuss frankly the relationship between town planning and air attack. Air attack has two dominant factors; the first consists of the potential performances of aircraft and of bombs; the other, of the natures, locations, and densities of target areas—that is to say, of town planning in its widest sense."[48] The bombing runs by Luftwaffe and R.A.F. forces could, in one sense, be seen as acts of "creative destruction," and in the vacant lots and flattened districts that remained blossomed the imaginary (and real) products of postwar reconstruction. *Town and Country Planning*, a survey of the field written in 1941, noted that "while directing relief operations after the bombing of Coventry, the city architect, Mr. D. E. Gibson, yet found time to point out to a friend, indicating this devastated area or that, the site of a new town hall, a new school, a new shopping center."[49]

What both the bombers and the urban planners now possessed was the aerial photograph, which presented a new and startling way of imagining the city in its entirety as a single organism with a network of interdependent

Hamburg fire storm damage, captured in U.S. Strategic Bombing Survey photographs

functions. As a manual for the newly organized "Industrial Camouflage Program" at New York's Pratt Institute put it, "a new element determines our planning —the bird's-eye view. Until now, we designed a factory with ground plan and elevation, but it is no longer unimportant how this looks from the sky."[50] Since the 1920s, the aerial photograph had fascinated town planners, and in the writings of Le Corbusier the bird's-eye view was given it fullest expression; finally freed from the city's iron grid and the myopia of the block-level view—"eyes which do not see," as he said in another context—the architect now had a transcendent means of envisioning the city. In *Aircraft*, he sounded his famous claxon: "The airplane indicts the city." The proof was in the pictures. "By means of the airplane, we now have proof, recorded on the photographic plate, of the rightness of our desire to alter methods of architecture and town-planning." In page after page, the "eagle eye" of the airplane bores into the city below. "The eye now sees in substance what the mind formerly could only subjectively conceive,"[51] wrote Le Corbusier, reaffirming the belief that there was no subjectivity present in the photograph.

Le Corbusier was quite aware of the dangers aerial attack presented to the city; the airplane could be "dove or hawk," he wrote. Indeed, Le Corbusier, citing "the first destructions of the Great War in Flanders in September 1914," had incorporated armored concrete into his own architecture.[52] "*Et la guerre aérienne?*" he had asked with the Ville Radieuse, whose dispersed concrete tower blocks offered a less direct and more resistant target to enemy forces (a French colonel had taken up Le Corbusier's call with a proposal to rehouse Paris in a series of "tower cities"). The old city, wrote Le Corbusier, was a "stifling accumulation of age-long detritus," and in offering his choice of "architecture, or revolution," he charged that "entire cities have to be constructed, or reconstructed, in order to provide a minimum of comfort, for if this is delayed too long, there may be a disturbance in the balance of society."[53]

The polemics of Le Corbusier, however utopian, were chillingly reflected in the war's aerial destruction. His maxim, "the American engineers overwhelm with their calculations our expiring architecture," seemed tragically poignant in the wake of Dresden; his charge that "men—intelligent, cold, and calm—are needed to build the house and to lay out the town"[54] took on a new meaning in the wake of the cold and calm men who "laid out" cities by bomb-sight. The feeling was hardly limited to Le Corbusier; modernism repeatedly foreshadowed the death of the city. Jose Luis Sert, whose 1941 book *Can Our Cities Survive?* originally featured the more ominous (as the war progressed) title *Should Our Cities Survive?*, was enchanted with the aerial view as well—"a perspective which had never before been known"—using it to forecast the obsolescence of the city: "For while man has gained, through the perfection of the airplane, a revolutionary means of abbreviating space and of discovering a new urban and world vision, he has also been confronted by a destructive weapon of greater power than any known heretofore. The very power of this destructive force now demands that the structure of cities be subjected to drastic changes."[55] Lewis Mumford had written, well before the war, that "the city, with its dead buildings, its lifeless masses of stone, becomes a burial ground."[56] Such attacks, as a historian of the Congrés Internationaux d'Architecture Moderne movement points out, "encapsulated the prevailing attitude toward existing cities held by radical architects, planners, and some sections of the public in the 1930s, where the 'dead' body of the traditional city was seen as a frustrating impediment to social change that must be swept away."[57]

The village, to be saved, had to be destroyed. After the war, the aerial view of the bombers was fully transferred to the planners. It had been a long time coming; after all, Maj. Gen. Curtis LeMay, who had presided over the aerial destruction of Japan, had photographed an aerial mosaic as part of a civil engineering degree at Ohio State in the 1930s. In the Fairchild Camera and Instrument Corporation booklet, *Focusing on Victory*, amongst the varied other uses of aerial photography cited was city planning. "Progress photos...showing 'before,' and 'after' this great housing development was completed,"[58] read the caption below a photograph that showed what looked like a park area converted into a teeming maze of buildings of the sort that would eventually be demolished at Pruitt-Igoe. The "before" and "after" seemed eerily reminiscent of the Strategic Bombing Survey's pre-and-post-attack comparison shots. Melville C. Branch, author of *City Planning and Aerial Information* (1971), served in the Navy's Air Combat Intelligence School ("where the author was introduced to aerial information") and would later join the city planning commission of Los Angeles. "Among the millions of air photographs exposed during the Second World War for many military purposes," Branch wrote, "There must be thousands of satisfactory quality and scale which show cities, towns, and small settlements in many countries of the world, including the u.s. Coupled with extensive information collected from other sources for strategic use, there must exist in the files of the armed services a wealth of background material for urban planning research."[59]

The aerial view that had depicted the city as a manageable target was now taken to be a more benign force for fostering greater understanding of the terrain below. "The present age is the first to proceed boldly with wholesale replanning of the centres of old towns," wrote the editor of the 1966 volume *The Uses of Air Photography: Nature and Man in a New Environment*.

Not only are our towns growing in extent, but as congested areas within them fall for "redevelopment," as old buildings reach the

U.S. Strategic Bombing Survey photograph of Nagasaki following detonation of atomic bomb

end of their useful life, or as space becomes available because of changes in ownership, or for other reasons, not to mention the devastation of war. Replanning within the heart of the old town is a difficult exercise because of the many different and often competing interests involved. Here the air photograph involves great advantages over a ground-plan for it enables the whole of a town to be seen and studied comprehensively when . . . the importance of individual buildings not only in themselves but in their setting becomes clear.[60]

Aerial photography was a "strategic" tool for planners, "the only way a municipality can be visually shown or simulated so that city planning decisions can be related as closely as possible to the three-dimensional reality in being."[61] Once again, the omniscient camera had arrived to record the defenseless truth below. In a passage reminiscent of Le Corbusier, E. E. Gutkin, writing in *Our World from the Air* (one of a number of books of aerial views to be published in the 1950s), observed that "an entirely new element is introduced into the building of our cities and the re-shaping of our environment. We have the choice whether the aeroplane of the future shall be the unerring instrument, the incorruptible recorder, of INDICTMENT or FULFILL-MENT." In a more prophetic passage, Gutkind contended that "the discovery of the third dimension, the conquest of the air, has made all national frontiers obsolete, and their defence senseless. Frontiers have been revealed for what they are in reality—historical incidents."[62]

At the very moment it had arrived to present an "image of the city"—a way of exposing what Kevin Lynch called "the hidden forms in the vast sprawl of our cities"[63]—the aerial view had revealed the grim truth that the visualization of a city in its entirety was a visualization of a city that could be destroyed; a city that had become, in the intercontinental range and satellite tracking of the Cold War, a target. The aerial view had, arguably, increased the palatability of urban holocaust—now viewed as a stage of historical evolution—by rendering it not as a human settlement or an organic entity but as a fixed image, an x-rayed set of parameters; so too did the large-scale modernist planning projects of the postwar decades promote a way of living that seemed more palatable from the air (and which took literal form in the airplane-shaped city of Brasilia). As one aerial photographer put it, "air photography... makes almost any pattern look pretty and tidies away the junk-yard."[64] If the modern city needed "legibility," as Lynch wrote, the aerial view provided a comfort—it reduced the expanding metropolis to one tidy agglomeration—as well as concern. Haunting those same aerial photographs were the pond-ripples of atomic destruction: Ground Zero, One Mile, Two Miles.... In either case, events on the ground only seemed to make sense from the air. "If we got nothing else from the space program but the photographic satellite," wrote Dwight D. Eisenhower, "it is worth ten times the money we've spent. Without the satellites, I'd be operating by guess and by God. But I know exactly how many missiles the enemy has."[65] Eyes that could not see were relying on eyes that could not be seen.

2.
SURVIVAL CITY:
This is Only a Test

If one were to require further evidence that the aerial campaigns of World War II were campaigns against the city, against architecture, against housing—"the primordial element of urbanization,"[1] as CIAM, the influential group of modern architects, put it—a worthy exhibit would be found in the vast, unknown expanses of the Dugway Proving Ground, a Rhode Island-sized tract of saltflats and mostly non-arable land southwest of Salt Lake City, which for half a century has served as an environmental test bed for some of the most elaborate and toxic chemical and biological warfare experiments ever undertaken in this country.

The very idea of a "proving ground" is indicative of the shift modern war had taken: Weapons had become so destructive, so unspeakably terrible, that even their speculative deployment required virtual states unto themselves. Dugway, which encompasses more than 800,000 acres, is still an intensely secretive place, a yawning geographical chasm. The day I attempted to visit I was told my intended area of inquiry was located in a region undergoing active testing; as I talked to the guard at Dugway's main gate, a car approached, and its occupant turned out to be a lone, rather confused French tourist who pointed repeatedly at a silver-dollar-sized chunk of *Rand McNally* that read, simply, "Missile Range." The map's white space showed no roads, and I was not sure how the traveler had intended to get to his destination, or what he expected to find once he got there—he seemed propelled by the sheer absence of it all.

The replica bombing village German Town today, Dugway Proving Ground, Toelle, Utah

In March 1943, with bombing attacks on cities being intensified by all sides, the U.S. Army Corps of Engineers began construction at Dugway on a series of "enemy villages," detailed reproductions of the typical housing found in the industrial districts of cities in Germany and Japan. The purpose of these "test villages" was to determine the effectiveness of a variety of incendiary bombs then under development by the National Defense Research Committee (NDRC). The NDRC's most significant contractor was Standard Oil, which had underwritten a series of previous tests in other locations on generic architectural structures. But since these tests had "served only to establish a relative order of effectiveness of the bombs,"[2] it was decided it was necessary "to conduct mortar tests on target buildings that would be exact reproductions of German houses."[3]

To help achieve this rather strange feat of building several blocks of German and Japanese housing in a barren stretch of Utah desert, Standard Oil and the NDRC turned to a number of architects, among them the noted expatriate German architects Erich Mendelsohn and Konrad Wachsman, as well as the Czechoslovakian architect Antonin Raymond, an expert in Japanese construction. Identified as "consultants," the architects provided a survey of leading industrial cities (to "provide reliable data regarding the roof area coverage of German types of buildings") and made recommendations on building materials. As an NDRC report notes, "no trouble or expense was spared in making all details of these dwellings correspond with authentic Japanese practice"[4] (the same could be said for the German structures).

As they constructed, they deconstructed, analyzing the component parts of the houses, looking for weak points even as they created ostensible shelters. The German structures were mostly brick and plaster, divided between the "slate-on-sheathing" roofs of the Rhineland and the "tile-on-batten" roofs of Central Germany. Coastal douglas fir and loblobby pine were deemed adequate substitutes for the scotch pine and European spruce used in Germany, steam radiators were used to bring the "moisture content" into line with its German counterparts, and the average "ignition time" of each structure was carefully calibrated. In the German buildings, it was noted that "unlike Japanese or American construction, the typical German structure utilizes little wood as framework or trim below the attic . . . for this reason a thorough study of typical furnishings was made so that proper fire severity would be reproduced in the floors beneath the attic."[5] In other words, if a bomb penetrated the attic, the furniture was the last best hope of starting a fire. Two members of the "Authenticity Division" of RKO Studios, who had created a version of Germany in its 1943 blockbuster *Hitler's Children*, were hired to help design custom pieces. Carefully plotted maps revealed "vulnerable zones" amongst the arrangements of beds, hi-boys, and the "simulated chaise lounge."

Against these archetypal houses, the military refined the design of incen-diary weapons such as the AN-M50 and the AN-M69, the latter a seminal form of napalm developed at Harvard University. Where the phosphorous-based AN-50 would simply ignite wherever it landed, the AN-M69 featured the more ingenious design innovation of landing on its side and then ejecting a stream

Photo 9 - Partial burn-out of row house construction. Note separating unparapetted fire walls.

Photo 10 (right) - Undamaged row house construction with fire walls below roof line.

Damage to German row housing, captured in U.S. Strategic Bombing Survey photographs of napalm—presumably, the theory went, in the wooden eaves of an attic. The bombs were tested as to their effectiveness *against architecture:* How well the bombs penetrated the roofs of buildings (without penetrating too far), where they lodged in the building, and the intensity of the resulting fire. While the Achilles' heel of German architecture was the attic, in Japanese structures it was the floor. As a Standard Oil report pointed out, "the tatami floor mats are the most important item of Japanese furnishing since they greatly influence bomb penetration as well as the inflammability of the test structure. The tatami used at Dugway are either originals made in Japan from the hard-packed rice straw or imitation mats manufactured from thistle which have been shown by test to approach the original mats in both bomb penetration and inflammability."[6]

While the United States had carefully distanced itself from the R.A.F.'s policy of bombing the housing of industrial workers, the overwhelmingly domestic emphasis of the structures created at Dugway reveals that restraint to clearly have been on the wane, at least in the minds of planners. The test village reports contain photos of a "typical dining room arrangement," complete with an overstuffed sofa in German dwellings; or, in the Japanese structures, the *tansu, futon,* and *zabuton.* The distinction was always drawn that these interiors housed workers, and were thus part of the enemy war effort, but looking at these photos, such distinctions seem to disappear. These are photographs of homes, and in the meticulous studies undertaken at Dugway, the intricacies and characteristics of their construction were used not simply to increase their efficacy as a target, but as a weapon. As the fire engineer Horatio Bond pointed out just after the war, "If one needs to be reminded that civilians were the real sufferers, he need only recall that the number of Japanese civilian casualties in the Japanese Homeland, inflicted entirely by your air force during a 6-month period, was nearly twice the Japanese military casualties inflicted by our combined Army, Navy, Air Force, and Marines during a 45-month period."[7]

And what of the architects, who had seemingly reversed their role as providers of shelter? For Mendelsohn and Wachsman, Jewish exiles of Nazi Germany who had joined Walter Gropius at Harvard and were perhaps among the first architects ever hired as consultants to the War Department, architecture provided a way—a way they might not have even imagined—of ending Hitler's reign. For Mendelsohn, who had been expelled from the "newly aryanized" Union of German Architects[8] and whose Jewish Youth Center in Essen, Germany had been burned in the 1938 *Kristallnacht*, the destruction of "traditional" German architecture—keeping in mind what the notion of "tradition" as postulated by the Nazis meant for Jewish citizens of Germany—must have been freighted with cultural and moral meaning. One wonders, too, if Mendelsohn as a modernist (albeit not a doctrinaire one) might have seen in the destruction of these densely compacted vernacular houses—the dead past "melted into air"—an opening for the building site of a better tomorrow, a resurgence of the vision that had animated the early German modernists, whose practitioners, as Kathleen James writes, "believed that a new style would rise out of a cauldron of pragmatism and symbolic effectiveness and give concrete form to a better world."[9] Mendelsohn's archives contain no direct reference by him to the Dugway project (his wife cautions his biographer, "I would not like to have any details mentioned in the book, as it was the most secret work he did"), but they do contain some glimmers of his mood, as in this 1941 letter: "Outside the concentration camps, away from the actual battle-field, the crowds are gathering, and will, finally, strike dead the past and all who ride with it."[10] As Mendelsohn's own buildings, along with the typical worker housing of Germany, went up in the flames of Allied bombers (and Nazi terror), the present seemed to offer that chance for the radical break from the "expiring architecture" of the past, in a country that had not been bombed. As architectural historian William Curtis writes, "with the dousing of the modern movement in Europe in the 1930s, it seemed as if the liberal generosity of America was allowing a flame to keep burning which might otherwise have gone out."[11] The psychic ground had been cleared. A new, unforgettable fire, however, was on the horizon, no mere destroyer of architecture, but of worlds.

If one could not write poetry after Auschwitz, as Theodor Adorno postulated, then after Hiroshima, one could no longer speak of cities. The u.s. Air Force bombing raids of Tokyo had exacted a higher cost in lives and property— "City's Heart Gone," the *New York Times* had gravely recorded—than the dual atomic Armageddon; but whereas the incendiary raids had seemed the logical, industrialized conclusion to a process that could be comprehended in terms of familiar urban devastation (indeed, fire, as in Chicago, had essentially created the modern city), the forces unleashed at Hiroshima by a "device" whose creators seemed reluctant to even call a bomb awakened a primal dread, a collective terror of death for all those who lived in areas of strategic density. General Henry "Hap" Arnold had argued that "three or four cities must be saved intact from the b-29s' regular operations as unspoiled targets for the new weapon"[12]; as Hiroshima and Nagasaki were made "model cities" of urban destruction, as the ashes of the city trembled in the wake of the *Enola Gay*, the realization dawned that no more could any city be "saved intact."

Exhuming the remains of the city, the u.s. Strategic Bombing Survey— which had since tried to distance itself from the policy of bombing population centers—divined this inchoate sense of doom. "The Survey's investigators, as they proceeded about their study, found an insistent question framing itself in their minds: 'What if the target for the bomb had been an American City?'" That the survey had seldom, if ever, felt compelled to ask such a question as it pored over the ruins of Germany spoke to the sheer psychic effect of the magnitude of the new weapon. "The casualty rates at Hiroshima and Nagasaki," they wrote, "applied to the massed inhabitants of Manhattan, Brooklyn, and the Bronx, yield a grim conclusion."[13]

In one stroke, the concept of what it meant to live in a city, the parameters of security and the contours of daily life, had been fundamentally reordered. Over every city hovered the ghostly afterimage of Dead City. As *Time* reported, "The U.S. thought about its dilemma on various levels. Some architects in Boston conjured up a design for a circular house (flat surfaces are vulnerable to shock waves), built of concrete, with double-thick windows and stainless steel doors. Washington realtors advertised houses and lots 'beyond the radiation zone.' Worried people in Atlanta inquired about insurance policies against atomic bomb damage."[14] As one participant of an M.I.T. symposium on "Building in the Atomic Age" described the new condition, "At one time, protection of cities meant protection against warring neighbors, and the most prominent features of city design were walls and moats. As time went on, protection of cities came to mean civilian police forces, fire brigades, health departments, and building codes. With the atomic bomb substantially cheaper than the airplane which delivers it, we are now completing the circle... City designs once more may have to reflect a real risk of military attack."[15]

For Lewis Mumford, war was one of the city's "lethal genes," dominant in one epoch, repressed in the next. Conflict was inscribed in its very structure:

> Both the physical form and the institutional life of the city, from the very beginning of the urban implosion, were shaped in no small measure by the irrational and magical purposes of war. From this source sprang the elaborate system of fortifications, with walls, ramparts, towers, canals... The physical structure of the city, in turn, perpetuated the animus, the isolation and self-assertion, that favored the new institution.[16]

If the walls of the city were no longer visible, for Mumford they had been erected on a grand scale in the Iron Curtain. The city, with its material and cultural riches, had been for Mumford "a visible object" for "collective aggression." Now Hiroshima was to be destroyed, to prove it *could* be destroyed— for what could a demonstration of war power mean if conducted outside of the city? It had been suggested the bomb could be detonated near the city, to prove its lethal potential; but outside the city, outside of civilization, the bomb might have been comprehended as a force of nature—there is, after all, a terrible beauty in the photographs of desert and atoll atomic testing—rather than of man. In the new, yet ancient, formulation, the city—as a form, as an institution, as a way of life—was the target. As one civil defense official warned a group of urban planners, "the concentrated form of our big cities not only fails to offer any security against enemy attack; it actually invites it, and places the lives and property of the citizens in jeopardy."[17]

The very thing that defined the city—the concentration of population— was now viewed as its greatest liability. In Strategic Air Command doctrine, the destruction of cities was now a "primary undertaking," while military targets were an "alternative undertaking."[18] The theorist Herman Kahn wrote in 1964 that "during the last few years some New Yorkers have exhibited an attitude which might be called a 'prime-target-fixation syndrome.' This is an expression of apathy or fatalism often found among those who believe that their city or location would constitute a prime target in the event of nuclear attack."[19] Now that the city was a target, was there a fatalism in the glass curtain wall, the transparent facade that was the signature of modern architecture? The modernist "man in the street" now worried about "the blinding flash of a terrible light brighter than a hundred suns," as *Time* put it, and every new building that went up was as much a reason for celebration as caution; the Massachusetts Mutual Life Building's completion on Fifth Avenue occasioned, in one magazine, a range of comments: A magazine editor noted that "people live happily on the sides of volcanoes"; another interviewee saw the building as a sign of peace, while still another said "a thousand buildings wouldn't be assurance to me."[20]

With its Freudian undertones, Kahn's "syndrome" seemed another reconfiguring of the various spatial anxieties that have haunted the city through history. Architectural theorist Anthony Vidler, describing the various late-nineteenth-century theories of "degeneration" and "estrangement," as well as such novel urban maladies as "agoraphobia" (and its symbiotic twin, "claustrophobia,") notes that for such theorists as Camillo Sitte, Freud, and the Berlin psychologist Carl Otto Westphal, "of special interest was the *space* of the new city, which was now subjected to scrutiny as a possible cause of an increasingly identified psychological alienation—the Vienna circle was to call it 'derealization'—of the metropolitan individual, and, further, as an instrument favoring the potentially dangerous behavior of the crowd."[21] Against the crowded dystopias ("the street wears us out...it disgusts us," wrote Le Corbusier[22]), which it saw as the generator of such conditions, the nascent modernist movement had postulated new solutions that, as Vidler notes, were "dependent on the erasure of the old city in its entirety."

   The threat of atomic attack seemed to provide that opening, as architects, planners, and civil defense officials rallied around the banner of "dispersal." Inheriting the banner of theorists like Le Corbusier and Sert, as well as the Garden Cities of planner Ebenezer Howard, the postwar planners argued that the only effective defense against an atomic attack was to rechannel urban development into a series of "linear" or "ribbon" cities that would, as one planner put it, "produce a dispersed pattern of small efficient cities much more attuned to the needs of modern living, modern commerce, and modern industry and far less inviting as potential targets."[23] Dispersal as defense mechanism was a fringe idea during World War II, but, reporting from the ruins of Hiroshima and Nagasaki, the Strategic Bombing Survey articulated what would become a mainstream concern: "Though a reshaping and partial dispersal of the national centers of activity are drastic and difficult measures, they represent a social and military ideal toward which very practical steps can be taken once the policy has been laid down."[24]

   The city, in the eyes of officials such as Tracy B. Augur, urban planning officer for the government's General Services Administration, was "obsolete" and "economically unsound and dangerous."[25] "Some cities," Augur wrote, "seem to feel they don't rate unless they contain at least one good A-bomb target."[26] The Commissioner of the Department of City Planning for New York City, Goodhue Livingston Jr., argued that "the building of new towns and the proper planning toward increasing moderately the size of smaller ones will serve the dual purpose of giving us immunity from atomic warfare as well as creating a better, richer, fuller life for all."[27] Town planner Clarence Stein, author of *Toward New Towns for America*, declared that "dispersal of industries and workers into limited-sized, low-density communities, surrounded by open country, is the only realistic protection against atomic attack."[28] *U.S. News and World Report* touted "fringe cities" as a counter to the bomb, noting that in New York City, where a million families would be added in the next several decades, "plans are already being made to guide the growth of these centers, so that they will conform with the needs of atomic defense."[29] "Net result of Russia's getting the atomic bomb," the magazine predicted, "is likely to be a gradual change in the pattern of city and country within the United States." Horatio Bond, of the National Fire Protection Association, went so far as to suggest that "it will be proper for our military establishments to veto further concentrations of urban centers. No more skyscrapers. No more concentrated housing projects. If slums are cleared, leave them clear. Build new buildings in such a way as to keep down the concentration of people. By these measures we may get more comfortable cities, not to mention badly needed parking spaces between buildings."[30]

In space was seen defense. Cities were targets; suburban dispersal represented safety. In planning exercises such as Columbia University's "Project East River," the theories of utopian town planning were intertwined with military contingency, and this development pattern was made clear: "[Project East River] has estimated that population densities averaging less than 8,000 persons per gross square mile—typical suburban developments of single family homes on moderate sized lots—do not offer high enough yield in death and destruction to attract enemy attack, and, with proper construction and spacing of buildings, will not provide the fuel for conflagrations or fire storms."[31] In some ways, none of this was new; dispersal as "non-military defense" simply augmented the sense among modernist city planners that the old city was congested, inefficient, and outmoded. "This municipal congestion already hurts productivity, and so causes us losses even *before* the first bomb has been dropped," noted one professor of city planning.[32] Planners adopted a Cold War style in their approach to the city; M.I.T.'s Norbert Wiener, the "father of cybernetics," whose theories helped develop the guidance mechanisms of atomic weapons, championed a defense plan that posited the city as a "communications system," whose efficiency lay in decentralization and rigorous planning. Cybernetics itself gained currency in city planning; as Peter Hall writes, "cities and regions were viewed as complex systems—they were, indeed, only a particular spatially based subset of a whole general class of systems, while planning was seen as a continual process of control and monitoring of these systems, derived from the then new science of cybernetics developed by Norbert Wiener."[33]

The Cold War's command-and-control mechanisms were seen as equally beneficial to cities as they were to defense systems. This is exemplified in a General Electric ad that appeared in *Fortune* in November 1961, opposite an article entitled "The Economy Can Survive Nuclear Attack." The ad is for the "GE 225" computer, which utilized something called "Critical Path Method" processing capability. What is striking about the ad, with its pictures of punch cards and flow charts, is the list of applications at the top of the page, which ranges from "highway construction" to "slum clearance" to "nuclear power projects" to "missile production." That these quite divergent enterprises should be lumped together is a telling indication of the mentality of an age in which any number of civic functions, from town planning to military defense, were being run via push-button. In his essay "Invisible City," the Japanese architect Arata Isozaki elaborated on this tendency in discussing the evolution of computer modeling in urban planning: "In the process of expressing these ideas in models and manipulating them so that they overlap with the real city, the designer acts as a pilot and must not be swayed by his own preconceived concepts, since he is dealing with constant mutual response between reality and hypothesis. His city designing resembles push-button warfare."[34] With the flick of a switch one could hypothetically wipe out blocks of slums, or far-off missile installations—it was all data, all systems. Again, it was Mumford who raised the most poignant objection: "To suppose that the abstract intelligence that proved so brilliant in developing nuclear reactors and supersonic planes will be equally successful in finding technological solutions that could be applied wholesale to the rebuilding of our cities is to misconceive the nature of the whole problem," he wrote in *The Urban Prospect*.[35] Both solutions were hopelessly locked in the closed-loop feedback system of what Mumford liked to call "the Machine."

Once the death of the city was assumed, survival was seen in the suburbs. Civil defense films depicting an atomic attack were invariably set in some small town or suburban setting, the housewife hearing about the bomb that had hit "the city," wondering if her husband were among the survivors. The pattern itself was viewed by one planner as an architectural fortification: "The walls of the modern city are to be found in a satellite dispersal pattern."[36] "Dispersal is good business," wrote Augur, arguing that "another indication of the economy of new construction is found in the increasing number of modern, well-planned suburban shopping centers that are being built to replace congested downtown facilities."[37] Not surprisingly, the shopping center, which was to become the surrogate "public space" in the new suburban formations, was also touted for its possibilities as a fallout shelter; studies by shopping center developer Victor Gruen for Detroit merchant J. L. Hudson depict four "huge regional shopping centers" dispersed in an arc around the city (the Office of Civil Defense would later sponsor a competition for model applications of fallout shelters in shopping centers).

In the planners' utopian schemes ran an undercurrent of violence, of "creative destruction." Non-military defense was a vehicle by which all other sorts of enormous schemes might be carried out, central among them the key missions of postwar planning, highway building, and "urban redevelopment." While Lewis Mumford said the effect of building highways through cities might be more ruinous than an atomic explosion, the civil defense planners were more optimistic. "Such a system of express highways cut through the built-up mass of our great cities will greatly increase our present slum-clearance and relocation programs," wrote one planner, citing the great costs of "housing those in the expressway rights-of-way, plus the housing of incoming defense workers."[38] Shopping center pioneer Gruen, in a telling comment, declared: "As we proceed with these various plans for many cities of the nation, it seems to us that here might be a weapon for a successful counterattack in the technological blitzkrieg. If we use the weapon and we can create large numbers of these clusterlike centers, we will be able to raze the tenantless strips of shanty towns along our roads and when the rubble is cleared away, we will plant trees and shrubs and grass and flowers where the suburban slums stood."[39]

With the atomic bomb came a new reason to distrust the city, and one senses in the myriad accounts of bomb destruction (e.g., "What Would Happen to Philadelphia?") a speculative wish fulfillment of a chance to start over, from ground zero, with a new city. The planners' prognosis of what would happen to the city in the event of atomic attack reflected their own visions of "urban redevelopment." Vincent Scully characterized them thus: "Cataclysmic, automotive, and suburban: these have been the pervasive characteristics of Urban Redevelopment in America ... [These redevelopment projects] derive, as we have already noted, from the same kind of combination of Le Corbusier's Ville Radieuse with Howard's Garden City which marked Wright's Broadacre City. As such, they are exactly in accord with the most persistent American myths and desires: the city is *bad*; tear it down, get on the road, be a pioneer, live in Greenwich like a white man."[40] On the road one would find survival, as promised in the Federal Civil Defense Administration's (FCDA's) pamphlet "Four Wheels to Survival," which noted that "your car can be your shopping center," and even that "the car provides a small, movable house. You can get away in it—then live, eat, and sleep in it in almost any climatic conditions, if necessary, until a civil defense emergency is ended."[41] The recurring accounts of urban destruction, and the promises of a better life in the great satellite-dispersed beyond, were on a continuum with the fantastic tales of urban destruction prophesied in science fiction, from H. G. Wells' *The War in the Air* (as Wells writes of New York, the "splendidest" and "wickedest" city: "men likened her to the apocalyptic cities of the ancient prophets"[42]) to the post-nuclear-attack bestseller *Alas, Babylon*, which saw in a small Florida town the chance "to build a new and better world on the ruins of the old."[43] In *Five*, a film about an atomic blast, a character declares, "I hated New York. I'm glad it's dead."[44] In *The Rest Must Die* (1959), the survivors of a nuclear explosion battle against each other for survival in New York's subway tunnels, and salvation is at hand only when they have escaped the city—airlifted to safety at a military facility in Virginia.

Since the various calls for dispersal and decentralization never took the form of any actual legislation, it is difficult to locate the influence of the atomic bomb in the suburban drift. In the case of the plans for dispersal of Washington, D.C., put forward by planners Augur and Clarence Stein (a fellow member of the Regional Development Council of America, or RDCA) in the 1950s, however, there is a suggestive relationship between the military threat of the Cold War and the eventual form of the city. In 1949, Augur was hired as urban planner by the National Security Resources Board to help formulate a plan that would "assure the continuous operation of Federal Government activities in time of emergency by providing maximum security through adequate dispersion."[45] Augur's plan called for the relocation of federal employment centers beyond a 20-mile arc from the White House, with a "new express highway serving the dispersed offices," as well as an underground "alternate seat of government" that would protect some 5,000 key personnel.[46] Because this plan would only protect employees at their offices, and not in their homes during a surprise atomic attack, the discussion was expanded to a wider concept of "new towns," as championed by RDCA members such as Stein and Lewis Mumford. The eventual plan, which featured a "related location of the living places and the work," was rejected by Congress. As historian Kermit Parsons later noted, however, "we find (almost forty years later) in the Washington region part of Augur's proposed pattern of Federal Government employment centers and new towns located more or less in the arc, northwest of Washington, where the 1950 plans' principal authors indicated they should be,"[47] while new towns such as Reston and Columbia were near centers of government employment.

Dispersal was not the only response to the nuclear threat; a concurrent strand of thinking was to fortify the everyday environment. In the damage photos of Hiroshima and Nagasaki, which used the aerial perspective to both heighten the enormity of the damage and lessen the perception of actual human impact, there seemed to be a story in the shadowy shells of concrete buildings that stood out among the prairie-like flatness of the demolished city. As the survey noted: "Men arriving at Hiroshima and Nagasaki have been constantly impressed by the shells of reinforced concrete buildings still rising above the rubble of brick and stone or the ashes of wooden buildings. They show... that it is possible without excessive expense to erect buildings which will satisfactorily protect their contents at distances of about 2,000 feet or more from a bomb of the types so far employed." The members of the survey already had on their mind, and their agenda, the future of the city in an age of the bomb; the Urban Areas Division had listed, on a June 1947 report, one of its purposes as, "To provide information to the United States Government in connection with possible future offensive use or defensive protection."[48]

Was there, in the concrete shells of Hiroshima and Nagasaki, the groundwork of a future society? War had killed the historic city and its architecture, but was there something in the materials and form of the new architecture that promised shelter in an atomic age? On a desert playa in Nevada some hours from the remains of the "target villages" of the Dugway Proving Ground, a new American village was being erected. If the villages at Dugway had been created as an offensive weapon to expose the weakness of the enemy, the village at the Nevada Proving Ground was being erected as a defensive weapon to demonstrate the strength at home. With the ruins of the Dead City still visible, a new "Survival City," as it was called, arose in the wilderness, the latest city on the hill, shining in the artificial sun.

To get to Survival City, I climb in a white Jeep Cherokee in the parking lot of the Department of Energy's (DOE's) offices in north Las Vegas. Riding with the DOE's LaTomya Glass and Bill Johnson, an archaeologist with the University of Nevada's Desert Research Institute, I drive north on highway I-15 out of the arid haze of the city, past the motel from whose window I have been listening to military jets from Nellis Air Force Base sear the late afternoon sky. Leaving the road at the "Mercury" exit, which bears the two most sinister words of desert travel, "No Services," we quickly arrive at the front gate of the Nevada Test Site (NTS). A sign dubs it an "Environmental Research Park," a tag that is accurate in the sense that the research being conducted generally involves letting all manner of toxic substances loose on the desert floor, and then seeing what is left of the environment. Approaching the gate, the first thing one sees at the NTS is, off to the left, a series of small pens, each containing, in the very center, a Port-o-San. Glass tells me the pens are used to house protesters, but what strikes me is the absurdity of these precisely circumscribed enclosures, each the size of a small backyard in the city, cordoned off in the middle of thousands of acres of endless vista.

The test site is a 1,350-square-mile landscape of fear, created by federal edict in 1950 when the conflict in Korea was seen as having engendered the "national emergency" that Atomic Energy Commissioner Gordon Dean had said required implementation of domestic nuclear atmospheric testing. A range of sites was considered, from Utah to the coastal Carolinas. This region, too, had its history, its original inhabitants, its bones and graves, but all that would vanish behind a cloak of secrecy. "What was once 650 square miles of Nevada's most useless desert wasteland," one newspaper declared, "today ranks among the most important areas within the confines of the United States, based on the viewpoint of national security."[49] Over the succeeding years, the nation's eyes would turn here, first to see the technicolor plumes of atomic tests from the predawn rooftops of casinos, then to see the epochal, Zapruder-like frames of images played out in a sequence that would reside forever in the American subconscious: the wood-frame house, first illuminated by the flash of the bomb, captured in an otherworldly light by armored camera, standing like a frontier house on a dark moonscape; then curls of black smoke creeping up the charring wood of the facade; then a brief clearing, the smoke gone, the damage visible, a momentary respite; and then the blast wave striking, the front buckling in, pieces of the roof peeling off; then the front disintegrating and the roof torn back; then the entire mass swirling in a torrent of splinters. "Down it goes...in 2 1/3 seconds!" marveled the FCDA.

Our first stop is Mercury, the town that at its fevered peak hosted some 10,000 inhabitants, making it briefly one of Nevada's largest cities—even bigger, in terms of actual residents, than the green-felt jungle to the south. Standing at the corner of the Mercury Highway and Buster-Jangle Road (Mercury is the only town in America where streets are named after atomic tests, or "shots," as they are called here), the place is dusty, hot, and still, as if it were another of Nevada's myriad ghost towns. In fact, one ghost town did exist among the bomb-scarred environs of the current test site: Wahmonie, a town that sprung into being after a 1928 silver strike. Some 1,500 people arrived, bringing the attendant shops and saloons, but within a year the town was gone. In Mercury, one half-expects to come across a marker announcing the details of the industry that occasioned its rise.

Mercury, however, is not entirely shuttered. Some 2,000 workers still call Mercury home, if only for the day. They eat tater tots in the cafeteria, a pristinely preserved den of 1960s institutional modernism, with color-chart fiberglass chairs and Formica tables, cork-lined walls, elliptical pendent lamps hanging with symmetric precision—a place bristling with the domestic promise of the space age. They can also buy condoms in a vending machine, or, from a neighboring machine, "Fernando's chicken chimichangas," dispensed from below a sign on which someone has superimposed the word "Nukeables" over a billowing and bright mushroom cloud (a photo taken, rather curiously, from the South Pacific rather than right down the block). A nearby sign warns, "Others are interested in your work." But the vast majority of Mercury is empty; street after street of low-slung cinder-block buildings, painted desert pastel with air-conditioning machinery lurking atop their flat roofs, evenly spaced aluminum lettering in a Futura-like font announcing some long-ago function. I have taken to calling such architecture "military moderne": buildings that are functional, flexible, and devoid of any ostensible martial purpose, erected in the great rush of the missile gap and then left to sit in the sun.

After obtaining our security badges, we proceed down Mercury Highway, past signs that read "Drive Carefully...Preserve Wildlife" (this in a place where penned animals were routinely subjected to weapons effects), and after crossing the first ridge of mountains that obscures the bulk of the test site from I-15 to the West, we come upon the broad playa of Frenchman's Flat, a shimmering field of white in the 105-degree August heat. We pull off the highway and onto the flat, parking amidst a strange scattering of concrete blocks, half-buried bunkers, junked automobiles, and scraps of metal.

Bailey Bridge, Nevada Test Site

Ruins at Frenchman's Flat, Nevada Test Site

Frenchman's Flat, or "Area 5," as it is labeled by the NTS, is the half-buried nightmare face of the fifties, a once-secret showcase of a dismal science. If the World Expo in Brussels in 1954 presented a vision of progress in nuclear energy (i.e., the "Atomium"), Frenchman's Flat was an alternative kind of World Exposition, a concrete-and-steel "White City" of the atomic age, a place where architecture and engineering and the new wonder materials came to be tested against the overpressures and drag coefficients and blast forces of a nuclear detonation, mere objects in an outdoor wind tunnel. As Johnson puts it, the flat was "one of the hottest battlegrounds of the Cold War," a place where hypothetical war was waged against the environment of everyday life.

There is a parking garage buried in the middle of the flat, now shuttered but once an engineer's dream of a perfect dual-purpose building. There is the "motel," which is actually not a motel but has been called so since the 1950s for its resemblance to a drive-up motor court. There are the pillars that once supported "Bailey Bridge," but instead of a bridge there are only the arched beams warped by blast (so uniformly distorted they seem built that way) and the tangled rebar that juts into the noonday sun, like industrial reeds frozen in the atomic wind. Concrete domes, some crumbling, some intact, dot the desert floor, and what look like flattened tires are actually the crushed remnants of aluminum domes. It is a place whose strangeness was obvious from the beginning—as the narrator of the FCDA's 1950 film *Let's Face It* says in a report from the flat, "it's a weird, fantastic city, a creation right out of science fiction. A city like no other on the face of the Earth. Homes, neat and clean and completely furnished, that will never be occupied. Bridges, massive girders of steel spanning the desert. Railway tracks that lead to nowhere, for this is the end of the line."

Armed with reinforced concrete and more recent materials such as aluminum, the official medium of the jet age—the sleek skin of supersonic fighters—engineers and architects, aided by such agencies as the Terminal Ballistic Laboratory of Maryland's Aberdeen Proving Ground and the Federal Civil Defense Agency, came to the flat to put forward their best theories against the leveling force of a thermonuclear explosion. It was a science with few precedents, save for the cities that had already been bombed. "Since the blast forces vary rapidly with time, and since buildings subjected to blast forces will respond dynamically," noted a professor of structural engineering at M.I.T., "this type of analysis is new to most engineers and architects."[50] On the new frontier of "radiological defense" and "atomic defense engineering," nothing was as it immediately seemed. "Even on the simplest structure, a rectangular box with no openings and whose walls and roof do not fail, there is some uncertainty at present as to the force-time relationship due to a known blast loading," said a Massachusetts civil engineer. "All told, very great uncertainties exist when one attempts to predict the loads that act on ordinary structures."[51] The shock wave created by an atomic blast, a swirling mix of pressures, particle velocities, and drag forces, was as complex a creature as the weapon itself. "In the first place, there is nothing intuitively obvious about a shock wave for it represents one of the rare events in nature, namely an approach to a true discontinuity of conditions," declared the head of Aberdeen's ballistic laboratory, adding that previous hydrodynamicists had doubted that such a thing existed. He added: "No instrumentation exists today which will resolve the rise time of a shock wave, so that for all practical purposes, it is instantaneous."[52]

The sheer mystery of blast effects no doubt explains the vast range of structures found at the flat, as well as their almost elemental quality: concrete cubes, sets of parallel walls, earthern-bermed bunkers, all lined with oscilloscopes and other instruments. In the smashed remains, the assembled witnesses hoped to find the blueprints of atomic defense: "Structurally, the high-pressure dome failed, as expected, providing us through the many instrument records a history of its brief life (a few thousandths of a second) and character of failure when severely overloaded."[53] In tests labeled "Effects of a Non-Ideal Shock Wave on Blast Loading" and "Evaluation of Nuclear Effects on AEC Test Structures," analysts probed the wreckage, speaking of "the air blast-induced environment within civil defense structures" or "the propagation of blast waves into chambers." The navy tested a "corrugated metal arch structure," with 8-gauge steel with "supply and exhaust openings for ventilation," while the Army Corps of Engineers analyzed blast results from various points on a "cast-in-place concrete arch," featuring 8-inch thick concrete walls buried by 4 inches of dirt. In 1957, one account noted, "test personnel in Nevada actually occupied a Navy corrugated steel arch shelter and emerged unscathed."[54] An exhaustive range of urban infrastructure was tested, ranging from manhole covers to electrical power substations to fire trucks. The Research Center of the Association of American Railroads tested timber pilings treated with flame-retardant agents, while the Society of Plastics Industry tested vinyl and other plastics, seeing in their products a non-shattering alternative to glass. As the narrator of a test site newsreel intoned in that dour tone of 1950s authority, "We're trying every angle and every gadget to find out what really does happen when an atomic bomb kicks out at the world around it."

The blast-resistant architectural profile that emerged from the battery of tests over the next several years was predictably dour, emphasizing shelter at its most fundamental, cavelike level; anything humanizing about architecture, it seemed—any considerations of light or ventilation or ornamentation—was potentially lethal. After Operation Plumbob, the Test Organization depicted the ideal building: "A full-size brick structure, 32 feet by 28 feet, which could serve as a school classroom, survived atomic blast forces with no apparent damage inside or out. No cracks were noted in the walls, roof, or at any joints...The structure had 10" thick reinforced brick walls, a reinforced concrete flat roof, and was windowless."[55] Windows, just as they were in space capsule design, were anathema to engineers, representing the weak point of structures, as well as apertures for the missile debris of blasts. Astronauts demanded the psychic comfort of windows; could terrestrial architecture do without them?

One of the things engineers at the various proving grounds learned early on is that windowless domed or cylindrical structures resisted blast pressures better than rectilinear forms, essentially for simple reasons of aerodynamics: *Architectural Forum* observed that "in Japanese cities exposed to blast, circular chimneys were left standing where destruction all around was complete."[56] Another technique that emerged at Survival City was the creation of Nebraska builder Walter Behlen, whose "Atomic Test Building" at Yucca Flats had been the only metal structure to survive at 6,800 feet from ground zero; according to *Popular Science*, the "novel structure...had the front of its roof deeply dented and its sides noticeably poked; window frames were empty and its wood door had been split into kindling. But the building still stood firm and ready to provide shelter."[57] Behlen attributed the building's success to the deeply corrugated, 16-gauge galvanized steel panels that comprised the walls and roof. "Corrugating them increases their strength 1,000 times," Behlen told the magazine. Behlen's atomic house was, like the houses of America, using clever engineering and modern materials to raise the standard of living. Behlen's corrugated steel panels were like aluminum siding or Formica, tested in America's only atomic-blast laboratory. The house, like a returning war hero, was brought to the 1955 Nebraska State Fair, a decorated shed viewed by thousands.[58] Not surprisingly, the Behlen Manufacturing Company of Columbus, Nebraska, would go on to manufacture blast and fallout "Community and Family Shelters" utilizing the same corrugation principle, endorsed by former Federal Defense Administrator (now Shelter Products Advisor to the Behlen Mfg. Company) Val Peterson, a witness at the 1955 tests. "Atomic-tested design," announced a Behlen brochure, showing a man with a briefcase and a woman and child descending toward a vault-like door, the shelter revealed in a cutaway view beneath a hill. "When mounding is necessary," the brochure advised, the "flat roof design of the Behlen Shelter permits a low silhouette, simple to attractively landscape."

The tests at Frenchman's Flat were more than an exercise in the engineering of passive defense. They were an attempt to bring the bomb into focus, to normalize it against the venetian blinds and bank vaults of everyday life—to achieve an "adequate understanding of nuclear effects on life in all of its phases"[59]—not to love the bomb, as *Dr. Strangelove* had, but to *live* with it. "In any case, peace or war, we are already well into the atomic age," remarked Robert L. Corsbie, director of the Nevada Test Organization's Civil Effects Test Group. "Learning to live with the by-products of nuclear reactions is now necessary and urgent."[60] At a press briefing a month later, Corsbie explained, "As people become more familiar with radiation levels as they are with reading an ordinary thermometer, it will become a matter of knowing how to live with radiation." Atomic war was simply the extreme of the lessons being learned at the test site, where activities proceeded not under the guise of war, but science. The peculiar discipline of "blast biology" was inaugurated here; conducted by the Lovelace Foundation, the experiments tested blast effects on various colonies of animals (typically swine, whose skin approximated that of humans). Before the Plumbob series of tests, the Test Organization noted that "Plumbob will provide equally valuable information on the problems associated with biomedical effects of static pressures and dynamic pressures sufficiently strong to translate bodies the size and weight of man from a state of rest to a state of motion."[61] There is an odd matter-of-factness to such statements, as if the "biomedical effects" of a blast were merely a phenomenon of nature. The position that the activities taking place in Nevada were scientific in nature, rather than military, was an issue from the beginning. In a 1953 report on the "Operational Future of the Nevada Proving Grounds," a participant notes, "I would like to point out that the name, 'Nevada Proving Ground,' is, to my way of thinking, both a misnomer and a confusion." The speaker was a scientist who felt the site, with its military exercises and civil effects tests, had deviated from its original incarnation as a "backyard" outdoor laboratory for the Los Alamos National Laboratory. The atomic bomb was no longer a military weapon, but a virtual condition unto itself; such distinctions as "civil" or "military" were merely "effects" of the bomb.

Although the relics of Frenchman's Flat are less than half a century old, it does not seem incongruous that Johnson, an archaeologist, should have spent the last few years studying them. For the shattered bunkers and Stonehenge-like arrays of pillars already seem the ruins of a lost civilization, whose secrets are not fully known, whose function and purpose is occluded. A report by Johnson on the flat lists page after page of architectural oddities, and what is striking is that for many of the structures, literally no information exists; one vainly attempts to fathom their meaning. One page lists a "Ferris Wheel Sign," standing near a concrete instrumentation bunker, which raises the perverse question: Was there a test carnival here, to determine the effects of a blast upon the amusement industry? Johnson records, "The name 'Ferris Wheel' does not indicate association with atmospheric testing." This void is the condition of all atomic ruins: the forgotten detritus of a war with no clear boundaries, no clear battlefields, a war of scientists and radar; a war waged in such secrecy that both records and physical locations are often utterly obscured. These ruins are the unacknowledged cenotaphs of that war, but instead of explanatory markers they bear merely the hieroglyphics of age.

We eventually rejoin the Mercury Highway, heading for the remains of Survival City. We skirt Area 23, where some form of chemical test is taking place ("We don't want to be spilled on," Johnson says) and drive north, the open land punctuated every few miles or so by an industrial-looking collection of buildings off to one side, or a sign reading "Toxic Gas Gate." We pass the Device Assembly Facility (DAF), a building remarkable for the fact that it, alone among all the buildings at the test site, actually resembles a

Atomic blast test houses from Operation Cue, Nevada Test Site

piece of military architecture. A solid low-slung white wall flanked by two 51-foot-high, gun-turret-equipped guard towers, the DAF, with some 100,000 square feet of mostly buried space covered by collapsible roofs that would drop in the event of an emergency, was in essence a $100 million expansion of the Department of Energy's primary nuclear weapons manufacturing site: Pantex, near Amarillo, Texas. The Limited-Test Ban Treaty rendered it almost instantly obsolete. It stands as the quintessential nuclear age fortification, built to protect a scientific process rather than men or a strategic position. The DOE's Glass tells me the twisting road leading to the building's entrance is intended to prevent "accelerative vehicle assault." Before proceeding to Yucca Flats, to the site of Survival City, we pause briefly at the Sedan Crater, the gaping hole left by the 104-kiloton "Plowshares" device detonated in 1962, which portended a world of heroic civil engineering powered by the atom. Beyond the crater, over a ridge of mountains, is the southern end of Area 51, whose gate I had been asked not to photograph. When I ask Glass if I can photograph the crater, she says with quiet officiousness, "You can photograph the crater, but you can't photograph the sky behind the crater."

"I took a walk up a dusty road to a dead city yesterday," began a writer in the March 18, 1953 *Las Vegas Review Journal.* "It was as dead as any Aztec settlement, yet only seven hours before it must have appeared—from the air at least—like a prosperous community."[62]

"Survival City," as newspaper datelines read, or "Doom Town," as it was alternately called, was hardly a city—merely two "typical colonial two-story center hall frame dwellings designed with input from the American Association of Architects"—but during its brief tenure it crystallized the pervasive anxiety of impending nuclear destruction into a tangible, if simulated, representation of that most potent of American icons: the single-family house. Placed, respectively, a half mile and a mile and a half away from Ground Zero, where a 15-kiloton atomic device was mounted to a 300-foot tower, the two houses captured the ambivalence of civil defense: One was completely destroyed, the other remained standing, its windows blown out and mannequin inhabitants jumbled on the floor. Some read the results as a sign of hope. The *New Mexican* observed that "Tuesday's spectacular detonation at Yucca Flats northwest of here demonstrates clearly that humans, properly sheltered and trained, can survive atomic attacks. After all, the bombs can't all be bulls-eyes, and a properly sheltered person even a short

Overleaf: Nuclear Family—residents of Survival City, Nevada Test Site

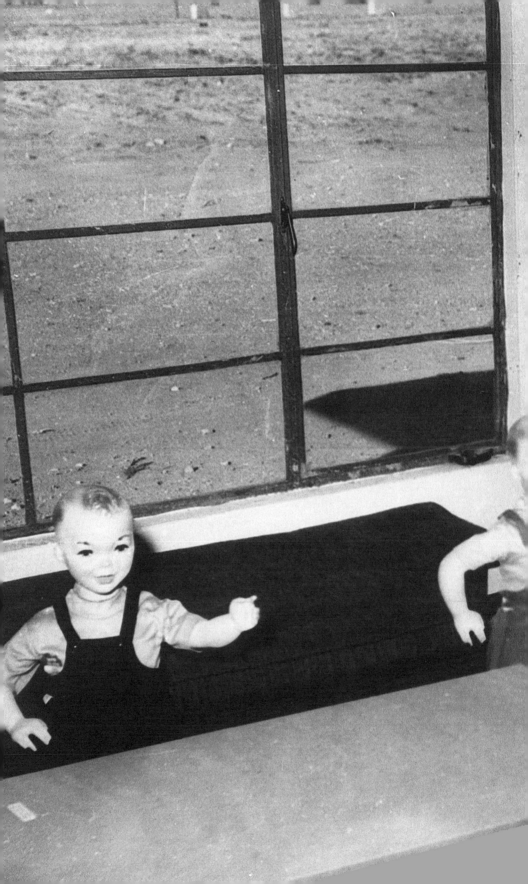

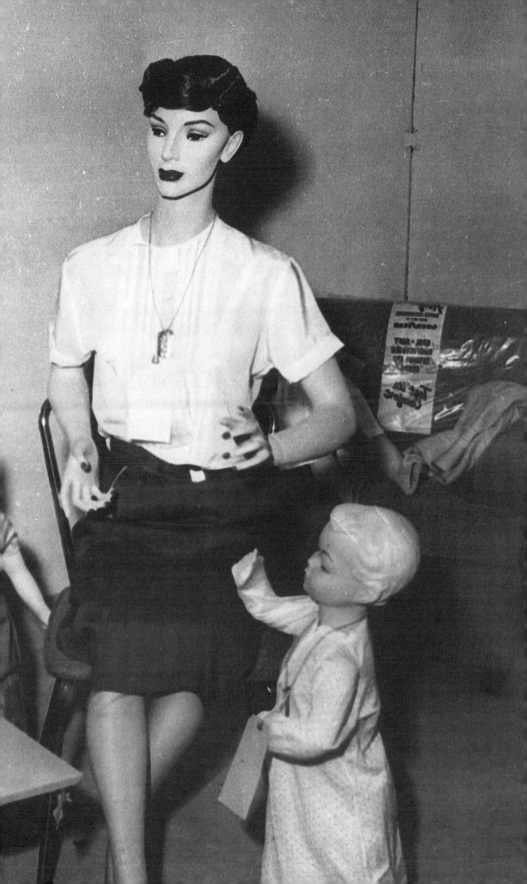

Project Ichiban, Nevada Test Site

distance from the point of explosion need not die."[63] Others were quick to note the weapons tested were not even as potent as those used in Japan, at a time when the weapons were growing ever stronger. "If civil defense authorities also gained additional information about structures and materials, so much the better," wrote *The Washington Post* on March 18. "Though as this newspaper observed yesterday, the explosion bore only a small relation to what cities would have to face in nuclear war. The prime benefit, civil defense-wise, was publicity."[64]

In the days leading up to the test, Survival City was depicted as the embodiment of all towns, an architectural stunt-double for the American way of life. "Operation Doorstep," the test series was labeled, as if in recognition that war could now be delivered, as a newspaper, to every front door in America. "A portion of your neighborhood will be put to the atomic test Tuesday," wrote the *Albuquerque Journal* on March 15, noting that "the Federal Civil Defense Administration had hoped to build a small, simulated town on the desert flat, but Congress failed to appropriate the money."[65] The *New Mexican* asked the same day, "If the Russians drop an atom bomb today on Sante Fe Plaza, what are your chances of survival?"[66] A day later, the *New York Times* published a preview photograph of the "International

Family" of test mannequins (supplied by L.A. Daring Co. of Bronson, Michigan), equipped with J. C. Penney clothing and inserted into a domestic tableaux that looked at once cozily familiar and presciently eerie. The living rooms, the television sets, even the well-stocked "Grandma's Pantry" were the very vision of 1950s television sitcoms and home magazines, but in the rigid eyes and blank expressions of the mannequins—the crash test dummies of the atomic age—death seemed already foretold. FCDA accounts are filled with curiously incongruous depictions of the events, such as "While some mannequins look comparatively undisturbed all showed marks from flying glass," and "the mannequin on the bed was undisturbed, except for loss of bed clothes."[67]

In the exacting recreation of materials and domestic arrangements, Survival City recalled the German and Japanese villages of Dugway, with a significant difference: Those houses had no occupants. In the formulation of plans for incendiary aerial bombing, the occupants had been literally written out of the picture, for what happened to the housing was of much greater concern than what happened to the inhabitants. Now, the inhabitants had been rewritten into the picture. The United States, after all, had been given a clear picture of the offensive effects of atomic warfare in Japan; the grim business now at hand was to determine what survival was possible. No consideration was deemed too minor. "In the Hiroshima and Nagasaki blasts, white or light colored clothing reflected the rays of the blast, thereby saving many people," noted the director of J. C. Penney's Research Laboratories. "Black, however, absorbed the heat and rays, inflicting painful burns."[68]

Hiroshima had come home, and nowhere is this more apparent than in one of the test site's strangest structures, the "Japanese Village" built in conjunction with the Atomic Bomb Casualty Commission's (ABCC) 1954 Project Ichiban. Intended to provide comprehensive information on the radiation levels of survivors of the Hiroshima blast, as well as to measure the "shielding effects" of buildings, a series of wood-frame houses—similar to those in Hiroshima, as well as at the Dugway Proving Ground—were built at the test site, then exposed to radiation from the tower-mounted "Bare Reactor," which essentially spewed radiation onto the houses like invisible spores caught on a dry gust. "ABCC studies were used to develop these 'analog' houses. Plans of rooms drawn during interviews with bomb victims and measurements of structures at varying distance from the bomb's hypocenters contributed to the design," notes one account.[69] As I stand with Johnson looking at the weathered, skeletal remains of the village, I realize that the house that had been built to be destroyed in Utah was metaphorically re-erected here, built from plans that themselves were drawn from the memory of survivors. Here was the real Survival City.

Atomic test house today, Nevada Test Site

A short distance away, on Yucca Flats, stand two houses from a later civil effects test called Operation Cue. Johnson calls them "Monopoly hotels," and there is an unreal quality to them: They are too spartan, lacking front porches, gables, or adornment of any kind, sitting impossibly in the middle of this scarcely inhabitable desert, spaced out at regular intervals from the former Ground Zero. They lack even the rudimentary signs of life one would come across, in however faint a form, in the abandoned homesteads one finds to the north near towns such as Rachel. Walking through the house, I see graffiti (left, Johnson tells me, by a CNN film crew) and the signs of animal infestation, but nothing else. The roof, once reinforced already, is beginning to collapse. The agencies involved are engaged in the curious task of trying to preserve a house whose purpose was to be subjected to an atomic blast. Whether or not the house survives, its lifespan seems insignificant compared to the many thousands of years for which the invisible byproducts of testing will haunt these lands.

The raw data and the lessons of the test site were transferred by the civil defense establishment into the thousands of other presumptive survival cities. The findings of blast-effects studies would be distilled into the fallout shelter handbooks distributed to American families, or the more arcane tomes of radiological defense engineering that were as much a part of the theoretical exercises of the Cold War as the game theories of the Rand Corporation. Taken as a whole, the images and facts emanating from Las Vegas were ambivalent: tinged with doom, but shot through with a glistening undercurrent of faith that the technological advancements of a confident society would win the day. Las Vegas itself seemed to embody the ambivalence. As the concrete shells and wood-frame houses were being erected at the test site, Las Vegas was entering its storied phase of exuberant streamline moderne, the city's casinos a radiant spectacle of burning chrome, sparkling glass, and towering neon signs, "the rich sleekness of modern design that suggests suavity and impermanence."[70] Las Vegas was a place where people came to turn their back on reality, a place where appearance outshone truth, a city that laughed off the precariousness of its survival in the desert with lavish fountains, an electric atmosphere, and air-conditioning. The American fear occasioned by the launch of Sputnik was here blended into giddiness: The 216-foot-long neon sign at the Stardust (whose "S" alone contained 975 lamps), a sign that *was* architecture, depicted Earth "ringed by a Sputnik off the front pages of the newspaper."[71] Was Las Vegas itself—the city closest to America's Ground Zero—the living incarnation of a culture in chronic denial, where roulette wheels spun as the atmosphere burned, where nothing ever closed because one never knew when it all might end? America was "learning from Las Vegas," but the lessons were wildly divergent.

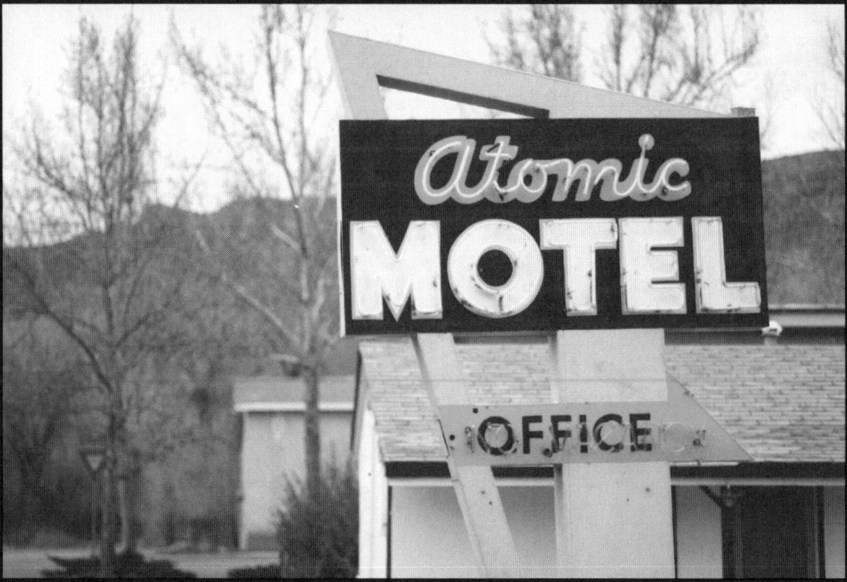
Atomic
MOTEL
OFFICE

3.
THE DOMESTICATION OF DOOMSDAY:
New Buildings for the Perilous Atomic Age

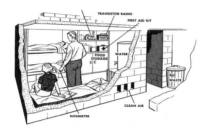

On the facade of any number of postwar institutional buildings in America one still occasionally sees a sign marked "Fallout Shelter." Once bright yellow and black, the signal colors of caution, the signs, after decades of weathering, are now typically a variant of ochre and charcoal. One often has to struggle to make out the iconic three fans that are the graphic symbol of shelter (a symbol that evokes, but is purposely distinct from, the radiation symbol); sometimes one can even discern the word "capacity" at the bottom of the sign, even though no number is usually visible.

The sign is a curious emblem. The space it advertises, in most cases, is no longer used for its original purpose, nor is it capable of being used for such a purpose, having been long since converted to some other function. Nor could any of the building's users typically direct the inquiring visitor to the advertised "Fallout Shelter" or report having been there themselves. The signs hang like a kind of architectural ornament, one that once connoted a common message (and, like precast concrete or the curtain wall, marked its building as being of its times), but they have since drifted into the repository of unnoticed urban symbols.

In early 1961, with the Kennedy Administration's inauguration of the National Fallout Shelter Survey, the signs began to appear on buildings that had been identified by a mobile army of atomic surveyors (many of them architectural students) trained in the new art of shelter design, as having sufficient architectural and infrastructural properties to serve as a fallout shelter in the event of nuclear war. Until 1964, when the government abandoned the

Motel near Moab, Utah

PA—578
Federal Extension Service, U S. Department of Agriculture
in cooperation with the Office of Civil Defense, Department
of Defense.

Wherever you are—at home or away—seek the best available protection and stay there as long as you can or until advised to come out.

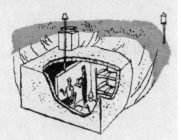

The best protection is an underground shelter with at least three feet of earth or sand above it. Two feet of concrete will give the same protection. If the shelter has an adequate door and an air filter, it will give you almost complete protection.

An ordinary house without basement probably would cut the radiation in half, if you stay on the first floor near the center of the house.

Staying in a house basement will reduce your exposure to about 1/10 the outside exposure. If you can sandbag the basement windows, there will be a further reduction.

If you arrange a basement refuge, with a mass of material around and above you, as shown, you can reduce your exposure to about 1/100 of the outside exposure.

Large buildings—apartment or office buildings—give good protection. Their masonry or concrete construction generally makes it harder for radiation to get through. Basements, inside rooms, or corridors are safest.

Outdoors, a culvert that can be blocked off at the ends will furnish protection. A trench or ditch also will protect you if it can be covered quickly with three feet of earth or other heavy materials.

practice, many shelters were stocked with an array of survival rations and dosimeters, the likes of which still surface in yard sales. In 1967, it was reported that "by the end of the last year, space for some 155 million people, in 172,000 structures throughout the country, had been located... [A]n additional two million spaces were found through a Smaller Structures Survey."[1]

As the years wore on, however, and civil defense drifted to the margins of the public imagination, the signs and the spaces they signified began to disappear. In 1986, for example, a report from Hartford, Connecticut, found that the number of identified fallout shelters had dropped from 177 in 1977 to 62 a decade later. The fallout shelter signs that remain seem to do so out of benign neglect, or a kind of invisibility—they have become part of the building—or the vague suspicion that permission from some unknown authority is required for their removal. The signs are now taken as a piece of Cold War kitsch, a cultural reference to a time better forgotten.

When the signs finally vanish altogether, an entire chapter of the architecture of the Cold War will disappear. The signs are a discreet reminder of a massive effort by the federal government to organize space—urban and suburban—for a defensive purpose. The policy codified existing sections of buildings or, more ambitiously, encouraged the creation of shelters in the design of new buildings. As a federal civil defense bulletin put it, "the program also provides today, the orientation that architects and engineers must have if fallout protection is to be considered at the critical point in the creation of a building—the design stage."[2] The signs represented a different way of experiencing a building; suddenly particular spaces took on new meanings, which were not always understood or trusted. As the *New Yorker* rather mordantly observed in 1963, "Whenever an air raid drill is conducted in our building, we descend from our office, on the nineteenth floor, to the corridors of the tenth floor, where we huddle with other baffled laymen. Someone, evidently, has figured out that the tenth floor is proof against explosions. Everything above this floor might be vaporized and everything below it smashed to rubble, but the floor itself, and all its grateful occupants, would waft gently down into the crater."[3]

A generic Survival City was taking shape across America, and architects and planners, the typical providers of shelter and shapers of cities, were called upon to help build it. In the end, the architecture they constructed was stronger than the social or moral conviction behind it, but in the myriad "Fallout Shelter" signs, and often in the architecture that they adorn, one can still glimpse the past of a future averted.

Speaking to a gathering of the American Institute of Architects in Houston in 1949, Rear Admiral William S. Parsons of the United States Navy, having just evaluated a Los Alamos National Laboratory report on the effects of atomic weapons, warned the assembled architects against a campaign of fortification building—what he called a "hysterical effort to buy absolute safety"—arguing instead that "we should make every effort to add atomic facts of life—subtle and obvious, pleasant and unpleasant—to our folklore." The only alternative to going underground, he declared, was to take a "calculated risk." This in itself was not outside of the folklore of everyday life: "We make these decisions each time we ride in a taxicab or go skating or skiing."[4]

Architects were suddenly on the front lines of defense. In the Cold War, all architecture was military architecture. An m.i.t. professor declared at a conference on "Building in the Atomic Age" that "I do not believe that the planners, the architects, the engineers—the builders of this country—have ever stood before on the brink of a situation where their efforts, their advice, their leadership, could conceivably play such a major role in the shape of

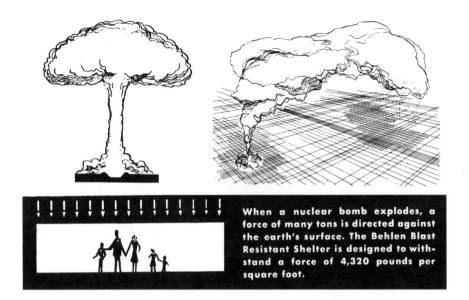

When a nuclear bomb explodes, a force of many tons is directed against the earth's surface. The Behlen Blast Resistant Shelter is designed to withstand a force of 4,320 pounds per square foot.

things to come."[5] In the new logic of atomic war, architecture that would be left standing, that provided sufficient shelter against little understood forces, was a strategic plank. "An effective civil defense is a deterrent to war," Civil Defense Director Leo Hough said. "The country which survives best will win."[6] It was presumed that architects, as traditional providers of shelter, would find the ways to help the country "survive best."

The "atomic facts of life" were presented to architects, in the wake of Hiroshima and the tests in Nevada, in a variety of architectural publications and through professional organizations such as the AIA, which worked from the outset with federal civil defense officials. With titles such as "Model Buildings with Fallout Shelter," the Federal Civil Defense Administration (FCDA) and other organizations set the parameters on a kind of architecture of defensive space, which one publication called "new buildings for the perilous atomic age"; they also tried to construct a profile of who the architect was and what their role in society should be. A consistent idea transmitted by these publications and forums was that the byproducts of the atomic bomb were merely an extension of previous "natural" forces with which architects always have had to concern themselves.

"The architect can be defined as that designer who, through his specialized training and ability, can most efficiently and creatively determine the environment in which man can live and function," stated the introduction to the Office of Civil Defense's (OCD) *Shelter Design in New Buildings.* "The definition is extended, for the purpose of this manual, to include the environment of fallout gamma radiation as well as the normal environments of wind, rain, and sun."[7] This logic was echoed in publications such as *Architectural Forum*: "Atomic radiation is a new building design element to be taken into account with wind, weather, and sanitation."[8] *Architectural Record* noted that "eventually, the inclusion of shelter in buildings will be a primary requirement as are fire stairs, exits, sprinkler systems, [and] safety treads."[9] In the civil defense film *How It Was Done*, "Sheriff Bob Russell" states "to build a new home in this day and age without including such an obvious necessity as a fallout shelter would be like leaving out the bathroom twenty years ago."[10]

The "atomic facts of life" were presented as a *fait accompli*, part of the natural order of things, an environmental condition as ubiquitous as sun or wind. Only a fatalist would not choose to counter the new forces with a new kind of design. "Protective construction" was the most modern form of architecture, employing the most up-to-date materials and engineering innovations. "Building against the atom" entailed a whole new host of engineering and design considerations, a litany of strange concepts—"reflected overpressure," "dynamic phase," "the totally engulfed house"—that had been tested in the proving grounds of the desert and were ready for domestic consumption. As the OCD itself admitted, it was difficult to build against the atom based on a small number of tests conducted under conditions that had already changed (i.e., the kilo tonnage of weapons was increasing): "In the design of a residence to conventional standards, building codes and good practice have established minimum design standards which a structure must meet to be considered safe. When designing to resist the effects of a nuclear explosion, relatively limited test data are available. An exact design basis for these new forces is difficult to establish."[11]

Still, a thoroughgoing effort was made to sketch the contours of a defense that was itself deemed possible. The first thing, noted the author of *The Bomb, Survival, and You: Protection for People, Buildings, Equipment*, was not to assume that every home had to be a bunker: "In considering the protective design of new buildings for potential target areas, many of us, layman and technician alike, tend to overshoot the mark first and fall into the common error of seeking something totally *bombproof*. And before we know it, we find ourselves with the vision of fortress cities of the atomic age, studded with great monolithic mastodons of heavily reinforced concrete and honeycombed with underground factories, offices, and dwelling places."[12]

In addition to naturalizing the presence of the bomb and gamma radiation, the government, and architects themselves, had to work to resolve the overwhelming paradox of civil defense, that architecture created to resist the effects of an atomic bomb would be incompatible with everyday life. How could architecture provide reassurance without merely reinforcing the notion that one was living under the threat of atomic attack? As historian Guy Oakes writes, "In the absence of civil defense, the public would be gripped by a nuclear terror. But once civil defense had done its work, the public would be even more terrified."[13] The solution was to meet the bomb on a purely professional level, as a physical force that could be withstood; the bulk of attention was placed on the survival of the structure itself, with less thought given to the mechanics of survival afterwards. The house had become an engineering problem, the "machine for living" placed in the wind tunnel. "In providing the proper stiffness against the one-sided lateral overpressures of the atomic bomb," one manual advised, "the designer may do well to think of the problem as an earthquake in reverse . . . in an earthquake the earth exerts a force against the building through the foundations, causing it to shake. A blast wave, on the other hand, takes hold of the earth by means of the building, and tries to shake the earth."[14]

Publications tried to emphasize the place for traditional architectural considerations—siting, materials, proportion—in protective construction. A civil defense manual on prototype houses touted the benefits of judicious landscaping ("use planters for barriers," it noted, adding, "trees provide thermal shield but are subject to burning") and advised the architect to "orient structure to receive least thermal and blast effects." How would one know from where the blast would be coming? "In many cases, especially in suburban areas, the most probable direction can be predicted: toward known defense installations, industrial areas, or the center of a large city."[15]

The overall tone of the atomic-defense/architecture conversation was sober but upbeat; this was architecture-as-propaganda. Reams of engineering data and the technological utopianism of postwar America created a hypothetical architecture that could not only help ensure survival against atomic attack, but provide ancillary benefits as well. One study noted that fallout-protected buildings better resisted other scourges of modern society, such as vandalism and noise.[16] Another civil defense document posited fallout shelters as a means to attract both tenants and employees:

> As large business enterprises become increasingly concerned over the need to protect key personnel and as competition for apartment tenants becomes more acute, the availability of shelter in apartment and office buildings may help them to obtain a favorable occupancy and a higher rate of return on the total investment. In turn, business enterprises may find it easier to obtain competent clerical help if shelter facilities form a part of employee benefits.[17]

The grim physical realities of defending against atomic attack could be dealt with in split-level ranches and other manifestations of what design historian

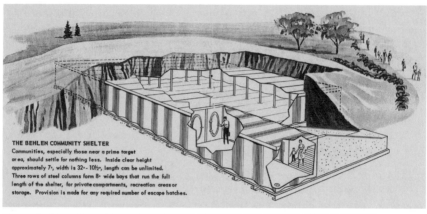

THE BEHLEN COMMUNITY SHELTER
Communities, especially those near a prime target area, should settle for nothing less. Inside clear height approximately 7', width is 32'- 10½", length can be unlimited. Three rows of steel columns form 8' wide bays that run the full length of the shelter, for private compartments, recreation areas or storage. Provision is made for any required number of escape hatches.

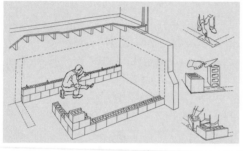

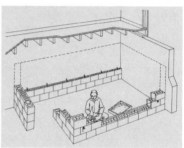

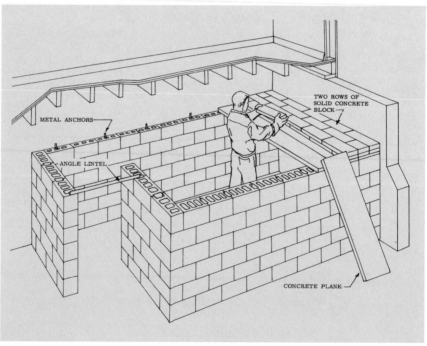

TWO ROWS OF
SOLID CONCRETE
BLOCK

METAL ANCHORS

ANGLE LINTEL

CONCRETE PLANK

Thomas Hines calls "Populuxe." The concrete bunker and the picture-window could be reconciled: "Populuxe nomenclature embraced such contradiction because it was designed to convince consumers that they could have it all. Modern and traditional, showy and tasteful, machine-made and craftsman-like, all these could be reconciled in the same household, sometimes in the same object."[18]

In Survival City, Nevada, the country had its nuclear-age Levittown, a blueprint for the future. "Houses *do not have* to be doomed by blast and fire," counseled *Architectural Record* as it unveiled "Survival House," a dwelling with a reinforced concrete roof and large windows and doors (to "permit partial balancing of the blast pressures") designed by New York architect Ellery Husted, for the Portland Cement Association. The house, the magazine pointed out, was based on the concrete masonry houses on the proving ground's "Doomsday Drive."[19] *Architectural Forum* offered "design lessons from Hiroshima and Nagasaki," noting that "for the atom age there is emerging a building design combining a normal exterior, adequate light and air for outside rooms and a blast-resistant interior of heavy sheer-wall and roof construction designed for plastic yield."[20] In a *Progressive Architecture* forum, the American Institute of Architects (AIA), in an article titled "Civil Defense: The Architect's Part," laid the groundwork for the new architecture: "Steel-skeleton-frame fireproof structures with steel-supported concrete floors, and monolithic concrete buildings, are structurally the safest and best," it advised. "Glass is one of the greatest sources of danger. It should be removed or replaced with non-shatterable material."[21]

In blast- and fallout-resistant architecture, the engineering criteria trump any aesthetic considerations. And they are quite specific and unusual engineering criteria; in what is called the "negative phase," for example, after a blast wave has passed over a house there will be a drop in pressure and a reverse wind, creating forces opposite to those a structure is designed to withstand. Idiosyncratic events occur when those waves enter shelter spaces: "If the blast enters what is called a 're-entrant corner' (for example, where a vertical wall meets a horizontal surface) the incident overpressure can be amplified by a factor of 10 or more with a corresponding increase in destructive effect."[22] As the Italian architects Paolo Bulli and Franco Vaccari have pointed out, "the atomic shelter, like the igloo and the nomad's tent, belongs to what might be called the architecture of extreme situations, i.e., the architecture that develops in environments that are so specialized as to reduce variational possibilities to zero. When environmental pressure reaches extreme values, possible solutions rapidly converge towards the sole solution."[23]

One favored solution for cloaking the "architecture of extreme situations" in a more everyday guise was the "dual-purpose" or "convertible" shelter, a fallout- or blast-resistant space that also served a non-emergency function. Civil defense officials and architects praised the spaces for their flexibility, cost-effectiveness, and inconspicuousness. As one book of plans put it, "[This] guidebook illustrates the point that integrated convertible shelters can be incorporated within conventional spaces of buildings without decreasing the efficient performance of normal functions or creating windowless monstrosities, and at little or no increase in cost."[24] By linking the shelter to another residential or industrial purpose (e.g., storage room, recreation room), the stigma—and the added cost and space requirements—of the shelter as merely a protective space were avoided.

Architects, as professionals, insisted that what they were doing was separate from the ethics of the bomb itself, or the nagging question of what kind of society would endure after a confrontation. Their task was pure design. A "design fête" at Rice University in 1963 illustrated the technocratic tendency. It was "not the purpose of the conference to reflect any state of alarm or even any trend or opinion about the possibility of nuclear warfare," the conference organizers said. Rather, the goal was to "demonstrate to both students and architects the simple, low-cost practicalities of shelter design—*where the shelter is a requirement of the architect's initial program*" (original italics).[25] The dual-purpose shelter, poised between war and peace, was a neutral space that seemed to resolve the paradox of spaces for living versus surviving, as well as the moral distinction between them. "Indeed, it was just that demonstration of basic simplicity which served to remove the whole question of dual-use, multiple-occupancy fallout shelters from the realm of emotional and ethical opinion to the realm of simple prudence."[26] In one hypothetical project, for a manufacturer of "nuclear detection devices," the shelter was placed in a space normally reserved for employee recreation: "Its location enables the moderately protected kitchen to resume service to shelter occupants soon after peak fall-out activity has subsided."[27] The dual-purpose space matched the Cold War duality of the mind, a compartmentalization that sought to reconcile the postwar boom with the threat of annihilation, spaces for nuclear defense with the family rooms of the Affluent Society.

In still another meeting of architecture and civil defense, a competition— "Awards Program—Building with a Fallout Shelter"—was cosponsored by the American Institute of Architects and the Office of Civil Defense beginning in 1968. The competitions strove to equate the dual-purpose shelter as a simple outgrowth of good design: "In most cases, the potential for fallout shelter in the award-winning buildings appears as a natural or inherent characteristic of the basic design."[28] Buildings stressed flexible, functional areas, often with "large windowless core areas as habitable space." Looking at the grouping of 1969 award winners, one is struck by the fact that the buildings, most of which adhere to the precepts of institutional modernism of the late 1960s, seem to take on a militaristic tone. Dominated by large slabs of reinforced concrete and selective groupings of windows, this architecture connotes little outside of sheer strength and a rigid geometric logic. It is unclear, however, whether the buildings would have looked any different were fallout shelters not part of the design. It is said of buildings such as the Library Building at the University of California, San Diego—what looks like a looming concrete launch pad, best approached by ramp—that they were constructed to "prevent riots," but such buildings largely predate late-1960s campus unrest. Paul Rudolph's Art and Architecture Building at Yale University, for example, with its masses of stone, narrow window slits, and restricted entryways, was completed in 1963—and thus can hardly be a response to unrest on campus. One senses a larger defensive impulse, whether literal or metaphorical, in such constructions; the overbearing islands of concrete and fanciful quasi-fortifications are examples of what Vincent Scully called "paramilitary dandyism"[29] more than a response to a specific set of conditions. *Architectural Design* charged in 1967 that "the form and finishes of military installations are being used for the most hallowed of new buildings—cultural and civic centers. Throughout Europe and even in America architects are setting up their culture bunkers."[30] Historians Keith Mallory and Arvid Ottar have noted that while it is impossible to claim a direct link between Le Corbusier's roughened and exposed concrete Unité d'Habitation and military bunkers of a similar finish, Le Corbusier's shift from precise, machine-finished concrete to the more natural "brutalist" form occurred during the period of coastal bunker building in Europe.[31]

On the home front, the dual-purpose shelter was taken as another reorganization of space for a more modern age, of a piece with the open-plan interiors of modernist homes. At the January 1960 Home Furnishings Market in Chicago, the American Institute of Decorators (AID) and the National Office of Civil and Defense Mobilization (OCDM) sponsored an exhibition featuring model fallout shelters that had been blended seamlessly into modern interiors. "There is nothing fearsome in the word 'shelter,'" said the exhibition's organizer. "It is a pleasant sounding word. Men seek shelter from any excessive conditions—shelter from the storm, the heat, the cold, the noisome pestilence, and in this case, from the 'blast of the terrible one against the wall.'"[32] A shelter built only on the OCDM's stringent requirements, the AID noted, "cannot easily be sold to the public, particularly on such a grim basis." The AID's "family room of tomorrow," on the other hand, was designed "so it can be and will become as necessary to tomorrow's living as is the central heating plant."[33] Colorful drawings depicted vibrant interiors that suggested nothing of survival: "By concealing all essential equipment behind random panels of walnut, Roy F. Beal, A.I.D., of Austin, Texas, creates a fallout shelter that has all the appearances of a library-study." One fallout shelter, disguised as a "colorful music room" with "shaggy carpeting" and "flexachrome blue vinyl tile," had a few strange accessories, such as a "First Aid Kit" and a "Forty Year Calendar"—a particularly dark, if unrealistic, bit of décor, given that most actual residential shelters were equipped for only a week or two of underground living. Decorator Barbara Dorn displayed a model layout for Shelters for Living Inc., in the lower level of Grand Central Terminal. "It will be informal in feeling, comfortable, and as cheerful as possible, with lots of buoyant colors. Why be drab about your shelter, when it's more fun, and costs no more to survive in style?"[34]

In these layouts, the home fallout shelter seems a strange corollary to postwar phenomena such as the "case study houses." Like those avant-garde houses, the construction of fallout shelters never expanded beyond a limited audience, but their presence in the American imagination far outweighed their actual numbers. The home fallout shelter was a new kind of space, one that tied the home to a hypothetical global confrontation—and to a new way of life, where the suburban nuclear family, relying on the ingenuity of industry, the doctrines of "preparedness," and their own strength as a social unit, could wait out Armageddon in stylish, if spartan, comfort. As the civil defense film *Walt Builds a Family Fallout Shelter* (sponsored by the National Concrete Masonry Association) put it, "no home in America is modern without a family fallout shelter. This is the nuclear age."[35]

That relatively few ever explored this "modern" way of living can be attributed to the vast amount of confusion in government policy concerning fallout shelters, uncertainties over their effectiveness and design (professional architects attempted to impose standards on a market that was quickly flooded by a range of "do-it-yourself" shelter kits), and even the ebb and flow of international tensions. "Civil defense is basically a crisis to crisis proposition," *Newsweek* observed in 1963.[36]

Architecturally, the fallout shelter was an admission that the traditional source of shelter—the home—was no longer sufficient *as it was*. At the same time, another message was being broadcast: the home was in fact the stronghold of national security. As the director of the Federal Civil Defense Administration put it, "for the first time, the personal defense of our homes is . . . being rated *as co-equal in importance* with our military defense."[37] The private space of the home was being opened to the contingencies of national defense—homeowners were urged to send in a survey in which they drew plans and answered questions about their house. In return they might get a letter on official u.s. Department of Commerce letterhead, signed by A. Ross Eckler of the Bureau of the Census, which stated: "Based on standards provided by the Department of Defense, Office of Civil Defense, the analysis of

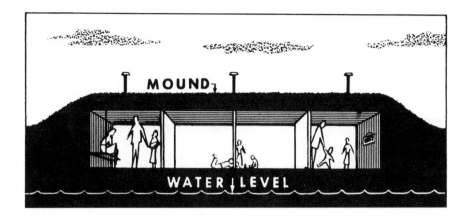

the information obtained from your Home Survey Questionnaire indicates that your home provides very little protection against fallout." The house was being codified, not merely socially but spatially. "The highest military authorities in our country," a civil defense official said, "stressed the fact that good housekeeping is one of the best protections against fire in an atomic blast."[38] Just as there was no doubt who was to do this atomic housekeeping (civil defense films that depicted an atomic blast invariably featured the woman at home, the man at the office), the civil defense authorities felt equally confident imparting advice on how the house should be ordered: "Attic a junk pile? Stairs or halls cluttered?" one pamphlet asked. In this new war, every broom was a rifle—it was even claimed the radioactive particles "were much the same as ordinary, everyday dust."[39] The lesson was taught by *Good Housekeeping* itself: "This is to remember: if and when a single bomb falls within 200 to 500 miles of you, your survival depends on a shelter—and the shelter depends on you."[40]

During the crisis in Berlin, the fallout shelter was touted as a wise response to the political climate and a novel consumer accessory for the modern home. A number of suburban builders included fallout shelters in new subdivisions. The developers at Edgebrook, in Framingham Center, near Boston, were "the first to announce the addition of a fallout shelter in this new community of homes";[41] while in the Sunset Conejo development of Thousand Oaks, California, builder Richard Doremus installed twenty fallout shelters between 1960 and 1962 to entice prospective buyers. The December 1950 issue of *Interiors* captures the mood well: A story about the "A-Bomb Shelter Corporation of Teaneck, N.J." is followed immediately by one about Hotpoint's "House of the Fifties," in which a "more hopeful attitude toward the future is indulged," featuring "an intercommunication system for mobilizing the entire family" and a large living room window that "sneaks into the basement at the touch of a button."[42]

A number of new subdivisions included fallout shelter space in their amenities, while the market was inundated with competing models, each with its own unique solution to the problem. The Con-L-Rad Company, asking "Are Your Loved Ones Protected?" announced "concussion chambers" with "no money down." The California firm Fox Hole Shelter Inc., a pool builder "that got into shelters two years ago by turning its original product upside down," had already sold more than 200 units in its two years of existence.[43] There was the "Lancer Blast and Fallout Shelter," recommended by the OCDM (it could be purchased using Federal Housing Administration financing) and able to accommodate a family of six "in comfortable although close" quarters, "comparable to a small pleasure boat."[44] There was the "Kidde Kokoon," an "entirely contained" 4,500-pound steel shelter created by the Walter Kidde Nuclear Laboratories, which "comes with an electric generating system, air blower, canned water, five bunkers with air mattresses, blankets, storage shelves, safety suits to emerge in." (In recognition of market segmentation, a "luxury" model was available for $500 extra). A September 1961 *Life* spread showed a shelter from Kelsey-Hayes—a manufacturer whose usual business was oriented toward automobile parts. The shelter "would even withstand the collapse of a house upon it."[45] An ad for this steel-paneled, 9 by 12-foot shelter noted that it could be "used as a storm shelter, photo dark room, game room, or office," and showed a family of three in an atomic-age Norman Rockwell setting: bunk beds, cabinet stocked with Campbell's soup, a short-wave radio, a girl playing a game, wife serenely gazing at a man holding a flashlight. More than the "family room of tomorrow," it seems a place to wait out a storm before returning to the split-level above—if it was still there.

There was a certain inherent "planned obsolescence" in shelters, which made them like other products of postwar affluence. "It was something more to be added, another room to be sold, another way of convincing the buyer to spend more money on housing," writes Thomas Hines.[46] The Situationist Internationale, the Paris-based left-wing collective made famous by member Guy Debord's *The Society of the Spectacle*, saw in shelters a mordant, subterranean reflection of the culture of consumerism: "The shelters, as a creation of a new consumable commodity in the affluent society, prove more than any preceding commodity that people can be made to work to satisfy highly artificial needs, needs that most certainly 'remain needs without ever having been desires' and without having the slightest chance of becoming desires."[47] Indeed, the fallout shelter was never perceived as something that one *wanted;* rather than a goal of one's life, it existed, like the threat of atomic war itself, as a vague possibility—something that someone else down the block might very well own. While actual shelters were usually dark, cramped, mildewed affairs, in the realm of subconscious desire they were always spacious, ridiculously well-stocked playrooms with artificial sunlight and state-of-the-art entertainment systems, inhabitable for years and years. Reports that shelters were being installed under cover of darkness—to keep them secret from neighbors—only heightened the speculation.

As the era of crises subsided into a more protracted sense of nuclear threat, the fallout shelter quietly slipped from the architectural imagination, becoming a time capsule of doomsdays past. They are another obsolete space, like the maid's room or the oversized pantry, to be explained away by real estate agents, humorously noted in the local paper as the symbols of a more dangerous (and somehow more hopeful) age, and due to be retrofitted for "modern" use, e.g., as a wine cellar. They are buried now, repressed, but in times of extreme fear they have resurfaced. In 1982, in the wake of the Chernobyl explosion and the Reaganite reawakening of Cold War tensions, a Utah developer named Lane Blackmore announced plans for a $10 million, 240-unit underground condominium named "Terrene Ark I." Blackmore quickly recorded sixty-five sales and discussed franchising throughout the country. "I'm getting doctors and lawyers in here, not kooks," he said. "These are really quite prudent people who know how to live in the nuclear age."[48]

The Reagan Administration raised the civil defense budget from $117 million in 1981 to $129 million in 1982, and was seeking nearly twice that for the following year. The Federal Emergency Management Association (FEMA), the heir to previous civil defense agencies, was touting a plan called "expedient shelter," namely, using ordinary household materials to construct impromptu fallout shelters. "The expedient shelter option has a number of attractive aspects," FEMA reported. "Perhaps the most attractive is that it requires little investment before a crisis."[49] In looking for a solution in sandbags, FEMA was acknowledging the difficulty in getting any purpose-built shelter program passed. FEMA and its predecessors had spent years, and countless millions of dollars, perfecting the art of fallout shelter building, only to arrive back at the hardware-store lean-to that had marked the early, optimistic days of civil defense. Like the utopian planners of large-scale housing schemes, FEMA was designing a better life for people without fully taking the needs or desires of people into account. The agency concluded in 1986 that "for the present, while we know how to build shelters, we have not solved the political problem of allocating the resources to get them built."[50] Shelters could be built to withstand the effects of a nuclear explosion, but without a social foundation, they sank into oblivion.

The building that would best seem to exemplify the Cold War's mandates for subterranean survival and brutal "building against the atom" is the now-shuttered Abo Elementary School and Fallout Shelter in Artesia, New Mexico, a dusty refinery town south of Roswell that proudly advertises its omnipresent industrial stench as the "Sweet Smell of Success."

Completed on April 20, 1962, the Abo school was billed as the nation's first all-underground school, a place where 460 pupils descended daily to climate-controlled, radiation-free surroundings. It was designed by Frank Standhardt, a Roswell architect who in 1959 built two energy-efficient windowless (but surface) schools in Artesia. The windowless school idea soon spread to other states, but in Artesia, that was not enough to keep out the Cold War chill. With Berlin on their minds, as well as the strategic proximity of Roswell's Walker Air Force Base and the White Sands Missile Range—in addition to the fact that the town lacked any public fallout shelters—the city of Artesia decided to replicate Standhardt's design, only underground (Abo's name was taken from a nearby, legendary historic site that was, as a school brochure noted, "possibly of one of Seven Cities of Cibola sought by conquistador Coronado, and certainly one of the 'Cities That Died of Fear' of Apache raids." Voters passed a bond issue covering the $400,000-plus school construction, roughly one fourth of which was dedicated to the costs of building it underground. The federal government subsidized the additional cost, since Artesia was presumably the pilot in a planned dual-purpose shelter-school project. Standhardt was also involved in a projected, but never built, underground shopping center-cum-fallout shelter, the "Del Norte Sheltered Shopping Center," to be located on a 10-acre tract near Roswell. The shelter's developers touted a variety of benefits in "near normal conditions," seeking initial memberships (like a nuclear-age Sam's Club) of $250 per person to finance construction. Roswell banks announced they would finance prospective buyers, but civic opposition to the shelter's members-only status eventually killed the proposal.[51]

The Abo school featured 12-inch concrete walls, topped by a 21-inch concrete slab that was capable of withstanding a 20-megaton blast from a distance of 10 miles. An air-conditioning system featured a filter to block radiation particles, while showers at an "emergency entrance" (the Cold War was all about trying to get in to places, not out) would wash off residual fallout traces. Three small blockhouses above ground served as stairwell entrances, and the playground was located on what was actually the school's roof. Inside, the school featured 14-foot central corridors (to prevent claustrophobia, it was said) and bright fluorescent lighting. As the Saturday Evening Post magazine described, "an air of quiet industry pervades the building, due partly to the insulation of acoustical plaster on the inside and solid earth on the outside, and partly to the somewhat sobering effect the school appears to have on its pupils."[52] Residents downplayed the school's subterranean quality. "I've lived in large cities," one resident said. "No one says anything there about becoming moles when they ride the subways. No one says, 'I'm going underground to shop,' but I never met a woman who wouldn't go into a basement for a bargain." The school itself noted in a promotional brochure that "students are happy, scholastically average or better and well-adjusted. Other localities apparently have been convinced, and other fallout shelter schools are being or will be built." One local resident without a child at the school asked: "Is driving our children underground to become a way of life? Is this the future we give them?" The New Mexico State Ophthalmic Association raised concerns over the effect that windowless schooling would have on children's eyes. But a brochure, headlined "Pilot Project for the Atomic Age," noted that the lack of windows ensured "no window breakage, washing, shade maintenance; usual window wall used for teaching display." A later visitor noted a sign on a door of the cafeteria that read: "Normal Conditions: Food Storage. Fallout Conditions: Morgue." In the intervening years, the school has gone from a controversy to a curiosity, a unique, if somewhat embarrassing, memento of the atomic age. Barrels of civil defense crackers were sold to a pig farmer for slop.[53]

Abo was not the only school driven underground by the Cold War. In 1964, the Lake Worth Junior High School, near Fort Worth, went underground in a new $495,000, 18-room structure, designed by the appropriately named Thad Harden. As with Abo, cost savings were cited, but the real reason had to do with the nearby Strategic Air Command's (SAC) Carswell Air Force Base. As reported by *Time*, the school lay directly in the flight path of SAC's incoming B-52 bombers; each day, teachers and students were losing 10 percent of teaching time. Building a new school on a new site was deemed too expensive, so Lake Worth opted for a sunken structure.[54] The Abo school — built to hide from bombs, not bombers —was particularly significant because, unlike the backyard fallout shelters of private homes, it was a public building funded through tax dollars—a referendum on atomic anxiety. And it was not alone.

There were myriad public or institutional buildings constructed to deter the effects of a nuclear blast or the subsequent fallout. In 1954, the Armed Forces Institute of Pathology built a laboratory some 5 miles north of the White House "designed to preserve the nation's vital file of military medical knowledge (e.g., 656,000 individual specimens, 6,000,000 pathological slides) and enable scientists to carry on their work despite atomic attack."[55] Described as a five-story gray concrete monolith, the laboratory featured a three-story basement that descended 50 feet; it also lacked windows except at its "expendable" north and south annexes. Doors were thick steel and walls reinforced concrete—the south wall, facing the White House, the likely direction of atomic attack, was designed to withstand nearly 35,000 pounds per square yard of blast pressure. There are similar buildings in nearly every city in America, usually with some military or infrastructural capacity. They are rarely noticed for their architecture. I see one every time that I cross the Brooklyn Bridge into New York City: the American Telephone and Telegraph Company Long Lines building, erected in 1974 and designed to withstand the effects of nuclear war (and to survive for two weeks afterwards). Where the original long lines building was an art deco "brick mountain," this building is a nearly windowless blank slab with a defensive shell of Swedish flame-treated granite, a looming obelisk of telecom equipment. As the editors of the *AIA Guide to New York City* put it, "Ma Bell, why didn't you leave the air for people and place your electrons underground?"[56]

What is most striking, however, in considering the architecture of the Cold War, is that most buildings did *not* become bunkers. In fact, quite the opposite occurred, at least in the corporate sphere dominated by the International Style. Despite the admonitions of the civil defense planners, the material that was considered most dangerous *vis à vis* atomic blast—both for its weakness and its tendency to transform into lethal missiles—proved the most enduringly popular: "The ubiquitous glass curtain wall turned out to be, paradoxically, a plane as absolute as the Iron Curtain," writes architectural historian Joan Ockman.[57] The Lever House was just the first of countless glass boxes; whether it was, as Lewis Mumford suggested, a "laughing refutation of 'imperialist warmongering,'" is difficult to say. After all, the building's architect, Skidmore, Owings, Merrill (SOM) had risen to prominence through the military-industrial complex (designing the "atomic city" of Oak Ridge, in addition to numerous military facilities). Lever's president, Charles Luckman, an architect in his own right, went on to plan, with William Pereira, the missile base at Cape Canaveral and a NATO base in Spain during Franco's regime. But in New York, where glass towers were beginning to reflect other glass towers, where even bank vaults were on full display, it was difficult to find a defensive architecture: "Unlike the new UN building in New York," one report counseled, "atom-resistant structures should have a minimum of glass and fancy decorative stone slabs. There's more danger from flying debris than from the blast itself."[58]

Architects, in embracing glass as a material, may have been rebelling against the Cold War's inexorable pull toward bunker living. Or perhaps they were erecting Crystal Cities of technological hope rather than mounting a futile defense, having already written off the city. Architecturally, the question was, what would building be in an age of American military and technological might, the new frontiers of science and exploration, and utopian models for a better tomorrow—all, however, tainted by a dread that the methods that helped create the "dreamworld" (as *Fortune* called it) of postwar America might also contain the seeds of its own destruction. "Struggling under the surface serenity and outward security of the mainstream cold war American mind," writes historian Margot Henriksen, "was an unstable and paranoid underground psyche in a state of panic."⁵⁹ This dualism could play itself out equally well in architecture: For every smooth-planed, glass-skinned, rationally ordered functionalist temple of the International Style—e.g., the Santa Monica headquarters of the Rand Corporation, the high priests of coldly calculated Cold War logic (a mathematician plotted special paths within the Rand building to foster random interaction among employees)—there was a hardened underground structure of concrete and steel doors, a place where Rand's game theories might actually assume real shape.

Following World War II, America had assumed a mantle of power; by the time radiation traces were discovered over Siberia—evidence of Russian atomic detonations—it was less than clear how that power should be expressed, politically, culturally, or architecturally. As architectural historian John Ely Burchard described the postwar situation, "at the highest level of response, architecture could find no fitting answer to the times. The mood of the West was strange, unreal, almost trancelike. It felt doom yet was unready to concede it."⁶⁰

It is not surprising that corporate institutional modernism should have emerged as the predominant Cold War style. It was, as Joseph Hudnut argued, an architecture based overwhelmingly on engineering: "Like the engineer we address our art, not to form—to a sensuous order of shapes and relationships set in space—but to a mechanical and clearly exhibited order of purpose and energy."⁶¹ The Cold War was a war of engineers, not soldiers, a war of plotted points and physics projections, not pomp and pageantry. The International Style and its derivatives presented a picture of cool efficiency and rational ordering, expressing power not as the function of any one organization or belief system but in the logic of the building itself. "Black boxes" with an overt transparency, these buildings were the civic equivalent of the room-size Cray and IBM "business machines" whose punch cards and magnetic tape were guiding the missiles and interpreting data on the radar horizon; these were buildings that could organize massive amounts of "data," bring organization and binary logic to complex problems, be plugged into the power grid of any city and be no more or less compatible than they would anywhere else. Outright power was cloaked in expressions of function and order— as Burchard writes, "not even the palpable presence of rockets, aircraft, radar, television, and automation could be immediately or obviously expressed."⁶² If overt references to rockets and radar were lacking, there was a larger sense in which a war that had been transferred to machines was echoed in architecture. "Because we have dethroned symbolism," wrote Lewis Mumford, "we are now left, momentarily, with but a single symbol of almost universal validity: the machine."⁶³ The United Nations Assembly building, the very representation of the fragile task of projecting order and unity in a bipolar world, was representative of this crisis of symbolism. As Mumford described it, "there is nothing in its shape, its position, its external treatment, or its relation to the two other United Nations buildings—to indicate its importance or that of the organization it serves."[64] Chastising its "arid neutralism" and "abstract composition," Mumford criticized the UN complex for not suggesting "in architectural idiom the dawning concept of world government or mak[ing] visible the love and cooperation that are needed for its success."[65] He described the building as a creation of Hollywood fabulists, an apt description when one considers that the speeches given within, in front of the lights and the cameras, often had the same kind of relationship to political reality as a Hollywood backlot does to the location it simulates. "We were not trying to make a monument," Wallace Harrison, the General Assembly Hall's architect had said.[66] Indeed, this was a stance entirely of the times and its architecture. Monuments were the dead symbols of an old, autocratic order—one only had to look at the fascist architecture in Italy and Germany—and neither their naked expressions of power nor highly charged ornamentation was deemed worthy of a new age of world democracy.

In one regard, the Cold War created its own monuments, if not at the United Nations then in another form of assembly, the Vertical Assembly Building (VAB) at Cape Canaveral. The primary component of launch complex 39, the VAB featured a 456-foot-high "T-opening" through which the Apollo and Saturn V rockets could be transported; the doors had to withstand winds of 125 miles per hour when sealed and be operable in winds of 63 miles per hour. Monumentality here was represented by the sheer bulk of the building, as well as the complexity of its moving parts. As chief architect Max O. Urbahn described it, "the VAB is not so much a building to house a moon vehicle as a machine to build a moon craft. The Launch Control Center that monitors and tests every component that goes into an Apollo vehicle is not so much a building as an almost-living brain."[67]

One building that tried to bridge the "monument gap" in a more self-conscious way, in which expressions of Cold War power were evoked in a style that was originally associated with a larger ideology that included anti-militarist leanings, was the U.S. Air Force Academy in Colorado Springs, designed by Skidmore, Owings and Merrill. The academy, a mix of low-slung glass boxes offset by the soaring, jagged aluminum spires of its chapel, blended the Organization Man, business-like architecture of the mid-century with a more dramatically overt reference to a squadron of swept-wing supersonic fighters. Upon its unveiling, it was denounced from all sides. The V.F.W. called it "experimental architecture, more suitable for a supermarket or factory than a service academy,"[68] while others wondered if the Chapel was "paganistic" or "not American"[69]; the *New York Times* noted that "a plan for the jet age it may be, but the suspicion in Washington is that Congress would breathe easier if the architects would come back with a variation blending Chartres Cathedral and Independence Hall."[70] As one historian notes, the academy itself represented itself a "cold war" in architecture over the modern movement: "The academy was widely seen as an opportunity to demonstrate once and for all that Modern architecture could rise to the grandest occasions, sweeping away the historical styles of the nineteenth century."[71]

The initial furor over the academy exemplified the difficulties in trying to put an enlightened face on Cold War power. On the one hand, it represented a co-opting of the International Style, a movement that had been "fashioned as a symbol of science's hostility to business" but had evolved into a "technocratic cultural symbolism" readily adopted by a military-industrial complex; as Richard Gid Powers writes, "business no longer claimed any divine rights derived from the competitive and Darwinian ideology of nineteenth-century entrepreneurship, but struck a new pose as the apostle of science; the courthouse, the corporation headquarters, and the military academy are all disguised as laboratories."[72] Segments of the military—outside this newest of its branches—seemed unwilling to part with the traditional visual trappings of military power and ceremony, unable to accept the picture of the armed forces as an industrialized organization whose most powerful expression now lay buried beneath the ground in missile silos. The military, after all, emphasizes tradition in the face of technology—it equips "cavalry" units with helicopters, "infantry" with mobile personnel carriers. The u.s. Air Force, with its aluminum-skinned aircraft, had few such historical associations and hence was in tune with modern architecture. som's Richard Owings hinted at this when he insisted the academy would be "as styleless as the most modern guided missile—timeless."[73] But was the machine a sufficient symbol in itself?

In an article entitled "Architecture in the Atomic Age," John Burchard, then dean at m.i.t., noted that under a system of mutually assured destruction, it was a natural impulse to turn toward a higher authority, whether governmental or religious. "So the atomic age can quite as well be distinguished by a set of architectural symbols of a 'Nineteen Eighty-four' or by a proliferation of temples and churches . . . Indeed, the multiplication both of totalitarian architecture and of houses of faith seems already to have begun."[74] Indeed, the Air Force Academy Chapel would spawn countless jet-age imitators—the architect Robert Des Lauriers, for one. He gained renown "as the creator of strikingly modernistic churches throughout Southern California," notes Mark Dery; the culmination was the Carlton Hills Lutheran Church in Santee, California, "a Jetsonian traffic stopper whose 'flying effects' exploit the hyperbolic paraboloid." ("everybody was thinking of doing space things," the architect himself confessed).[75] This strand of techno-theological faith would reach its apotheosis in the 1978 Crystal Cathedral, designed by Philip Johnson for the Rev. Robert Schuller. Located in

Garden Grove, California, in the heart of the military-industrial stronghold of Orange County, the cathedral (an updating of the original drive-in church, still located next door) is an immense structure of white steel trusses and glass-paneled walls. It features a massive "Tower of Power," made up of steel tubes thrust upwards that terminate in a set of jagged points, their metal surfaces glimmering menacingly in the sun like a phalanx of missiles at a desert military installation. A plaque inside reflects on the 1955 founding of the quite revolutionary church: "This was also the era of the birth of television, the building of nuclear weapons of warfare, an age of hope and fear."

Hope and fear, security and paranoia, "Open Skies" and "Black Ops," trust but verify; the Cold War was space age optimism and missile age anxiety. On the surface, things brimmed with exuberance: the split-level homes of booming suburban affluence; the glass towers of modernism; the Googie diners and other examples of vernacular architecture that gleefully absorbed the "atomic facts of life"—buildings that looked ready for takeoff and had names to match. Cold War-inspired architecture ranged from the "Satellite Motel" of Omaha, Nebraska (the city that was home to the Strategic Air Command) to an "Atomic Motel" near Moab, Utah (hopefully out of range from the fallout of the Nevada Proving Ground); to new shopping centers like the 1962 Topanga Plaza, in the western part of the San Ferdinando Valley, where amidst military contractors like Boeing and Litton Industries, "rocket trails regularly colored the Valley's sunset sky from the largest missile test site in the Western Hemisphere."[76] At Charles Luckman and William Pereira's (now demolished) Convair Astronautics Facility, a 579,000-square-foot plant built to manufacture the country's first ICBM, a crisp Bauhaus lobby with windows and high ceilings had as its centerpiece a floating corkscrew of a staircase that itself was a wonder of physics. Another Luckman and Pereira project, the LAX "theme building," that massive jet-age spider of steel parabolic legs that looks ready to abduct anyone hanging about below, provided a Cold War backdrop for Lyndon B. Johnson's June 25, 1961 dedication speech, in which he warned Soviet Premier Nikita Khrushchev not "to underestimate the United States' determination to honor its pledges to the brave and freedom-loving people of Berlin."[77]

The American rhetoric of democracy was accompanied by a bright and shining architecture, whether it was modernist—the "architecture of democracy,"[78] as Vincent Scully called it—or homegrown space age camp. Both emphasized display and access: Glass-curtain walls, exuberant signage, outsized picture windows, open-plan offices, sliding-glass patio doors and indoor/outdoor living, and drive-throughs. But there was a parallel architecture of doom, marked by a brooding, subterranean fear. Civil defense pamphlets show clip-art representations of stiff, blank-stared homeowners lining their basements with sandbagged lean-tos; almost entire underground cities were carved out, in which technicians and bureaucrats of the apocalypse would manage our remaining assets (in organizations like the "Assets Valuation and Equalization Corporation"); even the highway, that harbinger of freedom and fresh starts, was also seen as an escape route from targeted urban centers.

These divergent tendencies also emerged in the unbuilt visions of avant-garde architects. Archigram, the British collective that drafted plans for under-water cities and living capsules, "clamoured ecstatically over the rocket support structures at Cape Kennedy."[79] The engineers were unwitting innovators; as Peter Blake wrote in *Architectural Forum*, "it is unlikely the engineers who designed the various moveable structures at Cape Kennedy have ever heard of the Archigram group. Indeed, the idea of a walking city would probably hor-rify them. Yet these engineers have designed and constructed a couple of dozen structures, some the height of 40 story office buildings, that move serenely across the flat landscape . . . Yet in visionary architecture such concepts . . . are still considered impractical by most designers and builders."[80] In Kiyonori Kikutake's Marine City, inspired by the launching of Sputnik, underwater liv-ing is the last best hope: "Continental civilization has constantly spread bloody strife among that mankind fated to live on land. It may not be too much to say that continental civilization has been no more than a history of conflict. And today the world is being threatened with the final confrontation between the two continents."[81] The sphere, that "most resonant symbol" and futuristic form of the 1960s,[82] was open to many interpretations: as the faintly sinister "radome" glowering on far mountaintops near military bases, the all-seeing eye of continental defense, and in a quite different vein, as Buckminster Fuller's dome at the Montreal Expo. As described in *Interiors*, "It rests like a thistle above the waters of the Le Moyne Channel, an object dream-like and out of another world, an object that tells us that the space age might be an age of poetical contemplation and absolute tranquility."[83]

Even the utopian impulse rarely seemed completely free of Cold War thought. Some of the most grandiose architectural dreams of the 1960s came from Paolo Soleri, the enigmatic Italian-born architect and one-time disciple of Frank Lloyd Wright. Lured to the desert in the 1940s to toil at Wright's Taliesin West, Soleri soon estranged himself from the master and began developing plans for model cities based on a theory called "Arcology." Like the concepts of Marshall McLuhan, it was a somewhat fluid and elusive notion. Soleri's plans for towering cities that would house millions of people, sketched out madly on endless sheets of butcher's paper, became a *cause célèbre* in the art and planning worlds. Soleri's 1969 Corcoran show was catalogued by the *New York Times*:

> Lucite models of polyhedral cybernetic cities scaled higher than two Empire State Buildings; intricate representations of structures

resembling jet engines, only 2,000 times their size, and accommodating as many people as San Francisco, plaster casts of graceful, sculptured bridge spans; plans for floating cities, space cities, cities within bridges, megastructures so huge that their inhabitants would be able to build houses within their frameworks.

The year 1970 hardly was a propitious one for building a hyper-urbanized megalopolis. America's cities were seething with crime and social unrest, suburban flight was in full blossom, the model housing project Pruitt-Igoe was long demolished, and Lyndon Johnson's "Model Cities" program—which rebuilt blighted urban areas—had been abolished by Nixon the year before, its resources channeled into the Vietnam War. But on a basaltic mesa overlooking the Agua Fria River some 60 miles from Phoenix, Soleri broke ground on Arcosanti, which the *Times* described as "less an apartment building than 2,500-inhabitant megastructure with a volume roughly equivalent to that of St. Peter's in Rome...an alien body on the land, it will be an almost self-contained space colony, and its chief purpose will be to test whether man can build environments that have only a minimal effect on the ecology of his planet."[84] *Newsweek*, commenting in 1976 that "a magnificent, inspiring and doomed city is rising out of the Arizona desert," concluded that "as urban architecture, Arcosanti is probably the most important experiment undertaken in our lifetime."[85]

Today, Arcosanti houses roughly 100 inhabitants, and only an estimated 4 percent of the original plan has been built. The cruel irony is that the city itself is likely to be lost in the urban sprawl of Phoenix before ever being finished. The fate of Soleri's dream is suggested to me on a summer afternoon as I exit I-17 and head toward Arcosanti, past a cluster of gas stations. As the road turns to gravel, I see the sign, "Arcosanti: An Experimental Community." To the right, however, I see another form of experimental living: a group of "manufactured housing" units for sale. The trailer is the desert's most ubiquitous shelter form, its prefab mobility attractive to those likely to pull up stakes when fortune or water runs dry; the trailer succeeds where only a madman would install a permanent house.

The most memorable example of trailer living I ever saw came on a visit to artist Nancy Holt's *Sun Tunnels* earth sculpture, located on a remote stretch of arid Nevada grazing land. The trailer (certainly not present when Holt installed the artwork) sat like a Martian probe on the scorched flats, the only human reference point visible for miles apart from the cement cylinders that comprise the *Sun Tunnels*. The owner was an electrician with Semper Fi tattoos who told me he was going to dig 100 feet, tap the water, and start a Christmas tree farm. Where Soleri's utopia envisions communal living in densely clustered, rationally planned structures, the trailer, for all its lack of architectural merit, represents the way people have preferred to live in the desert environment.

Arcosanti experimental community near Phoenix, Arizona

Arcosanti surges into view only after I drive down a rutted and twisting road (a guide later told me a car company had offered to pave it in exchange for sponsorship—the offer was turned down); suddenly, I am confronted by soaring blocks of poured concrete, earth-colored apses, circular windows, and metal sculptures—as well as looming cranes and the other detritus of building. The scene startles for its sheer visual novelty, but then one's mind begins to play back previously acquired images of dream architecture, of projected future civilizations; suddenly, Arcosanti, with its vaults and creeping vegetation and amphitheater-like steps descending in a semicircle around one apse, begins to seem almost a ruin. It recalls the iconography of science fiction, particularly dystopic visions of the future—Arcosanti could be the city in *Planet of the Apes*, or the refuge on the hill in *The Omega Man*. Or perhaps *Logan's Run*: For decades, Soleri's workforce has been idealistic youth, an impression reinforced on this visit. From one apse comes the honk of an avant-garde saxophone. "They're practicing for Burning Man," a guide tells me. Burning Man, that Archigram-like Instant City and annual countercultural festival on the desert at Black Rock, is actually a useful referent for evaluating Soleri's utopia.

Arcosanti has a very small full-time population; the bulk of residents carry out short-term internships. With its perpetually replenished constituency of likeminded people, living and working under the eye of the benevolent dictator, it works quite well. Like Burning Man, though, it is essentially a temporary fantasy, a respite from the mainstream. One wonders what would be the consequences if Arcosanti were ever to incorporate a varied and large population, or assume any of the other elements of a real city.

Arcosanti, with its ecologically minded architecture and anti-consumerist rhetoric (even if it survives by selling its iconic bells and ceramics), would hardly seem a Cold War landscape, but Soleri's grandiose visions, with their redemptive faith in technology, reflect their time. As historian George Collins notes, the visionary strain of architecture was revived after World War II, owing in part to a larger impetus toward postwar reconstruction as well as the threat of atomic attack.[86] The Cold War's twin axes of technological hope and doom prompted visionary architects to respond with plans for cities that would use technology to survive on a planet—"Spaceship Earth," as the suggestive phrase went—that was no longer inhabitable. Ironically, many of the schemes were influenced by the Cold War's architecture itself (e.g., Archigram's Cape Canaveral influence, or the fact that Buckminster Fuller's Dymaxion domes and hyperboloid housing towers resembled radomes and nuclear reactors, respectively). Like Fuller, Soleri was a technological optimist, whose early plans called for "Cosmodomes" that featured self-contained environments and artificial suns. His theories bristled with unintended Cold War phraseology like "complex systems," or "miniaturization"—the notion that cities would miniaturize their inhabitants (one cannot help thinking of *The Incredible Shriking Man*, in which an atomic accident shrinks the protagonist, turning his own house into a battleground). Arcosanti was a survivalist project, a shelter from the society that would kill itself in one great flash of the bomb or in the slow strangle of resource-consuming sprawl. Where most visionary architects' projects existed only in theory ("The Radiant City is on paper," Le Corbusier had written; "When a technical work is drawn up (figures and proofs) it *exists*"[87]), Soleri had found a blank slate, a drawing board in the desert. Reyner Banham saw a dubious parallel between it and similarly ambitious projects: "Might this not be the proving ground for an architectural tyranny (25,000 souls in one building!) as potentially harmful to humankind as the atom bombs that were also tested in secret seclusion in these deserts?"[88]

The fantastic schemes for self-contained communities propagated by Soleri, Fuller, and others might be easier to dismiss were they limited to the visionary schemes of the avant-garde. Such speculations, however, became part of mainstream planning discourse. One example is seen in a project undertaken by graduate students at Cornell University's College of Architecture in 1961. Titled "The Schoharie Valley Townsite: A Protected Community for the Nuclear Age," the project envisioned a sort of New Town centered around the corporate headquarters of the fictitious company "E.M.F" (modeled on IBM, which had assumed a consulting role in the project). The choice of IBM was not accidental: "The heart of much of our military, governmental, and civilian operating machinery in the second half of the twentieth century might be said to be the electronic computer. If it is not the heart, it is no less basic to the functioning of our present system."[89] What is remarkable about the project some forty years later is its faith in the technological solution to a technological problem, the trust that "thoughtful planning" could help provide a way out of the nuclear dilemma, i.e., protection from man's own destructive forces: "Now, in the twentieth century, he has unleashed a power which can elevate or exterminate him. Nuclear energy places man in a position where he must intelligently and sensitively come to grips with his own abilities."[90] Significantly, the power source for the self-sustaining community of some 9,000 was to be nuclear energy.

The Cornell planners move beyond the idea of designing individual *buildings* with blast protection and toward an entire community—literally, a survival city. "Is it possible to design an industrial installation which can maintain its operations during and after a nuclear explosion? Is it possible to design a community which can continue to function as such in spite of thermonuclear attack? Is it possible to conceive a community and industry which can exist in a normal human manner in spite of the ominous overtones of being designed as 'bomb-proof'?"[91] Rejecting outright the idea of a completely subterranean facility, the planners worked under the dominant assumption of the time, that the dual-purpose space was not only more economically feasible, but more palatable to people. But mirroring the surface city was an underground city, a grouping of hardened cylindrical structures—not unlike that of the NORAD defense installation at Colorado's Cheyenne Mountain—connected by an automated "seatway." Streets above would correspond to streets below, normal activities would be transferred underground to "alternate hardened spaces." The facility would "button up" and continue to function normally, technology below affording shelter from technological fallout above. "With its library, museum, and auditorium, this hardened central complex is also the town's cultural center, and would provide such cultural and entertainment activities as could be expected during the refuge period. As in the case of the seatway, continued normal use of these facilities by the townspeople is expected to reduce the psychological reactions that one might encounter in entering them as disaster shelters for the first time."[92] Armed with the tools of space-time analysis and the blast-resistant specifications of the Office of Civil and Defense Mobilization, the planners left no consideration unaccounted for, no human or industrial need uncalculated; what was missing, as was generally the case in such speculations, was the presence of people. Humans were the unknown factor in post-apocalyptic planning, a variable whose psychological well-being could be estimated like dynamic loads on walls, but whose actual life in such conditions could only be imagined.

Nearly half a century later, the report's author, M. Perry Chapman, now a campus planner based in Boston, recalls the project as more of a fascinating intellectual exercise than a practical undertaking. "The city planning studios were set up with a little bit of unorthodoxy about them. They were conceived more to prompt some fresh thinking about town making than simply being a conventional New Town," he says, adding that the previous year's study had been for a New Town in Colorado based around the oil shale industry. As for the project's thermonuclear component, he says, "most of us took it for granted that it was just part of trying to introduce some unconventionality—at least to the physical context of the planning." In other words, creating a town as a survivable cog in the military-industrial machine was no more remarkable than creating a town oriented around raw materials extraction. "There was a weird kind of normalcy about that in the 1950s which was why it probably didn't seem remarkable to us at the time," he says, adding that the "culture of conformity" expressed in IBM's corporate ethos was as fascinating to the students as the exotic aspects of the protected community. Both were irrevocably of their time. Chapman did not build a bomb shelter, nor did he know anyone who did. "I think people didn't have too much motivation to rebuild cities and houses for the possibility of being blown up by a fusion bomb." Instead, people dwelt in a netherworld, overshadowed by the nuclear threat, but still imagining a future, guided by "thoughtful planning" and visions of progress. The Cold War was the environment itself. "We lived with the Cold War for some forty years," Chapman says. "It was almost like background noise in some respects. Yet it was the prism through which everything was seen."[93]

The Cold War was paradoxically both present and invisible. Architecture was no less complex: What was secret was often right in the open, and what was "bunkerlike" was often far removed from traditional connotations of defense. The Maryland headquarters of the National Security Agency (NSA), dubbed the "Puzzle Palace," is described as a "tan, nine-story monolith [that] might belong to the Social Security Administration or some other elephantine bureaucracy."[94]

Yet inside its anodyne shell lurked the heart of one of the Cold War's most crucial enterprises: "SigInt," or "Signals Intelligence." The Puzzle Palace was a
building that literally grew with the volume of its activity, to the point where it
had become a 1,921,000-square-foot "Taj Mahal of Eavesdropping,"[95] featuring
the longest unobstructed corridor in the world (980 feet) and its own $2 mil-
lion, pneumatic-tube-fed trash incinerator. Another Beltway glass box housed
the National Reconnaissance Office in Chantilly, Virginia. This agency, in
charge of satellite surveillance and other Cold War tasks, was so secret that for
years it was not even acknowledged to exist—appropriately, its headquarters
was an anonymous office building among countless anonymous office buildings. And then there are buildings whose bunkerlike appearance seems at odds
with their function. Marcel Breuer's Whitney Museum, an inverted stacked
cube on New York City's Madison Avenue, has a monolithic stone facade,
moated periphery, and gun-turret-like windows that seem built to the dictates
of ballistic engineering. But Breuer's defense of the building was not mounted
with blast-resistant principles in mind; rather it was a "*Kunstbunker*" that championed sheer sculptural form and mass in a land where shopping mall, office
building, and military academy all looked the same. As Peter Blake described it,
invoking the language of nuclear confrontation, "Breuer is about to mount a
massive attack against those who made the name of this avenue synonymous
with their racket. The new Whitney will be art's answer to the huckster: Where
the ad agencies operate behind flimsy glass walls, the Whitney will be wrapped
in concrete faced with granite."[96]

"Cold War architecture" was not a single, recognized style, but if one
wanted to find perhaps the atomic age's truest landmark, one could look to the
place where it found its most fulsome and theatrical expression: the 1964
World's Fair in New York City. Previous expositions had dabbled in the utopianism of the space age; Brussels had its Atomium, while the 1962 Seattle
World's Fair had gone from a regional celebration of Seattle to a Boeing-led
coronation of the space age in the wake of the Soviet launch of Sputnik[97] (the
Fair's most lasting influence, of course, is the Space Needle, whose revolving
restaurant was touted as a sign of western technological supremacy). But it was
in the World's Fair site in Queens that the atomic age achieved its grandest display. There it reached critical mass, so to speak, in a delirious mixture of kitsch
and confidence, premature postmodernism and decadence. The reigning
motif was what critic Herbert Muschamp has called "Monumental
Temporary," an expression of the crisis of modernist architecture, which was
caught between its original democratic and egalitarian ideology and its evolution into a symbol of moneyed good taste and corporate power. The fair's aura
of irony, writes Muschamp, "was an effect of the cold war, a strategy for coping
with the culture of mass consumption on which American prosperity

depended . . . [W]hile industry was pumping out the furniture of suburban life—cars, appliances, situation comedies—modern architects were trying to keep kitsch at bay."[98] In any case, the fair's monuments were monuments to the present, dressed up as futurism; this was cultural saber-rattling, whose brio (whistling past the nuclear graveyard) belied an uncertainty that had been lacking at the first New York World's Fair. Roger Rosenblum writes, "The World of Tomorrow we had counted on in 1939 had evaporated together with Hiroshima, and only fools and hopeless provincials could look with wide-eyed hope at the future of modernity and the blessings of the Machine Age."[99] "Monumental Temporary" implicitly asked, what kind of monument could capture an age in which peril and progress were so irrevocably intertwined?

Designed by New York City planning commissioner Robert Moses and Major General Thomas F. Farrell, the former deputy commander of the Manhattan Project, the fair was a carnival of technological utopianism— "Atomsville, U.S.A.," as one display went. "Without pause," the guidebook read, "man has rushed headlong into the nuclear age, the space age, and the age of automation." But anyone might have wondered about the underlying meanings in the displays' vision of a world of atomic progress. A self-propelled, atomic-powered road builder was featured mowing through dense tracts of the Amazon ("GM shows how improvements in current technology may clear the way for man to enter, exist within and develop lands which lie unused today")—and was similar to the massive boring machines the government was employing at its most secret installations to construct security refuges of various sorts. The "atomic-powered submarine trains" that sailed "beneath the ice shelf," as well as the plastic dome for "climactic control," all hinted at the necessity for finding new habitable worlds after a nuclear war or creating artificial environments capable of surviving such a disaster. The white-smocked scientists loading the missilelike time capsule at the Westinghouse exhibit (a major Cold War contractor) evoked the contingency plans to bury the primary documents of the nation's cultural heritage in case of atomic emergency. The U.S. Space Park, cosponsored by NASA and the Department of Defense, featured Atlas and Titan II missiles, while even the fair's public artworks were steeped in Cold War imagery: Theodore Roszak's *Forms in Space* looked like a molten swept-wing fighter, while Donald De Lue's *Rocket Thrower* was interesting for its mythological associations, like the missiles themselves—the Thors, Nikes, Saturns, Jupiters, Hercules, and Zeuses. The Futurama model city, with its soaring buildings, empty plazas, and vigorous traffic arteries, recalled not only Le Corbusier's Radiant City but the evacuation plans of dispersal prophets in the 1950s.

Perhaps the most powerful architectural expression of Cold War hope and fear at the fair was the "World's Fair House," designed by Texas builder Jay

Swayze. With the claim of "greater security-peace of mind-the ultimate in true privacy!", the house's most noteworthy feature was that it was underground. While later earthbound structures would tout energy savings as their primary virtues, the security aspects of the house were readily apparent. Swayze, commissioned in 1961 to build a fallout shelter for the city of Plainview, Texas, was so struck by the experience that he constructed his own underground house: "I saw the merit of utilizing the Earth as protection against radioactive fallout. As a former military instructor in chemical warfare, I knew that the three ways man could destroy himself were by nuclear fission, nerve gas, or germ warfare. Despite President Kennedy's assurance that the threat of war was only temporary, one thing was clear. The nuclear age was upon us, and long-range planning was necessary to protect humanity from possible ill effects."[100] A writer for *Holiday* magazine, who called the house a "glorious nightmare,"[101] noted that one of the books lining the shelves of the underground home, where one would presumably have much time to read, was a u.s. Air Force report on the ballistic missile.

Described by *Look* as a "10-room house with its own push-button climate," Swayze's Plainview, Texas house, built for $80,000, featured its own "emergency power plant," a lighting system that could "bathe the house in 'sunlight' or 'moonlight' at the flick of a switch," a fake window with an ersatz view of trees, and enough equipment to "hole up below for a full year if they had to." Swayze, the magazine reported, "is negotiating to build an underground chapel and a motel, and has plans drawn for entire subterranean communities." A handful of similar houses were built across the country; one, a few blocks from the Las Vegas strip, "spreads over 5,200 square feet and is surrounded by an Astroturf lawn, fake trees and an 'outdoor' grill designed to send smoke and fumes up a fake tree trunk."[102]

While naïve enthusiasm like Swayze's may have waned, the not-so-secret fears embodied in underground architecture persisted for decades. An Oklahoma architect reported designing several underground homes for clients in the 1980s who feared that the proximity of the state's Tinker Air Force Base made them a target for Soviet attack. "I got so many calls I started to get scared," he said. "The common thread that I would sense . . . was a fear, a mistrust."[103] As it turned out, however, few people ever sought underground shelter, lacking either the financial resources or the will to seal themselves off from the surface. There were, however, larger agencies, who inhabited the blurred fringes of the public imagination, that were burrowing deeper than Swayze—and, moreover, out of sight and off the record. As the government's civil defense initiatives gave mixed messages about the means of survival in an atomic attack, the government itself was carving out an underground state, a series of ghostly, non-democratic realms that were the subterranean doubles of the civic order topside.

4.
THE UNDERGROUND CITY:
The Architecture of Disappearance
and Three Case Studies

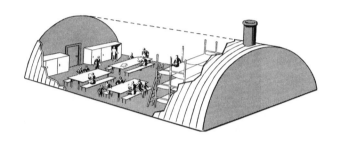

The underground is the paranoid aspect of the Cold War, the dark space beneath the symbolic order reigning above. It is a paradoxical netherworld of both security and insecurity, the place in which we seek shelter, store our possessions, extract wealth, hide our weapons. But it also is a place of fear—where we bury our dead, where criminality lurks, where the logic of the daylight world does not necessarily apply. In certain strands of psychology, the subterranean and the subconscious are parallel. Thus, one could not understand the Cold War period, with its superficial consensus, progress, and stability, without considering its subterranean chambers of reinforced concrete, locked doors, secret communication networks, and men with guns. In the underground world, complexes were built to replicate the governing structures above; the home fallout shelter promised security beneath the backyard; it was the only place eventually deemed acceptable for nuclear weapons testing; and tunnels were built to siphon information from hostile embassies. Finally, in the Cold War's aftermath, it was where we chose to bury the untouchably toxic residue that had accumulated.

After Hiroshima, American military planners began a far-reaching investigation into the creation of a kind of subterranean state, an emergency alternative to a world threatened by atomic destruction. A 1947 *New Yorker* article described a joint u.s. Army-Navy "survey of suitable subterranean sites"—in particular, natural caves—primarily in West Virginia. "People have got to be

Inside the North American Aerospace Defense Command, Cheyenne Mountain, Colorado

educated," an army colonel told the magazine. "They've got to become underground-conscious. I'd like to see industry start thinking about putting plants underground." The Army Corps of Engineers, working with the Bureau of Mines, made a "comprehensive survey of existing mines in the u.s. which had certain characteristics as to floor area, depth of cover, ceiling height, accessibility and other features which would indicate their value as potential industrial or storage sites."[1] A contract was given to a New York engineering firm, Guy B. Panero (which was later contracted to provide shelter space in Rockefeller Center), to determine the feasibility of actually adapting the mines to other uses.[2] Robert Panero, discussing the "exit problem" of underground spaces at one conference, made this distinction between the military and civilian installations: "If a military unit survives and operates during an attack period, it is not as important that the personnel operating the unit be capable of exiting; military people can be considered expendable. On the other hand, the civilian application . . . fails if the personnel or material cannot be removed after the attack or the war is over."[3] The Hudson Institute, in a report on "elaborate non-military defense," sketched out a new kind of Cold War space:

> Such a program might place a premium upon underground cities in solid rock and visualize the withering away of densely populated surface areas. One beginning to such planning was made in the Manhattan Shelter Study which developed preliminary plans for a deep (800-foot) rock shelter sufficient for all of Manhattan's population. Developments of this kind, of course, seem bizarre now, but are not impossible if, for example, some dramatic events should occur, such as the use of nuclear weapons in limited or general war.[4]

From Survival City at the Nevada Test Site, one witness to a bomb blast mused on the European example: "Word from Stockholm, for example, is that no permit is given for construction of a new apartment house unless it is built above heavily encased basement bomb shelters. Just about now the Swedes are completing six huge public shelters. One, in the heart of Stockholm, will take 20,000 people in five minutes."[5] Indeed, Sweden, where thousands of underground civil defense installations had been built (at a cost, in 1964, of $2 billion) for a nation of 7.7 million, was an apt model: "The Swedes, like 7.7 million moles in and out of uniform, have gone underground to create a wholly viable second nation in the granite."[6] (Ironically, it took only one man—Soviet "master spy" Air Force Colonel Stig Wennerstöm—to expose much of this dark space to light).

It is not surprising that planners turned to mines as they sketched the contours of this new underground world, for it was the nineteenth-century mine that helped create not only the modern conception of the underground, but the subterranean nature of the nineteenth-century city itself—Lewis Mumford argued that the industrial city—"Coke Town"—was literally an extension of the mine: "As one should expect of a regime whose key inventions came out of the mine, the tunnel and the subway were its unique contributions to urban form."[7] As the amount of underground economic activity increased in the nineteenth century, and with the increased sub-surface placement of essential urban activities, the idea of an entire life lived underground began to take hold. Jules Verne, in his 1877 *Les Indes Noires*, speculates on an underground "Coal Town," while H. G. Wells, in *The Time Machine*, imagined a race of subterranean "Morlocks": "Even now there are existing circumstances that point that way," Wells wrote, describing the "tendency to utilise underground space for the less ornamental purposes of civilisation; there is the Metropolitan Railway . . . there are new electric railways, there are subways, there are underground workrooms and restaurants, and they increase and multiply."[8]

As Rosalind Williams notes, accounts of underground life seemed to hinge on a fatal contradiction: "In most of them, the motive for going underground in the first place is to escape some natural disaster. . . . Once underground, however, society proves vulnerable to other catastrophes—not natural disasters, in most cases, but social ones arising from humanity's inability to live harmoniously in an enclosed environment."[9] This is a frequent theme in the fables of the Cold War. In the 1959 novel *The Rest Must Die*, the survivors of an atomic attack on New York city take to the subways, where internecine battles soon ensue; in Harlan Ellison's 1969 *A Boy and His Dog*, the underground is used to depict the Cold War conformism of the surface. In both cases, the confined underground space becomes a concentrated breeding ground for social dysfunction as the once-submerged id rages unchecked.

The massive aerial bombardments of World War II lent a new urgency to the idea of underground construction, whether the air-raid shelters and tube stations of London or the underground factories of Germany—the tunnel-connected v-2 complex near Nordhausen, or the Messerschmidt factory near Landberg, described as a "a four-storey factory sunk into the ground and then covered by a parabolic concrete cover some 5 m (16.5 feet) thick."[10] Fewer than 1 percent of German installations were subterranean, however, and as the English commander Sir Arthur Harris noted, underground factories, no matter how deep, still depended upon outside lines of communication and transport. "[Albert] Speer thought little of the German attempts to put essential industries underground," Harris wrote in *Bomber Offensive*. "One cannot meet air attack with the slogan 'Concrete versus bombs.' The opponent in the air is able to choose his objectives and in doing so he can plan to concentrate on any vital target such a weight of attack as hitherto has never been possible. There was consequently no means of defense."[11]

The fascination with—and ultimate futility of—massive underground fortifications reached its apogee in the Maginot Line, which entered the lexicon of history as a synonym for outmoded strategic thinking. Envisioned by its creator as a "subterranean fleet," the Maginot complex was described by one officer as "more like a submarine than anything except a submarine I've ever been in."[12] Indeed, it was buried in the earth deeper than any fortification in history, virtually out of the reach of enemy forces. As would be the case with later subterranean facilities, however, fact entwined with fiction. Stories of "concretitis"and other strange new "bunker" maladies competed for attention with enthusiastic tales that "the main section of the Maginot Line had been equipped with cinemas, barber shops (complete with white-coated attendants) even cafés with slashes of local colour from North Africa to make the Moroccan troops feel at home."[13] In one 1959 account, the "virtually indestructible" Maginot Line, described as a "trogolyditic city of extraordinary dimensions," was seen to have taken on a curious new role in the atomic age: "Today it may once more be impossible for a civilian to approach any of the forts, for after a period of neglect they have apparently come into use again. They make, it seems, perfect shelters from atom and hydrogen bombs and have been taken over as N.A.T.O. stores."[14] Although the enduring lesson of the Maginot Line was that fixed fortifications were outmoded in the age of *Blitzkrieg* (the mobile German forces had executed an end-run *around* the line), the spirit and technology of the Maginot Line would in fact be repeated —albeit with improved drilling technology and strengthened materials—in underground fortresses built not to hold a specific position, but from which to ensure the capacity for a retaliatory nuclear strike. In military architecture, form always follows ammunition—i.e., defensive architecture inevitably evolves and responds to advances in weaponry. As Herman Kahn pointed out in an address titled "Why Go Deep Underground?," "People are designing buildings for protection against single bomb drops, but the enemy may have thousands of ICBMs in the 1965–75 time period; people are designing buildings to survive inaccurate low-yield weapons, even though it is almost certain that the enemy will improve his accuracy and yield if he finds it necessary to do this to destroy an important target."[15]

Whether or not the new underground complexes were simply the Maginot Lines of the Cold War, the underground was touted as the last best hope for survival, and planners worked to naturalize the idea of an underground existence. "The attitude and expectations of many people about underground living," observed one Stanford researcher, "have been formed on the basis of thinking about crude caves and dugouts. However, a society that has and is building windowless factories, bargain basements, and congested apartment districts should be able to appreciate that underground accommodations can be adequately comfortable. With the application of architectural talent, developments of this kind can be aesthetically pleasant. There are, indeed, often a number of commercial advantages to construction of this type."[16] Accounts in the popular press presented a (literally) glowing picture of below-ground dwelling aided by technology; historian Paul Boyer describes a society in which "the populace lives underground in climate-controlled atomic houses, surfacing only for a dip in the above-ground swimming pool (which also provides insulation), for trips in large, transparent atomic-powered automobiles suspended from overhead tracks, or in airplanes propelled by high-speed particles emitted by U-235."[17] *Collier's* painted a similar picture: "The subterranean houses are heated and cooled by walls of radioactive uranium and illuminated by translucent panels aglow with fluorescence."[18] Proposals circulated for fantastic underground city concepts; as *Architectural Forum* noted in 1958, "The latest is Navy Commander George F. Bond, medical researcher at the New London Submarine Base, who solemnly proposes that underwater cities be built 150 feet down under the continental shelves off the coasts, equipped to support life indefinitely on algae, oxygen, and hydrogen from sea water."[19] Los Angeles architect and designer Paul Laszlo proposed an underground suburban settlement whose surface was camouflaged to resemble a park bisected by highways and whose mound roof would serve double duty as a landing strip. The power source was equally forward-looking: "Cheap atomic energy will be applied to all [the resident's] homely needs."[20]

Beneath the florid technological optimism lies a more ominous subtext: Once underground living had been made possible, it might become *necessary*. For Mumford, the rising investment in the underground city came at the expense of the above-ground city, which itself had begun to mimic its netherworld opposite: "With air conditioning and all-day fluorescent lighting, the internal spaces in the new American skyscraper are little different from what they would be a hundred feet below the surface."[21] The city, in other words, had become a bunker of sorts, a Survival City where the reproduction or augmentation of the environment through machinery was viewed not as an emergency measure, but an everyday condition. The city's survival became dependent upon the underworld, not only for the infrastructure contained therein, but for the womblike comfort of its labyrinthine passages.

In 1961, the city of Chicago began surveying a suburban limestone quarry—whose owners, looking to extract the last bits of raw material, had begun drilling "giant rooms" into the sides of the rock face—for possible use as a massive municipal fallout shelter. "The shelter could be tied in with the city's network of underground water pipes and transportation tunnels [an abandoned underground railway] and be connected to the downtown area where we have 1.3 million people working every day," said Chicago's director of civil defense. "It would easily shelter 500,000 people and a lot of lives could be saved . . . if people could get to the quarry."[22] The underground society that Jules Verne and H. G. Wells had prophesied, tied to the mine and the hidden veins of the industrial city, had been reborn. America scrambled for this metaphorical rabbit hole. The underworld was not merely shelter; it was also the stronghold from which wars would be fought and if not won, at least survived. "The masters of the underground citadel," wrote Mumford, "are committed to a 'war' they cannot bring to an end, with weapons whose ultimate effects they cannot control, for purposes that they cannot accomplish."[23] Having committed themselves to the endgame of massive retaliation and mutually assured destruction, the only place to go, it seemed, was down. Nearly half a century later, I went in search of three of these subterranean refuges, which became three case studies of the post-nuclear-attack future. One was intended for Congress, one was intended for the President, and one was intended to carry out the war itself.

Emergency entrance, Congressional Relocation Facility at the Greenbriar Hotel, West Virginia

Case Study #1: Project Greek Island

All wars end in tourism. Battlefields are rendered as scenic vistas, war heroes are frozen into gray memorials in urban parks, tanks and other weapons bask outside American Legion posts on suburban strips. That the Cold War, the so-called "imaginary war" that was never actually fought (apart from proxy conflicts)—its Atlas missiles never launched, its atomic cannons never fired, its massive retaliations never employed—makes its tourism somewhat odd. This tourism curiously combines "what if" with "what was"; as one tours never-before-seen secret installations that seem familiar, one is looking at abstract doomsday scenarios poured in hard concrete.

If war becomes tourism, it seems appropriate that its warriors become tour guides. And so it is that I find myself on a fog-enshrouded West Virginia hillside, standing in a light spring rain, listening to Paul "Fritz" Bugas as he prefaces his tour of Project Greek Island, the once hidden "Continuity of Government" bunker, located under the four-star Greenbrier Resort, which would have served as the emergency relocation center for the 535 members of Congress in the event of a nuclear war.

For decades, Bugas, a spry, bearded ex-intelligence officer (formerly with the Office of the Assistant Chief of Staff of Intelligence), ran the bunker's cover operation—a Virginia-based TV repair firm with the dubiously overblown name of Forsythe Associates. In reality, Forsythe only spent about one-fifth of its time servicing the hotel's hundreds of television sets, instead focusing on fulfilling its primary mission, which was, in Bugas's institutional patois, "operating the facility and keeping it on a ready basis." Standing in front of a conspicuously large, steel-plated door set into the mountain and with a sign warning "High Voltage" at its center, Bugas gestures at distant peaks, blithely detailing facts that he had once sworn to conceal. On top of Greenbrier Mountain, for example, more than 3 miles away, a 100-foot tower bristles with antennas and monitoring devices (called "nudets") that could have detected the effects of a nuclear detonation from a 100 miles away. On top of Kate's Mountain, across the valley, AT&T microwave telephone towers were linked by cable to the Greenbrier; along with two 80-foot radio antennas, normally buried in silos, these were the connections to a post-nuclear world, a network of secret transmitters installed across the country that would have crackled to life while all else was white noise.

How did such a mammoth bunker as Project Greek Island escape detection? To build it, the Greenbrier Resort, with federal assistance, embarked in 1957 on construction of a "West Virginia Wing," using the ensuing commotion as a screen. The presence of what locals called "the big hole," which

Air intake valve, Congressional Relocation Facility at the Greebriar Hotel, West Virginia

seemed to suck up an endless supply of poured concrete, fuelled almost immediate speculation: a 1959 *Charleston Gazette* article announced: "Greenbrier Rumor Denied: No Presidential Hideout Planned." Rumors swirled, and inquiries were met with a diffident evasion: "You might have gotten a letter to the president of the Greenbrier," says Bugas, "indicating that a board member or confidant had heard about a bunker, asking if there was any truth to it. This would be answered in a nebulous way, attributed to the idea that so many presidents had visited here." Strangely for a secret complex, even the plainest exposed details, such as the bunker's ground entrance with its industrial-looking steel facade, seem out of proportion to anything the West Virginia Wing might have required in its operation. Curious too are the т-shaped green smokestack and cordoned-off shed found in the woods near a set of tennis courts (indeed, these were the confirming details when a *Washington Post* reporter, following years of investigative work, exposed Greenbrier's secret in 1992). Otherwise, Project Greek Island, once known as Project Casper, is a purloined-letter kind of place, hidden in plain sight, its vents and external trappings blending obliquely into the surroundings. A section of the bunker adjoining the hotel was occasionally used as a conference center; the participants remained unaware that they had strayed into a bunker. A 1962 brochure touts the "Governor's Hall," featuring "continental style, permanent seating for 475"[24] (a capacity suited to the House of Representatives) and the "Mountaineers Room," hosting 125.

Atomic architecture is architecture that asks not to be noticed; ornamentation is replaced by pure blast-resistant engineering, never visible except in blueprints. Even then, the untrained eye is likely to be baffled by these self-effacing structures: In Graham Greene's novel *Our Man in Havana*, a vacuum cleaner salesman in Cuba submits drawings of a new space-age vacuum cleaner to British intelligence as plans of a top-secret missile base. This is not as far-fetched as it seems, for architecture with a Cold War purpose was nothing if not mechanical.

Standing on the hillside with Fritz Bugas, I watch the door to the bunker groan open. As it turns out, the entire facade *is* the door. Some 10 feet wide by 12 feet high by 18 inches thick, and weighing 25 tons, it is one of several "blast doors" made by Ohio safe manufacturer Mosler, which ran a "protective construction" division specifically for atomic architecture. A Mosler safe had survived partially the attack on Hiroshima and in atomic testing on the Nevada Proving Grounds. The company also manufactured doors for the Union Carbide Nuclear Company's Oak Ridge, Tennessee facility. Where most doors of this size would be of seamed double-leaf construction, this blast door is single leaf, i.e., essentially a solid slab of steel. It locks only from within; the point being, as Bugas says, "to control ingress and egress from within the facility itself"—meaning, to keep out unwanted visitors. The door itself was shipped from Mosler's Ohio factory on a custom flatbed railcar (made easier by the fact that the owner of the railroad that ran from Greenbrier to Cincinnati was the Chesapeake & Ohio Railroad, later csx, the owner of Greenbrier). Unlike other post-detonation redoubts, the Greenbrier is what is known as a "cut-and-cover" facility; it is not meant to survive the near-miss of a nuclear weapon, but rather to shield its inhabitants from a more distant blast and the ensuing fallout—the nearby mountains were considered added shielding from an explosion that would have targeted Washington, D.C. The real strength of the Greenbrier lay in its seclusion.

The inside summons every Cold War cliché imaginable, from *Dr. Strangelove* to *Get Smart*: a 400-foot tunnel receding into the distance, illuminated by overhanging metal-shaded lamps spaced at regular intervals. Above the entrance, Bugas points to a series of round exhaust vents; usually open, they would automatically seal (in u.s. Army Corps of Engineers lingo, "button up") if a radioactivity sensor sounded. Lining the tunnel are a handful of boxes bearing the brand name Mountain High, with labels reading "scrambled eggs" and "creamed cottage cheese." At one time the entire tunnel would have been lined with such rations, intended to feed occupants of the shelter—depending upon the number that had actually made it from Washington—for upwards of sixty days. Air would have entered through a variety of filters (against radiation, as well as chemical and biological agents), swept down the pressurized tunnel, and exited through exhaust vents on the far side of the bunker. "I want to know where we were supposed to go," a woman from the assembled group says, staring down into the disappearing gloom. "That's what I want to know."

There is a heavy air of grim utilitarianism as we walk through the two-floor bunker, which Bugas describes as "two football fields stacked on top of one another." The setting mingles 1960s gray-steel office modernism with power-plant rooms that mimic the service floors of high-rise office buildings, but embellished by peculiar "atomic" touches. At the end of the hallway, there is a set of blue-tiled showers through which entrants would pass for a fallout-cleansing scrubbing (one cannot help but think of concentration camps). Down the stairs are three room-sized black storage buildings, which could each hold 25,000 gallons of water; the various filtration systems to pull radioactive, biological, and chemical elements from the air; and an incinerator that, while not intended as a crematorium *per se*, does, says Bugas, "burn with an intensity that could be used for a human individual." Back upstairs, one walks through a broadcast room featuring a backdrop of the Congressional building, to be used as the virtual set in issuing communiqués. The tour concludes in the Governor's Hall, the 440-seat amphitheater that would have served as the chamber for the House of Representatives. Throughout the bunker, there are none of the sybaritic trappings rumored about these types of spaces—well-appointed sitting rooms or lounges stocked with an endless supply of fifteen-year-old scotch. There are indeed few soft edges whatsoever, nary a concession to the subterranean homesick blues; the feeling is of concrete and steel, of industry. The bunker looks like a factory; survival is its product. As death would presumably have been raging outside its doors, it was a "machine for living" of the most literal sort.

Touring the Project Greek Island bunker, it is difficult to escape the cultural connotations of Cold War kitsch—one wants to place a red hotline phone somewhere—and to wonder about the process by which the facility was conceived, engineered, and maintained (not to mention the feelings of those who kept fresh rations on hand underground, or updated the names of Congressmen on the dormitory beds when new members were voted into office). To revive an old phrase, it was a permutation of the "banality of evil," the rational response to an irrational policy. That engineers planned a 12-foot thick door speaks less to the strength of the facility than to the rather sobering question of what would have happened to everyone beyond the door.

Later in the evening, after touring the bunker and walking on the grounds above it, I settled in with what seemed like appropriate reading: the 1995 publication, *Underground Bases and Tunnels: What Is the Government Trying to Hide?* Written by Richard Sauder, the book is actually not as sensational as its delicious subtitle would suggest; its sources are droll government reports on the order of "Workshop on Technology for the Design and Construction of Deep Underground Facilities." Sauder's inquiry ranges from advanced tunneling technology to secret underground railway systems said to connect various nodes of the military-industrial complex in the southwest. As a student of ufology, however, Sauder cannot help but leave the door slightly open to speculation about what the "true" nature of these facilities might be: "And while there are stories floating around in UFO circles about bizarre, Nazi-style genetic engineering programs being conducted in underground facilities by 'Little Grey' aliens and the U.S. military, I can offer no proof that such programs exist. They may exist; they equally may not."[25] In this equivocation, and among the legions who believe the "truth is out there," exists the real legacy of places like Project Greek Island: Designed to protection constitutional government, the government's underground architecture actually undermines the faith of its own citizenry. That they look for alien threats in this architecture of doom only reminds us that the all-too-terrestrial truth is the most fantastic thing of all.

The President (played by Henry Fonda) in his underground command post in the 1964 film *Fail Safe*

Case Study #2: Project Hotel (The John F. Kennedy Presidential Fallout Shelter)

In the late afternoon on the eighth day of the Cuban missile crisis, President John F. Kennedy and his best-and-brightest-and-Brylcreamed circle of advisers (the hastily assembled group known as Ex Comm) huddled in the White House Cabinet room and mulled the rapidly constricting options of the escalating conflict. Talk turned from the steely language of brinkmanship to the question of what might happen to u.s. citizens in the event that the Soviet-installed, Cuban-based medium-range ballistic missiles were launched. "What is it that we ought to do for the population in affected areas, in case the bombs go off?" Kennedy asks, in the recently published transcript, *The Kennedy Tapes: Inside the White House During the Cuban Missile Crisis.* "Is there something we can do?"

Civil defense in America during the Cold War was always something of a fiction, an act of collective hope that produced rituals of civic drama but never generated the government funding its proponents sought nor ever unleashed the presumed mania in fallout shelter building (in 1960, a House committee estimated that in thirty-five states, only 1,565 home shelters had been built). But it is no surprise that of all presidents to serve during the Cold War it was Kennedy—the one who skirted the edge of the abyss—who was the strongest proponent of shelter from atomic attack. In an infamous issue of *Life* that assured a 97 percent chance of survival if the country was adequately sheltered, a letter from Kennedy stated that "the ability to survive coupled with the will to do so are essential to our country."[26] Before the Cuban missile crisis, as one story goes, Kennedy called his wartime friend and Navy assistant secretary Paul Fay to ask if he had built a bomb shelter for his family. "No," Fay answered, joking, "I built a swimming pool instead." "You made a mistake," Kennedy responded. As Fay recalled: "He was dead serious."[27]

On a small island near Palm Beach, Florida, a five-minute motorboat ride from the former Kennedy estate, one can get a visceral taste of life in the atomic age when, at its most terrifying extremes, nearly 10 percent of the Strategic Air Command's nuclear force was airborne and loaded at any given time, the nation's armed forces were on standing five-minute alert under DEFCON2, and anywhere—including the president's Florida vacation outpost—was a potential target. Here, on Peanut Island, a tiny "spoils island" formed in 1919 out of dredge material from the newly formed Lake Worth Inlet, the u.s. Navy Seabees came in December of 1961—almost a year before the missile crisis—covertly to build an emergency fallout shelter for Kennedy and his family.

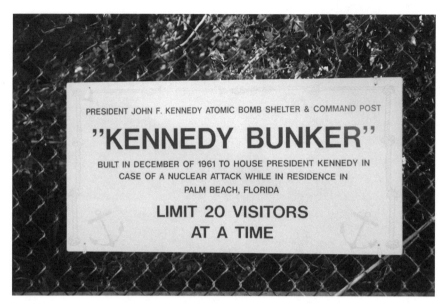

PRESIDENT JOHN F. KENNEDY ATOMIC BOMB SHELTER & COMMAND POST

"KENNEDY BUNKER"

BUILT IN DECEMBER OF 1961 TO HOUSE PRESIDENT KENNEDY IN
CASE OF A NUCLEAR ATTACK WHILE IN RESIDENCE IN
PALM BEACH, FLORIDA

LIMIT 20 VISITORS
AT A TIME

Presidential fallout shelter, Palm Beach, Florida

These days, the bunker is owned by the Palm Beach Maritime Museum and open for weekend tours. On a bright December day, the air sagging with moisture, I am taken to Peanut Island on a small pontoon boat by Bill Rose, a museum tour guide and scuba-diving instructor. As we slowly motor to the island, with the north tip of Palm Beach off to one side and the more rambunctious Port of Palm Beach to the other, Rose reflects that during the missile crisis, over 200,000 military personnel came to Florida. "You think it's crazy down here in the season?" he cackles. "Luxury hotels were told to send their guests home—and the military moved in." On October 22, 1962, the *Miami News* noted that the state "bristled with armed might."[28]

The shelter is found a few hundred feet past the old Coast Guard station, an expansive white Colonial opened in 1936 and shuttered in 1995. The shelter entrance, a blunt tunnel-like aperture with a door and two round openings, peeks out from the side of a small ridge atop which, as Rose notes somewhat conspiratorially, "the trees are shorter than all of the other ones." The shelter's official cover was that it was a munitions depot, and Rose pokes through a tangle of mosquito-clotted underbrush to show me a weathered sign announcing the same. There are several pieces of architectural evidence, however, which reveal the structure's true nature. The first are the "buttons," or adjustable air valves that flank the door. In the event of an explosion, the valves would have been shut, allowing for weeks of self-sustaining, presumably fallout-free underground living. Inside, down a length of corrugated-pipe hallway (itself another giveaway, as the main space is found angled off the hallway, which would become a trap of sorts for the incoming blast wave), comes another telltale bit of Cold War architecture: a drain on the floor of a small chamber just before the entrance to the main room. As with the Greenbrier bunker, the decontamination shower is the symbolic welcome mat, the thermonuclear boot scrape, the first thing one sees past the blast door and the blast deflection tunnel.

The main room is somewhat anticlimactic. Picture a musty Quonset hut with a few scattered pieces of furniture and radio equipment, and a 3-foot water line still visible on the wall from a severe flood in 1995. No flickering global wall maps, no hints of any post-strike opulence. At the far end of the room, a ladder leads to an escape hatch above—this too is an essential piece of bunker architecture. As an Oak Ridge National Laboratory civil defense report puts it, "As a matter of prudence and psychological acceptability, any underground space expected to be used for shelter of more than a few people should have at least two methods of egress."[29] As the bunker, which Rose describes as "one of the worst-kept secrets in Palm Beach County," was a near ruin when the museum acquired it ("It literally became home to homeless people for a while," notes Rose) in 1995, it has taken great license in attempting to recreate the flavor of those doomsday days. The red hotline phone on a desk is not real, nor is the desk (in fact, observes Rose, the hotline wasn't established until after the Cuban missile crisis), nor is the presidential seal painted on the floor. What is real are the infrastructural remnants that attest to the site's real purpose: a carbon-dioxide air filtration system (similar to that

Blast deflection tunnel, presidential fallout shelter, Palm Beach, Florida

used on submarines) and its overhead piping, the shower drain, the escape hatch, and the building itself, buried under 10 feet of dirt and coated with lead, which the museum discovered as it excavated for the required wheelchair entrance. Ironically, a space once reserved for a lucky few has now been modified to admit all.

John Grant, president of the Palm Beach Maritime Museum, tells me later that the Kennedy Library is not aware of the bunker's existence, nor will they even acknowledge it. But Grant, an old Cold War hand himself, having moved to Palm Beach in 1964 to serve as the civilian head of the U.S. Navy's Atlantic Undersea Test Evaluation Center—an agency that was charged with developing torpedoes and other underwater lines of defense—says a number of people have come forward who either helped build the bunker or report having seen it in operation. He waves a photocopy of a set of Seabees orders describing "Detachment Hotel," in which members of the construction battalion are to report to Palm Beach in December 1961, with a "secret" clearance. Another document shows the Port of Palm Beach giving permission to the U.S. government to "erect improvements" on the site of the bunker. "It was definitely a fallout shelter," says Grant, who notes that Kennedy spent "about every weekend" in Palm Beach—including the one before his assassination. Built in seven days, the site has become a historical footnote, so secret there is hardly anyone to remember it. "I talked to [Kennedy speechwriter Theodore] Sorensen, and he didn't know about it," says Grant. "There's supposed to be another one for Kennedy up in Nantucket."

While the Kennedy vacation bunker is something of a special case, every president since Eisenhower has had recourse not only to a White House bomb shelter ("the White House, to be sure, is equipped with a yawning bomb shelter that dates back to Franklin Roosevelt's day," *Time* wrote in 1961[30]), but to Virginia's Mount Weather, the legendary "special facility" now managed by the Federal Emergency Management Agency. FEMA, which uses the site as an emergency management and conference center, tends to politely eschew any mention or acknowledgment of the site's status as a presidential bunker.

Mount Weather, a reputed "underground city" of some twenty office complexes, an on-site waste management system, and a television studio once plugged into the Cold War-vintage Emergency Broadcast Network, was built in 1958 by the U.S. Army Corps of Engineers, part of the so-called "Federal Relocation Arc" of structures to which the various branches of government would repair in the event of a national catastrophe. It was described by one official as "otherworldly—just the size and weight and massiveness of the doors. It's a mini-city—like a space station."[31] By the time the Cold War thriller *Seven Days in May* was published in 1962, Mount Weather was not much of a secret; that book described "Mount Thunder, where an underground installation provided one of the several bases from which the President could run the nation in the event of a nuclear attack on Washington."[32]

The Federal Relocation Arc is a covert constellation of still-classified underground facilities stretching from Virginia to Pennsylvania, a zone where the civically harmonious architectural symbols and ceremonial pomp of the nation's capital is replaced by concrete openings into hillsides on large wooded tracts behind a wall of razor wire; hardened, austere "facilities" that for decades have played host to a fantasy government-in-waiting, rewriting scripts for the end of the world. These are negative spaces, defined by what cannot be seen; they are pieced together by rumor, blurred aerial photographs, and glimpses of vents and other infrastructure that peek out from their peripheries.

One of the most legendary sites is "Site R," the Alternate Joint Communications Center (known now more generally as the National Military Command Center), buried some 650 feet down and inside the mountain of Raven Rock, in the Blue Ridge Summit area of southern Pennsylvania. Work on "the Rock" began in 1950, prompted by the Soviet detonation of a nuclear bomb. The details of Site R remain classified—even though it has now been reduced to caretaker status—but it has been described as a set of five three-story buildings, totaling nearly 265,000 square feet, each occupying its own cavern set deep inside the mountain's greenstone—a variety of granite thought to be the world's fourth-hardest rock. From Site R, "watch teams" connected to the Pentagon acted as a kind of computer backup system; "if anything hiccupped," said one official, "they were supposed to be in step, following anything."[33] From unofficial reports, one can compose an image of the interior of Site R: cavelike, with well-lit hallways, period furnishings, a cafeteria named "Granite Cove" (to feed the handful of remaining "molies," as they are known), and "Sensitive Compartmentalized Information Facilities" that provide even more secretive enclaves for classified meetings.

There were myriad underground installations established by the government, ranging from the Federal Reserve's bunker near Virginia's Mount Pony (each Federal Reserve branch maintained emergency quarters; as a Fed brochure put it, "victory in a nuclear war will belong to the county that recovers first"[34]) to Nelson Rockefeller's "Emergency Operating Center and Alternate Seat of Government," a space of 6-foot-thick walls and a 7.5-ton blast door (where the bathroom mirrors are polished metal to prevent shattering in an explosion) located under Building 22 in the Albany complex. A 1973 inquiry by the *Village Voice* found the space to be the active home of Rockefeller's "Public Security Agency," even though the civil defense commission itself had been abolished two years prior.[35]

In the private sector, the subterranean expansion was equally fervent. In 1951, a New York entrepreneur named Herman Knaust established the Iron

Mountain Atomic Storage Company in a former iron mine near Hudson, New York. Knaust, who himself had purchased the mine in 1936 and converted it into a mushroom cultivating operation, reasoned correctly that corporations would be interested in preserving vital records in the event of atomic attack. "If an atom bomb burst right on top of us, it wouldn't even make a Geiger counter flicker here in the vaults," Knaust boasted.[36] Gradually, Knaust, who had installed a 28-ton bank vault door and incorporated other hardening measures, expanded the business, moving from the mere storage of records for companies such as IBM and Metropolitan Life to the establishing of full-fledged emergency survival spaces featuring offices, showers, and dormitories. As *The Nation* noted, "Iron Mountain has become a '20th Century Noah's Ark' for several thousand employees of banks, insurance companies, advertising agencies and every manner of enterprise, including a modeling agency and a dance band." The magazine described "an exact reproduction of a modern financial cathedral, glass door and all," as well as a "large lounge area furnished in Early American, a dining area that can handle sixteen at a sitting from an up-to-the-minute kitchen."[37]

Iron Mountain was replicated in Kansas City's Underground Vaults and Storage, housed in the former Carey mine; the Kansas City Federal Reserve leased two rooms. In 1960, the Bank of Boston built a survival center in Pepperell, Massachusetts, called "Location x," that featured a 426-foot artesian well, over 100 tons of reinforced steel, and an escape hatch from the nuclear submarine U.S.S. *Nautilus* (the site was later sold to a records management company).[38] On the West Coast, the Bekins Corporation announced in 1969 that it was considering the construction of a "corporate survival center" on a 200-acre ranch near Coalinga, California; the emerging Chinese nuclear capability was cited as one reason.[39]

All of these sites had the power to excite fantastic visions on the part of those who had not actually been inside. Speculations on the site's interior blueprints fell into two patterns: those who described overly elaborate, excessively lavish pleasure domes for post-apocalyptic survival, and those who saw in the security cloaking the cover for something more ambitious than mere federal relocation. For years, sites such as the Air Force Logistic Command's Kirtland Underground Munitions Storage Complex, a hardened bunker for storing nuclear weapons that was designed by the protective construction division of the Army Corps of Engineers (and built at a cost of $36 million, including $7 million for the blast doors alone), have been fertile terrain for hypotheses of covert laboratories housing extraterrestrial remains. Iron Mountain itself became the stage for the colossal hoax, "Report from Iron Mountain," published by the *Dial Press* in 1967, in which a Rand-like think tank, sequestered in a secret bunker, theorized on the eventuality and indeed the desirability of a nuclear war (the report, intended as a left-wing critique, eventually gained currency as an authentic document on the far right). Devoid of a map of these classified environments, the cartographers of conspiracy are left to color in their own fanciful regions, in a process that recalls a scenario Philip K. Dick presented in his 1967 novel *The Penultimate Truth*. To escape nuclear war, much of the population is sent to live in underground tanks, existing in a state of regimented deprivation until the fateful day they learn that the tales of an uninhabitable surface are a hoax; a handful of feudal lords have since divided up the quite-hospitable Earth to their liking. Under the nuclear shadow of the Cold War, it was the underground that was fetishized (the sprawling underground base was a staple of 1960s espionage and science-fiction literature) far beyond its quite spartan reality.

The set of circumstances that brought places like Site R or Mount Weather into being has long since passed into history. For one, the "Continuity of Government" program established by Kennedy (National Security Action memorandum no. 127 places "particular emphasis on the plans for insuring the survival of the Presidency" in the "event of nuclear attack on the United States") was changed under the first Bush administration's tenure to a program known as "Enduring Constitutional Government," notes John Pike, a global security policy analyst in Washington, D.C. With the cessation of the Cold War, places like Mount Weather have seen their budgets cut and their roles altered (the Federal Reserve's bunker in Culpepper, Virginia, now belongs to the Library of Congress). Since the 1960s, military planners have assumed that the Soviet Union had located and targeted its most hidden bastions; the weapons, too, had increased dramatically in strength. And now that anyone with Internet access can sneak a glimpse at Mount Weather or Area 51 via satellite, many view such secret redoubts as strategically obsolete, like hulking mainframe computers in an age of distributed networks. The planning now, says Pike, is "much more focused on things like an anthrax attack on the Washington metro subway system that shuts down the federal government rather than an 11,000-megaton lay-down general nuclear exchange."[40]

But Pike suspects the contingency planning is still in place for a nuclear attack. "I mean, think about it—how could it be otherwise?" he says. "The U.S. government is about the single most expensive thing there is—how could they not have a backup copy?" There is a White House fallout shelter, but beyond that, apart from Mount. Weather, Pike says any national park near Washington could serve as an emergency relocation center, now that the necessary communications hardware can fit in a fleet of trucks. And then there's the legendary National Airborne Operations Center, the fleet of Boeing 747s headquartered at Offut Air Force Base in Nebraska, which Boeing describes as "a survivable command post for control of u.s. forces in all levels of conflict including nuclear war."[41] As one nuclear warfare analyst describes it, "on any given day, duty officers at underground bunkers, in flying command posts, and on two 'survivable' ground mobile command centers (built into specially configured 18-wheel tractor-trailers stationed in Nebraska and Colorado), brush off the seven-volume 'Emergency Action Procedures,' particularly 'Volume IV: Authority,' which sets out the procedures for nuclear retaliation should a worst-case scenario ever occur."[42] The idea of a personal fallout shelter for a contemporary president in a vacation retreat, however, is retrograde, according to Pike. "The challenge for emergency war operations is not to ensure the survivability of *the* president, the challenge is to ensure the survivability of *a* president," says Pike. Hence the line of designated successors. "It doesn't matter what the guy's name is, doesn't matter what his title was one minute before the war started. The only question is: Can we find somebody who is the current commander in chief?"

As the once-hidden underground chambers of the Cold War are brought to light, their blast doors open for all to see, there is the lingering suspicion that there are other, as-yet undiscovered places where the executive body could ride out a nuclear threat. "I don't necessarily assume that we've found all of the big Cold War bunkers," says Pike. One place that still puzzles Pike is the National Communications System complex in Warrenton, Virginia, another Cold War-era facility home to such activities as intelligence cryptology. One site, "Station B," on top of a mountain, looks strikingly familiar to Pike. "When I look at aerial imagery of the thing it sure looks like Mount Weather to me. But is there a bunker in there? Nobody knows." And so we face one of the lasting legacies of the Cold War: the Architecture of Conspiracy. The subterranean state and the black budget created a world without walls and without boundaries—everything was possible, everything potentially connected—and, in the absence of visible lines of power, the paranoid draftsman steps in, sketching an Escher-like world of interlocking secret tunnels and furtive conduits of power. In such darkness, the only light to guide the way is a fervent, unblinking belief in disbelief. Whenever a space is opened or a document declassified, the inherited Cold War logic states that this must have occurred only because there is some other space, some other document, buried even deeper, belonging to an even more secret agency, that remains out of view.

Case Study #3: Cheyenne Mountain

From the window of my La Quinta Inn, a beige tower complex adrift in a sea of parking lots just off I-25 south of Colorado Springs, I look out at "Tinseltown USA," a sprawling concrete multiplex cinema adorned with illuminated towers and neon accents.

Beyond the arc lighting and curving drives of this somewhat recently suburbanized section of Colorado Springs, looming over Tinseltown's electric rainbow, is Cheyenne Mountain, home of the Combat Operations Center of the North American Aerospace Defense Command. The mountain is dark now, its presence marked only by a series of lighted antennas posted at the summit. They are not, as common local myth would have it, performing any nefarious function; rather, they are simply beaming the films that debuted last year at Tinseltown, USA, to the television-viewing public of greater Colorado Springs.

The mountain is dark. But the mountain is always dark, even during the brightest Colorado summer's day. As one in the endlessly unfolding peaks of Colorado's front range, Cheyenne Mountain is not particularly distinctive, and not nearly as high as nearby Pike's Peak. What makes Cheyenne Mountain so compelling is the peculiar fact that it essentially does not exist. As another in the Cold War's negative spaces, it exists only as a cover for something else. Its slopes cannot be traversed; hikers cannot scale its summit. When people refer to Cheyenne Mountain, they are not actually referring to the geological entity, but rather the space *inside* Cheyenne Mountain, its symbolic heart. From the outside, this space has always been black, as black as the background on the radar screens the officers of NORAD scan for anything that might tilt the "threatcon" (or "infocon") away from its standard "normal" and down the alpha-bravo-charlie continuum toward global thermonuclear confrontation. Inside of Cheyenne Mountain, there are lights everywhere, of course, but they are only seen from within. Cheyenne Mountain began as a hole drilled into the side of the mountain, but it contains more than infrastructure and systems; at its heart was the myth of a new age, a faith in an unseen defense network that linked remote polar radar stations to underground sentinels.

In the folklore of the indigenous Ute tribe, Cheyenne Mountain was described as a "sleeping dragon," its nose facing south, its curled tailed pointed north. According to Ute mythology, after a great flood sent by the vengeful Great Spirit drove the people to the top of Pike's Peak, where they were stranded, a dragon flew in and began to drink the water, so much so that it lost its ability to fly.[43] Cheyenne Mountain also was central to the mythology of the Cold War, in which America's nuclear arsenal might be seen as the sleeping dragon (or, if you will, a great flood). As a NORAD press release put it,

"Survival for North America's 220 million citizens is linked to a hollowed-out mountain in the Colorado Rockies." Buried in its underground lair, it was always there, like an idea buried in the subconscious, only coming to light during moments of extreme anxiety.

After driving the snaking path to the guardhouse outside the tunnel opening to Cheyenne Mountain, I am met by Captain Jeff Dean, a NORAD public affairs official dressed in a blue flight suit—once one goes inside the mountain, the flight suit is the only thing that reminds you this is an *Air Force* installation. Dean is crisply courteous, but his brow furrows when I present a tape recorder. "Has that been cleared?" he asks sharply. Indeed it has not, so two other officials disappear with the small black Sony into a back room. After a few minutes, when the tape recorder and myself have been assigned security clearances, we board what looks like a school bus and drive into the mountain, down a tunnel with no light at its end. Some 4,400 feet inside the mountain, we pass through a massive blast door and enter into the complex itself, leaving the rocky environs for what could be a school, hospital, or any other institutional setting where space and light are dear. One comes to NORAD expecting the technocratic flamboyance displayed in the James Bond films, but the reality is a place where normal people are simply going about their work, albeit without natural light, some 9,000 feet below the peak of the mountain. In a small office down a warren of hallways (in which I later get lost with a novice public affairs official), I find Ben Borth, a bearded civil engineer who for the past three years has served as the structural caretaker of the facility.

"The toughest job is myth control," Borth says of Cheyenne Mountain. "You talk to one guy and he'll say it will survive a 70-megaton blast and the next guy says it's 5 kilotons. You've got to find something that's more reasonable. Over the past few years, we've basically come up with some stuff that's more believable." (He demurs, however, when I ask for the specific figure on what sort of nuclear impact NORAD could theoretically absorb). When NORAD came online in 1966, the myth was in full bloom. Noting that the "nuclear age has dictated that these men carry out their responsibilities inside a solid granite mountain," the Defense Command wrote: "This is the NORAD city under a mountain today; modern, efficient, an awesome blend of skilled manpower, sophisticated computers and electronic equipment."[44] *U.S. News and World Report* said that "the complex is also considered close to indestructible by missile or bomber attack because it is nestled so deep within Cheyenne Mountain."[45] But according to historian Paul Bracken, the defensive capability of the site—he estimates it anywhere from 500 to 1,000 psi (pounds per square inch of pressure)—was never as great as some would have desired. Cheyenne Mountain, which replaced a concrete block building at the nearby

North American Aerospace Defense Command, circa 1966, Cheyenne Mountain, Colorado

A technician checks one of NORAD's nuclear blast-resistant shock absorbers, about 1960

NORAD, mid-1960s, Cheyenne Mountain, Colorado

Ent Air Force Base as the headquarters of the nation's air defense, was embroiled from the beginning in a disagreement between the air force and the planners of the Rand Corporation over the degree to which the site should be hardened. "The civilians," wrote Bracken, "wanted hardened sites in order to be able to wage limited nuclear war with protected leadership and control...They argued that NORAD should be built deeply *beneath*, not *inside*, Cheyenne Mountain."[46] The U.S. Air Force, on the other hand, which had yet to adopt the idea of limited nuclear warfare, saw the potential destruction of Cheyenne Mountain as simply a warning signal to launch a full-scale nuclear retaliation; the Omaha headquarters of the Strategic Air Command, which were never hardened, served a similar function. In the end, NORAD was hardened, but not to the 10,000 psi scale envisioned by Rand.

Whatever its true survival capabilities—declassified reports revealed that increased targeting capabilities of Soviet ICBMs had rendered the site vulnerable the day it opened—the engineering mastery behind the complex (NORAD was designed primarily by Parsons Brinckerhoff Company, a New York-Denver architectural and engineering firm with much military experience) becomes clear as Borth takes me through the vast service catacombs of the site, the places where the normal office environment gives way to dank cave walls, gouged out by "smooth-wall" blasting, a then-radical technique for avoiding excess fracturing of the rock behind the surface. Thousands of cinch-anchor rock bolts drilled into the walls literally hold the facades together. "We have a rock bolt maintenance crew that literally spends the entire year checking and retorquing rock bolts," Borth says. Essentially, the complex is a series of "steel cans," built inside of a hollowed-out space and supported by a series of springs—known as the "Shock Isolation System"—that weigh roughly half a ton each and were placed to help the building ride out the vibrations of a shock wave (the metal would deflect the electromagnetic pulse waves). If the building were "dead," or empty at the time the springs were installed, ballast was added to simulate the desired 26,000-pound load. Borth points to a series of tubes draped between two of the buildings. "All the connections from building to building or building to ground include flexible joints," he says. "If everything was hard and tight from building to building, you'd bust a pipe." We pass under the "B-2" dome, at the intersection of hallways "b" and "2," an enormous cap of steel and reinforced concrete engineers erected after they discovered a fault in the ceiling at a crucial juncture. "These were on-the-fly solutions that today, between the EPA and OSHA and political complications, would be impossible," Borth says.

Today, the concerns are somewhat more quotidian. "Air quality is a big issue," Borth says. "Right now we're trying to get diesel smoke from the buses on a separate path from the air that we breathe." Borth wants to generate a surplus of air within the complex, "so that if anyone was able to bring in a chemical or biological agent, the general drift of the overpressurization would force that air to go out." At the very end of the tour, we crawl into the dark space beneath Building 8, where I see a large cedar tub filled with water. The water, it turns out, is from the top of the mountain, having percolated its way down into the subterranean complex. "We could disassociate ourselves from the water supply and use the water supply that comes in," says Borth, who also suggests it could be bottled and sold as "NORAD water." Built to withstand the effects of man's deadliest invention, the facility is less secure against nature. It seems an appropriate coda to the Ute myth—the water seeping into the belly of the sleeping dragon.

At NORAD, I never saw the huge room where dozens of personnel sat rigidly before a wall-size map of the world, the satellite-fed panopticon that gave these blinded moles their extrasensory perception. That room is the product of Hollywood. Strangely enough, I found a much more compelling vision of that scenario not in the Colorado Rockies, but in the pastoral suburbs of New Jersey. There, near the sleepy town of Bedminster, New Jersey, off a highway exit marked simply "AT&T," sits the eye of the telecommunication giant's global network: the World Wide Intelligent Network Control Center. Housed in a building designed by the architectural firm HOK, the Center's signal feature is a 250-foot long, 146-screen "data wall," across whose spectral panorama dance the rhythms of the globe's daily flow of voice and data. "We have our thumb on the pulse of everything that's going on, all the time," says Dave Johnson, the AT&T spokesperson, as he leads me through the complex. "We have a total view of everything in the network, whether it's service to Afghanistan or whether a contractor cuts one of my fiber optic cables in Massachusetts." On any given day, some 280 million calls are monitored, which equals, Johnson tells me, some 75 terabytes of information, or thirty times the contents of the entire Library of Congress.

That AT&T's network showcase should seem flashier and more high-tech than NORAD's reflects not only the difficulty the once-pioneering secret government agencies had in keeping pace with the private sector after the fall of the Berlin Wall (heading into the new millennium, the National Security Agency was looking for outside computer consultants to overhaul its systems, while the Central Intelligence Agency had launched its own Silicon Valley startup to recruit high-tech talent), but AT&T's experience in keeping the lines of communication to places like NORAD open (and nuclear war-survivable) during the Cold War. In 1961, AT&T won the contract to operate AUTOVON (Automatic Voice Network), the military's electronic command-and-control communications system, installing more than sixty switching and relay stations across the country—roughly a third of which are underground, hardened facilities—in a clandestine network that, like the Greenbrier bunker, was hidden in plain sight. In towns such as Fearrington Village, North Carolina, the AT&T sites drifted into local lore; in this case, residents dubbed the AUTOVON site "The Big Hole." The sites attracted the usual Cold War commentary, i.e., that the roads leading to the site were always paved, that a strange cloud was sometimes visible over the site, that the building itself went down some thirteen storys. "I don't know nothing about it," a neighbor of the site said. "It's none of my business and I don't ask about it."[47]

With nuclear conflict no longer an imminent threat, AT&T, like NORAD, has been retooling its Cold War facilities for new purposes. The company's Internet Services Data Center in Redwood City, California, for example, a facility designed to ensure consistent Internet communications, is housed in a 1967 building intended to withstand a nuclear blast. With 1.5-foot-thick concrete walls and a 2-foot-thick concrete floor, as well as a column-based foundation that drops 138 feet into bedrock, the building is designed to endure a 25-megaton blast at a distance of .3 miles from the blast epicenter. The New Jersey site itself is heir to a previous facility designed with nuclear protection in mind, but now that it has come in from the cold, its role has been transformed into a more general "emergency management" function. In the event of a large-scale tragedy, Johnson tells me, the facility, as part of the shadowy Federal Disaster Recovery Network, becomes a nerve center for ensuring that communications remain open. For that reason, he says, AT&T maintains parallel centers in Georgia and Colorado. "I can't think of anything that would hit New Jersey, Georgia, and Colorado at the same time," says Johnson. "If anything that catastrophic does happen, a dial tone is probably the last thing any of us are going to be worried about."

NIKE GUIDED MISSILE

5.
TWENTIETH-CENTURY CASTLES:
Missile Silos in the Heartland

My first visit to Wall, South Dakota, came on a childhood trip *en route* to Wyoming, when it finally loomed into view after what must have been dozens of clamoring billboards and endless miles of anticipatory highway. Wall is little more than an overgrown rest stop that has mythologized itself into existence on the strength of its sole attraction—"Wall Drug"—but to my seven-year-old self it seemed the alluring gateway to the West, a place where the fables of itinerant prospectors, brave pioneers, and Indian chiefs began to come alive, thanks to the myriad trinkets on offer.

What I did not know at the time, as we drove down the Interstate past vast stretches of cattle country, the thin white jagged ridge of the Badlands shimmering on the horizon, was that just outside the tourist precinct of Wall, off one of the exits that did not advertise Dairy Queen or free coffee, a number of Minuteman intercontinental ballistic missiles sat stored in concrete silos under the pale grasslands, aimed toward a similar cluster of Soviet missiles on the other side of the North Pole. As I dreamed of historic prairie fortifications and epic battles between the cavalry and renegade bands of Sioux, I had no inkling that all around me, invisibly, was a ring of modern fortifications—castles for the twentieth century—and that the hostile frontier that I envisaged in my Louis L'Amour novels was in fact still extant, although in the form of an electronically monitored balance of nuclear countermeasures. Unlike the duels of western towns, in this standoff, who pulled the trigger first did not matter, because the catastrophic outcome would be the same.

Artist's depiction of Nike missile battery

Minuteman missile silo near Wall, South Dakota

A quarter-century later, I again find myself in Wall, not to buy coonskin caps and arrowheads but to visit a defunct, yet intact, Minuteman installation. In fact, it is the nation's sole surviving Minuteman II silo, which the National Park Service, working with nearby Ellsworth Air Force Base, is planning to turn into the country's only Minuteman museum. Having spent the night in Wall among the countless carloads of tourist families, I drive early the next morning 6 miles down the interstate, to exit 116. Wending my way over gravel roads and through a herd of grazing cattle, I reach Delta Nine, formerly of the 44th Strategic Missile Wing. The site is a fenced-off square in the middle of a pasture, and what is inside looks not unlike an electrical substation—several concrete platforms, three-phase power transformers, an antenna or two, and hooded vents scattered here and there. I meet Tim Pavek, a former missile engineer at Ellsworth who is now working on the site's interpretation and preservation. In short sleeves and closely cropped hair, with glasses that turn dark in the piercing prairie sun, Pavek looks the part (i.e., he could have stepped out of a 1960s Lockheed advertisement). He sounds it, too, speaking in deliberate, measured tones peppered with engineering jargon.

As Pavek turns on the power for the site and prepares to open the hatch, he begins to reflect on the history of the Minuteman—named for the Revolutionary War soldiers who were always ready at a minute's notice—as cattle shift nearby and trucks thunder down Interstate 90. "The Minuteman was really made possible by the development of solid rocket fuel," Pavek says. "It enabled them to be deployed in remote-control fashion, dispersed 3 to 5 nautical miles apart, so you couldn't get two for the price of one." Places like South Dakota were sparsely populated (yet contained sizeable government installations) and far enough inland to avoid the reach of Soviet nuclear submarines. Where the previous liquid-fueled Titan and Atlas missiles had been extraordinarily complex machines of hundreds of thousands of parts, requiring what the *Wall Street Journal* called "the desperate and constant attention accorded a man receiving artificial respiration,"[1] the Minuteman (initially dubbed "Weapon System Q") was a comparatively simple weapon that could in essence be mass-produced and remote-fired. "With the successful utilization of solid propellants," wrote historian Ernest Schwiebert, "the Minuteman could hide in its lethal lair like a shotgun shell, ready for instant firing."[2]

Construction on Minuteman began in 1960, and by the first week of the Cuban missile crisis, the first wing of Kennedy's "Ace in the Hole" had come online at Montana's Malmstrom Air Force Base (initially, the air force envisioned a 1500-strong "missile farm," but eventually opted for a strategy of dispersal). "By September of 1961, all 165 sites were declared fully operational," Pavek says (by 1967, there would be 1,000 Minuteman sites spread across the plains in six formations). With the presumed missile gap looming, construction crews worked in three shifts a day, seven days a week, building what amounted to a silo a day. "That's an incredible engineering undertaking, to build all those sites at a cost of $56 million in construction money, not counting the missiles themselves," says Pavek. "By contrast we've spent $18 million in ten years on deactivation of the sites." The American landscape was being transformed: *Time* noted, "from New York to California, in a total of 18 states, the U.S. is hard at work on the biggest, most complex and crucial military construction program in its peacetime history: the installation of attack-proof, underground launching sites for the nation's Atlas, Titan, and Minuteman intercontinental ballistic missiles."[3] As *Fortune* saw it, "never in military history has such a concentrated assemblage of destructive firepower been so completely masked in a setting of utter pastoral peace and tranquility."[4] New industries sprang up in remote hinterlands to assemble and test the emerging missile force; as *Time* reported of Thiokol's new Minuteman assembly site north of Salt Lake City: "Strange lights glare in the night, making the mountains shine, and a grumbling roar rolls across the desert. By day enormous clouds of steam-white smoke billow up in a few seconds and drift over the hills and valleys. Monstrous vehicles with curious burdens lumber along the roads."[5] Not all the activity was so cryptic: "Ranch-style homes for engineers, chemists, physicists, and mathematicians are spreading into the beet fields. This is only a beginning." In South Dakota, Boeing prepared mobile housing for the thousands of construction workers expected to descend upon the state, while the state's Highway Department was granted more than $600,000 in federal funds to improve roads leading to the missile sites.[6]

As Delta Nine's personnel hatch, some 10 feet in diameter and seemingly as thick (made of steel and concrete, it weighs 13,000 pounds), silently opens, Pavek spins the dials on a combination lock set into the ground. After unlocking several other mechanisms (the process, including several security precautions, would generally take forty-five minutes), we descend by ladder—climbing past the shed skin of a bull snake that has managed to work its way into the chamber (a not infrequent occurrence)—into a small lobby which itself leads into Launch Access Room 1, 20.5 feet below grade. Here a circular metal catwalk surrounds the now vacant 80-foot-long launch tube, reinforced concrete plated with quarter-inch steel; the outer ring of the walk is lined with banks of massive, long-obsolete computers. A stenciled sign reads: "No Lone Zone. Two-Man Concept Mandatory." A set of degree etchings notched into the wall, known as a "collimator bench," would have been used for missile targeting, as would two cement "azimuth" posts aboveground—a strange recourse to traditional celestial navigation in the age of push-button warfare (a computer was later used). Shock absorbers support the lower of the two tiers of catwalks, while the water hoses and electrical wires all feature flexible connections, the mark of a structure that was meant to survive a hit. The whole structure seems some kind of terrestrial submarine, with its naval infrastructure and metaphors: the hatch, the metal catwalks, the preponderance of battleship gray, the "lanyards" fastened to the silo door by which men would descend into the "hole."

Standing again on the surface, Pavek describes the layout: the 90-ton silo door, resting on four wheels and opened by hydraulic engine; as well as the variety of intruder-detection poles and "antenna silos" that provided hardened enclosure for the high-frequency antennas that, as Pavek points out, "were capable of receiving launch commands from the airborne command post that orbited this area on a constant state of alert." When I ask him what the siting criteria were, he shrugs. "The missile launcher door always faced 8.5 degrees off of south," he says. "That's because the missiles were flying over the pole. Other than that, if someone were to spin me around and pull a curtain around the fence I couldn't tell if you were one site or another." In fact, Pavek notes, some spots "are the worst you could ever think of in terms of drainage, where if you went a hundred yards, there wouldn't be a problem at all. Sometimes I wonder if they didn't just take a dartboard and throw darts at it." He concludes: "They were designed by California architects. Maybe that was part of it."

Pavek is referring to the Ralph M. Parsons Company, who along with Bechtel Corp. (designer of the Atlas "E" silo, among others) and Daniel, Mann, Johnson & Mendenhell (the architecture firm responsible for the Titan installation), was one of the architecture and engineering firms to enter the emerging field of missile installation design. It was a task that had seen no precedent in technology, funding, or scheduling. As *Architectural Forum* noted in 1960, "not only have completely new kinds of buildings had to be designed, but they have usually been designed and built under an incredible pressure unknown in private building jobs."[7] That architectural-engineer firms were chosen was no surprise; as one executive described it, "our architects are only involved to the extent that the project deals with people—personnel quarters and such facilities. The vast majority of missile installations involves straight engineering work."[8] It seemed the ultimate incarnation of the modernist dictum that buildings were machines; the missile silos, in their earliest incarnation, were disposable—once the missiles were fired, the structure was useless.

The missile silos were literally taking shape around the missiles: The air force's policy of "concurrence" dictated that the launch facilities be built simultaneously with the weapons. "Thus, even such an important element as the dimension for housing the missile 160 feet underground could not be finally determined until the shape and the size of the missile, being built by The Martin Co, was known."[9] By April 1962, the Army Corps of Engineers, which supervised the entire missile construction program, had issued 2,676 modifications and change orders for the Atlas D, E, and F silos—adding some $96 million to the overall cost.[10] The missile silo was a unique structure in military architecture—both an offensive tool for launching a weapon and a defensive fortification for protecting the ability of the weapon to be fired. As military architecture its design shifted fluidly as technology, and strategic considerations, evolved. The country's first Atlas missiles, at California's Vandenberg Air Force Base, were stored in the open or in "soft" enclosures, and ultimately "semi-hard" horizontal "coffins," concrete-encased boxes aboveground out of which missiles would be raised to vertical firing position. This approach shifted in favor of underground silos topped by gigantic "clamshell" doors, but engineers feared that engine vibrations from the enclosed missile would literally shake it apart, so elevators (designed by DMJM) were installed that lifted the missiles for surface firing. The Titan I, which featured a sprawling, "superhardened" underground launch complex designed to withstand 100 pounds per square inch of overpressure, looked like the experimental drawings of a utopian architect—an ant colony-like assemblage of tunnels and subterranean domes. With the Titan II, the air force had its first underground stored, fueled, and launched silo; designed by DMJM, working with Silas Mason and Leo A. Daly, the Titan featured a three-stage system of shock absorption designed to withstand a blast impact three times the force of gravity. The approach was perfected in the first Minuteman system, which represented the smallest silo yet, requiring just one-fifth of the concrete and steel of an Atlas F.[11] This configuration too changed with nuclear strategy. As the u.s. shifted from the doctrine of "massive retaliation" to "flexible response"—Secretary of Defense Robert McNamara's strategy for a series of limited nuclear attacks—the Minuteman installations were altered in two ways: The first was to allow the firing of individual Minuteman missiles, rather than the entire "flight" of ten missiles; the second was a hardening of the silos and their support functions in order to extend their useful life in a protracted nuclear exchange. As we stand in Delta One's subterranean power room, he explains: "They made this 'soft' support building capable of withstanding nuclear effects. Beginning with Wing 3 you see a little harder one, and by the time you get to Grand Forks, this same structure will be 30 feet underground, a concrete capsule with a hardened vault door and a floor suspended by shock isolators."

Later, we drive 11 miles down 1-90 to Delta Nine, the launch control Facility that would have controlled (by wire—a total of 1,532 miles of cable connected the 165 South Dakota Minuteman silos) the ten sites in the Delta flight. Looking like an anonymous ranch house, with a two-car garage and a basketball hoop, Delta Nine has remained unchanged since the day it was shuttered, an eerie time capsule of the long and quiet hours of nuclear stalemate. Inside the musty lobby, a poster announces: "Winning the Cold War was one challenge. Now we face a new challenge: Deactivation." A sheet near the phone gives instructions on handling bomb threats (one recommended question: "Can you

Minuteman Launch Control Center near Wall, South Dakota

Inside Minuteman Launch Control Center near Wall, South Dakota

tell me what kind of bomb it is?"), while a logbook lies open to May 23, 1991, the day Delta Nine was deactivated. In the suburban-style rec room, a magazine rack is too frozen in time—*Rolling Stone* has Dana Carvey (the George Bush years) on the cover. "There was a lot of waiting going on," Pavek says. "At other times, it could be rather tense." What distinguishes this otherwise bland interior is an elevator located just behind the guarded entryway. It drops 31 feet into a dark chamber, whose gloom is relieved only by a vivid piece of "blast door art," the nuclear age equivalent to the vibrant cartoons painted on the noses of World War II bombers: On the giant steel door that leads to the launch control capsule, someone has painted what looks like a Domino's Pizza Box, but with a missile emblazoned across it and the words "Delivery in 30 Minutes Guaranteed or Your Next Order Free."

Pavek swings open the 7-ton blast door, and we enter the launch control center, a 54-foot-long, 29 feet in diameter capsule with four-foot-thick concrete walls lined with steel. If Delta Nine resembled in structure and feel a submarine, the manned launch capsule of Delta One has more of an aeronautic feel, with radar screens substituting for windows, as if the pilot were "instrument flying" (the missileers, appropriately, wore air force flightsuits). The missile command chairs come from airplanes, as do the safety harnesses. A stainless steel coffee pot is bolted to a countertop, in the event that the capsule encountered the unexpected turbulence of nuclear blast effects. On the walls are racks of communication equipment such as the "Survivable Low Frequency Ground Communication System," while the primary console (along which the moveable chairs slide) features the eerily familiar toggles and keys and "Missile Status Indicator Panels." When I ask Pavek how long the missileers could remain underground, he says, "It depends on whether the support building was still present above. But down below there are 16 emergency power batteries. There are various scenarios under which you can stay in operation for an extended period of time."

Walking through Delta One, one feels safely ensconced in a history that did not happen. The look and feel reminds one of *The Day After*, the Reagan era's *On the Beach*, and the technology, advanced for its day, seems whimsically outdated. Seeing silos interred in the fertile fields or mummified into a Cold War museum (or mausoleum) is almost enough to make one forget that under other green fields and in other airspace there are still active missile silos, and radar that sweeps the sky looking for unknown aggressors.

With the destruction of the missile silos in North Dakota and elsewhere, an underground architectural network of sweeping proportions is vanishing. Even as those are destroyed, however, there are myriad silos, in other places and in other missile systems, that were not destroyed, but "abandoned in place." Stripped of military equipment and function, these former installations revert to a primitive, almost cavelike existence—underground utility spaces that once might have fulfilled any other civic function (e.g., providing power or water). Veiled in secrecy, never venerated in the landscape, today they are barely legible, their distinguishing marks (e.g., vents, power poles, or perfectly paved roads in the middle of otherwise uninhabited land) visi-

Atlas missile silo turned would-be Mars simulator near Roswell, New Mexico

ble only to the motivated eye. Not surprisingly, their myth-filled histories and subterranean mysteries have lent themselves to conspiracies—even the underworld itself. In November 2000, a former Atlas F missile silo near Wamego, Kansas was discovered to be the site of an LSD laboratory so productive it was said to supply one-third of the nation's traffic. For years, rumors had swirled about the former missile silo's occupants, who explained away the strange nighttime truck deliveries and excessive security as part of their work manufacturing equipment for the space shuttle program.[12] Near Roswell, N.M., a place where the military's historic presence has helped spawn theories of extraterrestrial conspiracies, I saw a strangely fitting potential adaptive reuse of an Atlas F missile silo: On a dusty desert road north of town, behind a fence marked "No Trespassing," painted onto the distinctive entrance chamber of an Atlas silo, were the words "Terraform" and "future construction site." Terraform, it turned out, is a joint venture between Jon Farhat, a Hollywood special effects artist, and Bob Lazar, a onetime Los Alamos physicist who gained renown in UFO circles after claiming to have seen aliens while working on a top-secret project at Area 51.[13] According to a news release, Terraform is planning a two-phase renovation of the silo: "Phase 1 will test the integrity of the facility by sustaining a sealed biological Earth environment for a period of approximately 6 months... [P]hase 2 will be the conversion, operation and maintenance of the Silo Chamber into a stable equatorial Martian environment." The Cold War had helped propagate the idea of extraterrestrial colonization, so it seemed an altogether proper encomium for a nuclear missile silo to be transformed into a Martian habitat; not to mention the fact that its new owner was a creature of Cold War myth himself.

In the Cold War, the Atlas and other silos were shrouded in darkness, their official secrecy breeding unofficial folklore; with the Cold War ended, they still draw power in their ominous enclosure. Other silos, however, have assumed more benign functions, as communities have found in their raw, virtually indestructible spaces the foundation for new beginnings. A school in Holton, Kansas occupies a former Atlas E complex (purchased for $1 from the government in 1968), while a company called "20th Century Castles" advertises a variety of former silos as "historic, collectible underground properties." The company's website touts the security features of silo living (mentioning germ warfare, for one), passing comment on the irony that one should now seek shelter in a space whose missiles were the cause of so much shelter-building elsewhere. The silo as house is a sign that architecture does not discriminate: Walls that provided protection for missiles against incoming missiles provide their own benefits for homeowners; a blast door is still, in the final analysis, just a door. The silo as house is something approaching the old school of brutalism, with its rough concrete surfaces and shamelessly exposed ductwork; twentieth-century castles they may be, but that means they are *industrial* castles, and instead of ramparts and bulwarks we have launch tubes and bundles of electrical conduits.

On one winter day I drove north from New York City to Plattsburgh, N.Y., a town so close to Canada the radio crackles with Quebecois. Here, a few miles west of town, I found what might indeed be an overlooked icon of modern architecture: an Atlas F intercontinental ballistic missile silo. With its 8-foot-thick walls and austere steel catwalks, its perfectly round two-story underground launch control center, its earth-ambient year-round temperature of 58 degrees, its ability—thanks to four giant hydraulic shock absorbers—to ride out the tremors of a nuclear blast, the Atlas sits buried like a time capsule of the year it was built, 1962, a mixture of state-of-the-art engineering and neo-brutalist strength, a synthesis of form and function, a minimalist shell that seems to cry out for a Mies chaise. It is also, it turns out, for sale. Asking price: $2.4 million.

Billing it as the "Most Unique Real Estate in the World," Connecticut real estate developer Bruce Francisco, in the final stages of converting the Atlas site into a 4000-square-foot-plus home, had in the month prior to my arrival recently begun showing the property to prospective tenants. One client, he noted, had flown in with a friend (the silo is now part of a twelve-plot subdivision, called Adirondack Airpark Estates, that boasts its own runway), to whom he had told nothing about the property's unusual subterranean features. "He just wanted to blow his friend's mind," he told me. "That's just the type of person this place is going to attract."

From the outside, there is little to suggest that the property was once part of the only ICBM system located east of the Mississippi. Driving through a gate marked "NY-17," one pilots down a runway to a wood house that looks like, for all intents and purposes, a bucolic mountain retreat. Even from here, though, there is evidence as to what lies below: Francisco points to a small fissure in the pavement running along the cleavage of the former missile silo doors, sealed tight years ago; nearby, a series of vents—akin to city sidewalk grates—push through the snow. Behind the house, a small sealed hatch covers a former "antenna silo," an 8-foot-wide, 40-foot-deep passageway from which an antenna would emerge to track the North Star—its signal relayed to the launch control center through a system of mirrors, where computers would interpret the data for missile tracking. "The whole launch control center could now be fit on a laptop," says Francisco.

Francisco takes pains to show me the above ground house's stainless-steel circular fireplace, or to point out where the slate tile will be applied in the kitchen, but he soon catches my apprehensive glances toward a set of stairs that, in most normal cases, would lead to the basement. As we walk down the stairs, he recalls that when he was first shown the property—some ten years ago after it was purchased through government auction by an enterprising cousin for $7,000—one could not safely walk past the first set of 2,000-pound blast doors that sit at the bottom of the stairs. In its dormant decades the silo had become a rusting cavern filled with water and disintegrating drywall. "You don't know how bad it was," he says. "It was like raising the Titanic."

After passing through two blast doors—set at different angles to mitigate a blast impact—we enter the former launch control center. Known by military engineers as the "Crib," the center is essentially a two-floor capsule, hanging inside of a 42-foot-wide cement structure and suspended by hydraulic shocks; in the structure's center a massive concrete pillar rises from floor to ceiling. Formerly, the space was divided into small rooms, which contained the guidance and firing instruments of the Atlas missile. When Francisco began the conversion, the "Crib" had been completely gutted, so he fashioned a sort of inner shell that mimics the curvature of the hardened exterior. Set into the walls are rows of plate glass, which are lit from behind by strands of fiber-optic light whose color changes every so often. Around the central support pillar, Francisco built a spiral staircase, which required cutting through the 3 feet of iron and steel that formed the floor of the Crib.

As we stand bathed in the dim glow of blue light, it is hard to imagine we are in anything other than a particularly well-insulated space-age bachelor pad, Bucky Fuller meets Austin Powers. Cold War architecture has become a subject of kitsch; e.g., MTV's use of a fallout shelter for its "Y2K Bunker" New Year's Eve special. In its day, however, the space would have held a crew of missileers, stationed round the clock, who waited out long days underground as America endured the tense days of the Berlin Blockade and the Cuban missile crisis, absorbing such abstract Cold War phraseology as "the missile gap" and "massive retaliation." The nation's first ICBM system, the Atlas was dispersed throughout the U.S. in locations within target range of Soviet cities (later missiles would be targeted at Soviet missiles); the silos also required the support of nearby military installations—in this case, Plattsburgh Air Force Base, shuttered in 1995 in the wake of congressional base closing and realignment.

Built at an approximate cost of $29.2 million, Atlas bases such as Plattsburgh's were rendered obsolete virtually by the time they were completed—Francisco's silo was closed in 1965, just three years after opening—supplanted by next-generation warheads such as the Titan, Minuteman, and ultimately, the mobile MX "Peacekeeper." As we sit in the bedroom ("I've never slept better," says Francisco of the sepulchral space), located down the spiral stairs on the second floor of the launch control center, Francisco screens an old military instructional video of the Atlas. As the narrator, speaking of the "missile stronghold," intones that "it would take a direct hit to put the missile or launcher in a no-go condition," Francisco nods excitedly. "You've got 3 feet of epoxy resin concrete stainless steel mesh," he says. "If a bomb hit, even though you've got 8 feet of dirt above you, that's the support for the whole facility," he says, glancing upwards. On screen, an Atlas test missile is launched from California's Vandenberg Air Force Base, a bright steel lance piercing the azure sky. Suddenly, it veers awry and explodes. "After only sixty-eight seconds of flight," the voice notes, "the range safety officer had no choice but to destroy the missile." The narrator vows the missile will be ready by the end of 1962—the year it was phased out—which prompts a slight smirk from Francisco. "I talked to someone who really knows these things, and he told me 'it wouldn't have worked.'"

With that, Francisco leads me to the unfinished centerpiece of the facility: the silo itself. Heaving open a discrete steel door adjacent to the launch control center, we enter a 50-foot-long, eight-foot-wide corrugated steel tunnel, again with a series of blast doors, this time to protect the crew from accidental detonation. The tunnel opens into a space that is made all the more surreal by the fact it is underground: a 185-foot-high towering chasm, around which are arrayed four levels of gridded-steel platforms, staircases, and, on the walls, a rusted tangle of hoses, clamps, and a bewildering variety of infrastructure. At the bottom, a pool of water some 20 feet deep murkily reflects the arc lighting above. It resembles a factory, absent its sole product: the Atlas F. Standing 82.5 feet high, the missile, which weighed 267,000 pounds when fueled, carried a W38 warhead with a 4-megaton yield (the Hiroshima bomb, with a total yield of 13 kilotons, was minor by comparison). Its maximum range was 9,000 miles. In fifteen minutes, the missile—and launcher—would have been hoisted by counterbalanced system to the top of the silo, where the two 45-ton doors would have been opened hydraulically. The doors now sit sealed shut, with remnants of hay strewn nearby—as Francisco explains, the army stacked bales on top of the doors, lit a fire, and let the heat fuse the doors shut.

"It's whatever you want it to be," Francisco says, gesturing at the damp abyss. By stripping the space bare, making floors by pouring concrete on the metal frames, and building walls, he envisions a four-level condominium. He is not sure who would take up residence. "I have another silo," he suddenly tells me, as if remembering a sundry fact. "I have an option on it. It's up the road. I'll only pre-sell it though. I'm not going to start it unless someone wants it." Some years ago, New York's Storefront for Art and Architecture held a competition for the adaptive reuse of Plattsburgh's missile silos, which were then being sold. Entrants, who included Neil Denari and Elizabeth Diller, proposed everything from a mushroom farm to a "Nuclear Heritage Theme Park." Yet there is something reassuring in the fact that this silo—as have dozens to the west of the Mississippi—is accommodating that most primal of human needs: shelter. It is the ultimate antithesis of the "un-private houses" on view at the 1999 exhibition at New York's Museum of Modern Art, the dark flip-side of the aggressive transparency that marked so many of its glass-skinned architectural contemporaries. And unlike the missile crews, residents here will have the luxury of "sunlight rendition" back-lighting to counter the effects of living without natural light. Security aside, underground dwelling has its particular attractions: insect-free living, for example. "Bugs are a surface thing," Francisco tells me.

Like any owner, Francisco is house- (or silo-) proud, which is not to say he is free from the affliction of missile-launcher envy. He speaks with awe of Titan I launch silos, of which he has heard near-mythic tales. "It has a huge launch center, with three launch centers off of that, with three tubes that are 60 feet wide and go down 240 feet. They're huge—they're like cities. You can't even touch those for less than $500,000, plus they're contaminated." Invited to the home of an Atlas E site owner in Kansas, Francisco noted that it was stocked with a "quarter million dollar sound system" and piles of opulent

Overleaf: Nike missile scrap at Fort MacArthur, California

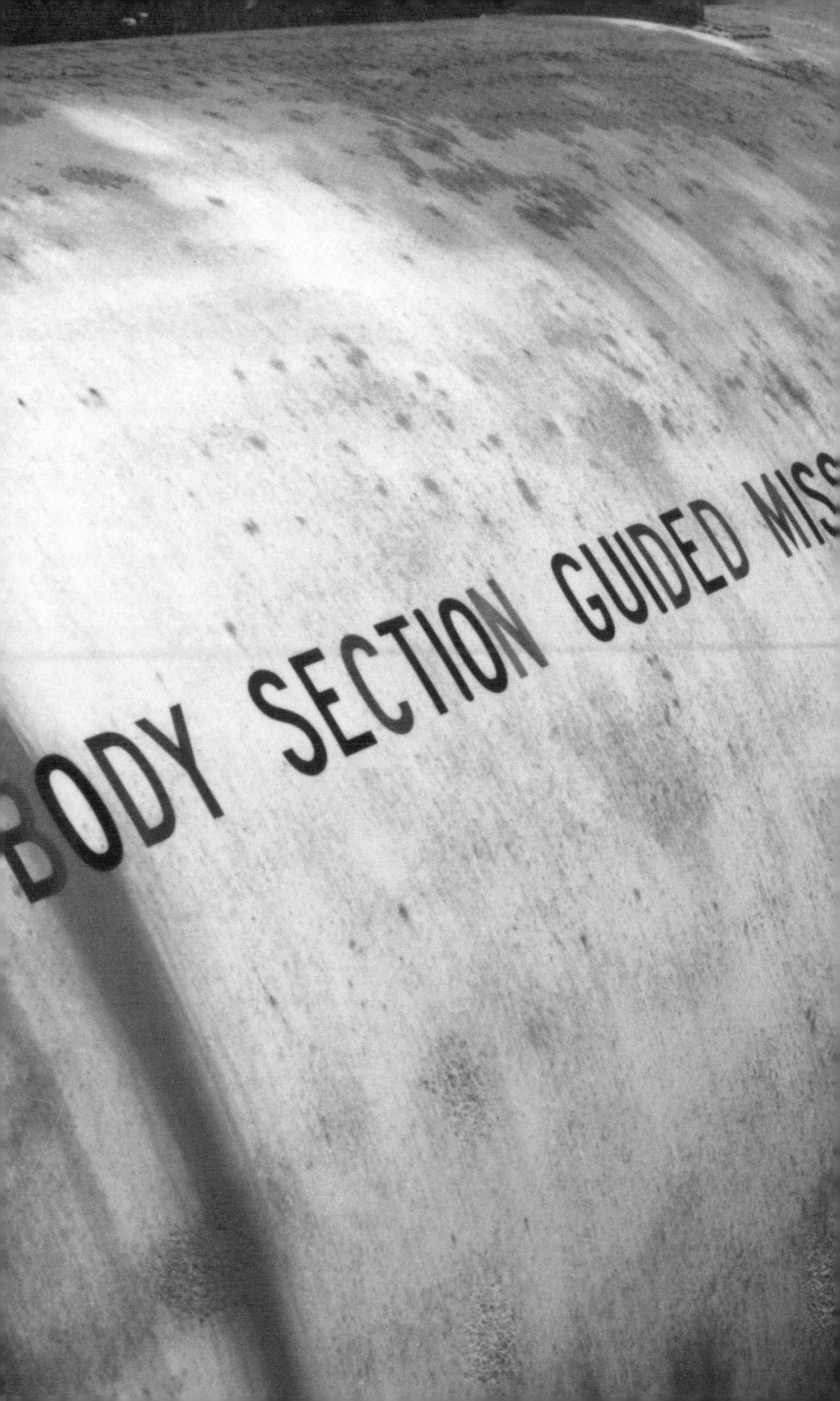
BODY SECTION GUIDED MISS

rugs. "This guy was waiting for the world to end," he says, shaking his head. "I just did this because it was there."

In a 1966 book titled *Wonders of the Modern World*, Joseph Gies, in an account of the building of a Titan missile site, asks: "Will the underground complex, with its beautifully efficient machinery so painstakingly mounted on springs, be the Stonehenge of America?"[14] This was a device that represented the pinnacle of human capacity for technological innovation; it was also the means for altering the world so dramatically that this same shining symbol of the space age would be transformed into the ruin of a lost civilization. The missiles were not launched, the sites were deactivated, and turned into ruins that were not of a lost civilization, but were lost *in* civilization, sepulchral spaces for which a few pioneering souls could find some new use—in Roswell, New Mexico, residents welcomed in the new year by sending laser-guided "messages" into outer space, beamed from a former Atlas silo (*not* the Terraform silo). The sites, unveiled as technological marvels, had in the course of several decades become nearly undecipherable traces on the landscape. The Titans and Atlases and Minutemen, however, are only an archaeological layer of civilization in this regard; to discover the earliest of Cold War landscapes, one must dig deeper, to another layer of weaponry that too takes it name from Greek mythology.

Walking one day among the shuttered coastal defense bunkers in the sprawling complex once known as Fort MacArthur, the centuries-old military bastion located in the Los Angeles suburb of San Pedro, I spied a man in uniform.

At first, I paid him no heed, assuming him to be some segment of a lingering detail assigned to safeguard the fort's historic integrity. As I shot him a second look, a full minute later, I noticed that the man in uniform, sitting on a stair and reading a mass market paperback, was in fact Adolf Hitler.

A man dressed to *resemble* Adolf Hitler, of course. He rather sheepishly explained that a History Channel documentary was in the process of filming, using the bunker as a stand-in for Hitler's Berlin redoubt, the 16-foot-thick concrete *Führerbunker* Albert Speer buried underneath the German Chancellery. As I walked down a fog-enshrouded passageway a few moments later, it seemed no surprise that a tall, trench-coat wearing blonde woman should emerge and, in a clotted-cream English accent, mockingly declare herself to be Eva Braun.

The "Good War" continues to claim enormous attention in American popular culture, its memories kindled with a seemingly endless march of documentaries and reenactments of the sort witnessed here filling the ranks of cable television channels. Its battles were not fought domestically, of course,

LA-43 Nike missile site near San Pedro, California

Warhead Building, LA-43 Nike missile site near San Pedro, California

Fort McArthur, California

Nike Hercules missiles, location unknown

so one does not find spectators paying homage to battlefields as one does with the hallowed grounds of the Civil War; still, though, World War II occupies a far vaster geography of the imagination. Its heroes and villains are etched in the mind's eye, so much so that to see them in any bunker—even one half a world away from the bunker in question—seems somehow natural.

I thought of the episode later that afternoon as I pursued my real objective in the area: locating the ruins of LA-43, a Nike missile site that was once one of eleven similar sites comprising the "Los Angeles Defense Area." Located minutes from Fort MacArthur, the Nike site has little in common with its historic predecessor. At LA-43, there are no interpretive markers, no refurbished cannon, no historical reenactors who come once a year to restage some military outcome. There were no battles fought here, no causalities, no heroes whose names are fetched with easy recall. The name "Nike," coming from the Greek goddess of victory, is at once lost to history and reborn, albeit as an athletic shoe; the name "Nike," in connotation with a nuclear-tipped missile finishes a distant third to its classical and contemporary meanings.

Driving past LA-43 on the coastal highway, one would in fact be at a loss to comprehend the exact nature of the patch of decrepit land and derelict buildings enclosed by barbed-wired security fencing and surrounded on all sides by the advancing encroachment of suburban housing tracts. Ducking through a gash in the fence, mindful of the myriad "No Trespassing" signs, one can walk through the abandoned buildings, their simple cinderblock exteriors etched with the ravages of salt air and graffiti. Large paved areas are choked with plants that have sprung through cracks in the concrete, obscuring the array of rusted metal ducts, caps, and doors that lie sprinkled about, the only visible footprints of an underground presence that was long ago sealed. Only minute signs, such as the stenciled logo "Warhead Bldg.," betray the site's historical meaning. On a high ridge behind the Nike site, one can find the remains of a World War II-era coastal defense bunker, set into an embankment. This too is unmarked and abandoned, but its form and function are clear—as historian Quentin Hughes notes, "the main fascination of military architecture lies in its honesty."[15] The Nike site, in plain view, is nonetheless occluded, an apt metaphor for a war that was real yet imaginary, abstract yet concrete, everywhere and nowhere.

For a brief period in the twentieth century, the Nike achieved notoriety as the "last-ditch defender of our cities." Built in defensive rings around major cities and installations of strategic importance, the Nike was a short-range radar-guided (and eventually nuclear-armed) missile designed to intercept incoming nuclear-armed Soviet bombers. As a weapon, Nike represented a kind of threshold: It was a high-tech equivalent of the kind of defensive military architecture found at Fort MacArthur, relying upon radar and nuclear detonation rather than periscopes and reinforced concrete walls; "the whole sky," as a piece of Nike literature noted, "reduced electronically to a sheet of paper." Yet if it represented novelty in terms of the strategic defense of the United States through conventional and nuclear missiles, it also represented the last of its kind. A decade after it was built, its defensive purpose had already in essence been rendered obsolete by technology—the invention of the intercontinental ballistic missile—as well as a far more comprehensive, if precarious, defense: the Cold War doctrine known as "Mutually Assured Destruction."

What seems remarkable today about the Nike sites is their sheer ubiquity—anyone who has lived near a major city has in all probability been in the vicinity of a former Nike site—as well as the sundry fact that missiles once comprised part of the urban landscape; the ramparts, walls, moats, and buttresses of the ancient city had returned, albeit invisibly. On New York City's Hart Island, a former Potter's Field located near the Bronx, it is possible to view the New York City skyline standing on the ruins of NY-15, the Nike Ajax battery built in 1956 (looking in the other direction, one sees unmarked graves and a large white monument built by the island's former prisoners that reads "Peace"). Near Hartford, Connecticut, I found Nike site HA-48 at the end of "Country Squire Road," a suburban-like street lined with homes. From inside HA-48, a site nearly overgrown with thick brambles, with the ghostly skeletal outlines of radar towers shimmering through the tangle, one can easily see homes in any direction. In the small town of Catawissa, on the outskirts of St. Louis, the Nike site is made easier to find by the simple fact that a number of former barracks have been turned into classrooms; on a hill behind the "Nike School," as it is called, the former missile battery serves as a parking lot for school buses, while the Warhead Assembly building houses a maintenance shop. Near my own childhood home in Chicago's south suburbs, Nike site C-54—located, appropriately enough, across from a "Target" store—houses both an army vehicle repair shop and a section of the city's administrative headquarters.

In front of my hometown's "Park District" building, where I used to spend weekend afternoons playing basketball, there in fact sits a disarmed Nike Ajax missile, a relic of the period when the army donated defunct missiles to be used as civic monuments in an effort at building goodwill with the communities in whose backyards they were erecting these battle emplacements of the Cold War. Like the old CONELRAD sirens or yellow and black "Fallout Shelter" signs, I never paid much attention to the missile, nor understood what exactly it was doing there. Like most boys of my age, I was preoccupied with G.I. Joe figures and other vestigial traces of what Tom Englehardt refers to as "Victory Culture," the kind of triumphalist American myths born out of western expansion and strengthened in subsequent in the subsequent military victories in the world wars.[16] The battles in my imagination were at Dunkirk and Anzio; the weapons were Stukka bombers and Thompson submachine guns; the military architecture such fabled installations as the Maginot Line or the fortification made famous in the film *The Guns of Navarone*. Amidst the storied exploits of comic books and *World at War* documentaries, I never imagined that fifteen minutes' drive away, on a street that had since become lined with the fast food restaurants and shopping malls of suburban outmigration, was a missile base. In the protests over America's involvement in Vietnam, the war was said to "have come home." But on flickering radar screens and in underground missile bays, located on the edge of urban parks and in bucolic small towns, it had always been there.

In *The Nike Hercules Story*, a film produced by the U.S. Army, the opening shot is of a white Colonial house, with a white fence, on a tree-lined street in a small town. The setting is autumnal, the colors faded with age, a scene out of a Douglas Sirk film. A man is demonstrating to a group of children how to fly a small model plane; the next shot shows one of the children excitedly hurling the plane upon its trajectory. As the plane soars through the air, the camera focuses on the accompanying shadow the plane casts on the ground, and then on the face of the father figure. "For a moment he thinks of Hiroshima," a narrator's voice says in eerily hushed tones, "and the toy casts over Elm Street a thin shadow of dread."

The father, it turns out, is "Joe Griffith," and he is no disinterested observer. "What might happen here," the narrator continues, "is on Joe Griffith's mind. Because his job as commander of the local Nike site is to turn the shadow of dread that hangs over us all into a shield that will protect us all." The film, which goes on to explain the "secret atomic device" at the tip of the Hercules, is rife with the trappings of Cold War mythology: the small town, depicted as the bulwark of American moral order and civilization, living with the perpetual fear of atomic attack (a blinding flash, then *Duck, and Cover!*); a belief that the advances of the same science that inaugurated the threat will prove capable of defeating the threat (the "shadow" turned into "shield"); the sense that military contingency was now an accepted fact of domestic life—i.e., the image of the sanctified small town nestled comfortably against the sweeping radar arrays and the "small new atomic device" of the Nike site; the front lines of the battlefield had shifted, metaphorically and strategically, to the nation's backyard.

Unlike the capitals of Europe, American cities had given comparatively little thought—a bit of industrial camouflage here, a few antiaircraft cannon there—to aerial attack or defensive military architecture during World War

II; Pearl Harbor heightened fears, of course, but even in the wake of that incursion the continental u.s. endured the war in relative security. The dawning of the atomic age, however, seemed to awaken a new and almost inherent sense of vulnerability. As early as 1944, inspired by German rocket advances, the army had already commissioned Bell Laboratories to develop a radar-and-computer-guided antiaircraft missile capable of destroying high-altitude bombers; by May, they had submitted a preliminary report on "Project Nike."

For several years, the Nike was a fringe prototype weapon, almost speculative. A series of escalating Cold War tensions, however—the discovery of long-range TU-4 "Bull" aircraft in the Soviet Union, the later Soviet atomic bomb detonation, the Berlin blockade, and the outbreak of fighting on the Korean peninsula—brought a new impetus and resources to the Nike (and other fledgling missile programs). As one military historian notes, "A succinct example of the change in attitude can be seen in the missile budget. From 1945 to 1950, the missile program in this country averaged about $70 million a year, gradually going up to $135 million by 1950. The first year of Korea saw $800 million spent on missiles, and the second more than $1 billion."[17] By 1951, the army had tested its first fully operational Nike battery at White Sands Proving Ground, New Mexico, with a Nike Ajax missile intercepting a remote-controlled drone; three years later, a Nike battery was installed at Maryland's Fort G. Meade, the first of more than 300 to come in the next decade.

The arrival of the Nike prompted a variety of responses, from relief to dismay. For the *New York Times*, the Nike represented "a triumph of electronic science, a winged messenger of death to the attack and a symbol of ultimate victory over aggression."[18] Its purpose was clear: "If enemy bombers have penetrated to within shooting distance of the Nike emplacements around our great cities, then Nike has to be good—or there won't be any more cities." *Business Week* called it an "Umbrella for the u.s. Homeland." Describing the sketch of a proposed Nike battery as a "scene from some fantastic science fiction movie," the magazine noted that "the strange, half-buried building in the foreground will be a common sight in a number of places two years from now."[19]

Viewed in the abstract, the Nike was a technological marvel and a much-needed defensive mechanism; the reality at ground zero, however, was a bit less glimmering. Erecting Nike bases required land; initially, the army proposed 199 acres were needed for the launch control facility, the battery itself, the clear "line of sight" between them, as well as barracks and other facilities. Securing such significant urban parcels proved so difficult, however, that the army decided instead upon underground installations, which required only 40 acres of land. Still, this represented a militarization of the landscape with which the populace was not entirely familiar. *Time* pointed out that "while doing their defending duty, the Nikes will not be desirable neighbors. The boosters that bounce them into the air are big enough to do damage when they fall to the ground, and so are the Nikes themselves."[20] *Business Week* noted a year later that "people don't want mysterious push-button weapons in their backyards, even if it means protection for them." A 1955 article in the *Chicago Sun-Times* summarized the civic response to Nike: "The reaction has varied from vigorous protest to indifference and ignorance of what is under way. But the Army is making a valiant public relations attempt to tell the public what it's up to and to temper the shock of the American civilian population's first direct contact with radar and guns."[21] The Cold War's suburban debut was satirized in Max Shulman's 1956 novel *Rally Round the Flag, Boys!*, in which the author used the deployment of a Nike battery in Westport, Connecticut, as his source material. The sentiment is captured in a scene at a town meeting, in which a realtor has asked the army's official about the Nike's effect on property values. The official responds: "I can assure you that property values will not suffer one bit. You will hardly know the Nike base is here. The buildings will be neat, low, and inconspicuous. We will landscape the base to blend with the surrounding countryside. We will only have one hundred troops. There will be no noise, no smoke, no fumes and no dust."[22]

When Nike site NY-53, located in the New Jersey town of Middletown (a memorial plaque now stands at the site, which was also known as "Leonardo"), exploded in 1958, causing eleven deaths, the full awareness that Nike was more than a vaguely industrial presence on the landscape dawned. As *Time* pointed out, "In the wake of Leonardo's explosive afternoon, It was going to be hard to convince the neighbors in New Jersey—or around the Nikes guarding 22 other U.S. industrial complexes—that living alongside atomic warheads was still like living beside a gas station."

It was technology, though, not public opinion, that signaled the eclipse of the Nike. From the beginning, it represented a fragile defense, despite the best assurances of the military and its manufacturers, Western Electric, who cheerily vowed in an advertisement that "whatever tomorrow brings, Nike will be watching, always ready." On September 1, 1953, the same day the *New York Times* reported that the Atomic Energy Commission had detected the fifth test detonation of a Soviet atomic bomb, the newspaper also announced that the army's new chief of staff was warning that "the country could not afford to install enough launching stations to make all cities invulnerable even if perfect protection were possible"; the general preferred, the account added, to engage "the enemy as far afield as possible and not be tied down to a static defense, or some sort of Maginot Line, in his own country."[23] The situation was summed up by one defense observer: "Advances of destructive over defensive techniques, which became quite apparent even during the Second World War, have increased so much in the age of the nuclear bomb and the long-distance rocket that any defence measures seem completely hopeless."[24] The advent of long-range intercontinental ballistic missiles rendered the Nike ineffectual (a prototype anti missile Nike program called "Zeus," and another called "x"—intended as a defense against the emergent Chinese nuclear threat[25]—never reached operational status, although the latter can be seen as a predecessor to the Safeguard ABM complex in North Dakota), and by the late 1960s a process of decommissioning had begun, explained in a Department of Defense memorandum: "As the United States has relinquished the option for continental defense against strategic missiles, the Department of Defense has placed a lesser priority on maintenance of the existing posture for defense against manned aircraft."

Just as Mohammed II had seized the walled city of Constantinople in 1453 by building a special cannon, the *Basilica*, which could fire 800-pound balls, so too did the new missiles render the idea of a short-range, anti aircraft urban strategic defense system obsolete. Nike had made the Cold War manifest in cities across the United States, but whatever relief its urban neighbors might have found in its closing was tempered by the knowledge that there was no longer any defense.

In an essay titled "Landscape as Seen by the Military," the writer J. B. Jackson remembered how the battlefield landscapes he surveyed under the guise of military intelligence during World War II possessed the same classical ordering as the eighteenth-century European landscape. Years later, he wrote: "I still find myself wondering if there is not always some deep similarity between the way war organizes space and movement and the way contemporary society organizes them; that is, if the military landscape and military society are not both in essence intensified versions of the peacetime landscape, intensified and vitalized by one overriding purpose which, of necessity, brings about a closer relationship between man and environment and between men."[26]

In the Cold War, which was neither accurately war nor peace, the boundaries of organization were entirely blurred. Regions such as Southern California, with its concentration of aerospace industries, were on a kind of permanent Cold War footing (*Fortress California*, as Roger Lotchin's book calls it), while the interstate highways were nothing if not a military landscape onto themselves. The lines of defense could be as remote as Lonely, Alaska, where a Distant Early Warning Station tracked incoming aircraft; or a short drive away from "Elm Street," where the Nike site sat as an uneasy neighbor, integrated into the landscape with such self-effacing ease they seemed as unremarkable as any other urban feature, despite even the best efforts of the Army to attract attention. As a National Park Service report noted, "although they were located near major population centers, Nike missile bases were low-scale and relatively obscure facilities. Nike battery commanders held open houses at their bases, and worked to build community relations. Still, Nike installations were often closed and abandoned before many local residents understood the full extent of what lay behind the security fencing."[27]

With their wholesale deactivation in the early 1970s, the majority of Nike sites were simply turned over to local governments. Many underwent some form of adaptive reuse, reemerging as low-income housing, underground storage facilities, county administration centers, school buildings, parks, even individual residences, as other local governments pondered what could be done with a grouping of cinder-block buildings and an underground chamber sealed behind welded missile bay doors. In Hamburg, New York, a Nike site became the "Hamburg Senior Citizen Center." The North Chicago suburb of Addison has a "Nike Park," while in Seattle, the "Midway Nike Manor" was used to house low-income families. At another Chicago Nike site, the housing was used for military dependents. "No, I don't know why they were built here," one resident told the *Chicago Tribune*. "But we really like it here, and it's a good place to raise children."[28] Stripped of their original context, the Nike sites were reinserted into a landscape that had changed— suburban housing was creeping to their very periphery, while the cities they had been erected to guard were in many cases no longer major manufacturing centers or of "strategic importance."

Other sites, "abandoned in place," as the military says, simply began to decay, places lost in the transition from past to future, gutted spaces where youth play out their transgressions in an environment to which they could hardly relate. And so the sites sit, vacant memorials to a war that never happened, mute sentinels to a threat that never came. Possessing neither recognized architectural significance nor entirely positive historical connotation, they lie beyond the reach of historic preservation. Built with obsolescence and mobility in mind—the buildings are essentially prefabricated and the missiles designed to be transported if necessary—they paradoxically exist with the permanence of ruins on the edges of our cities. With proposals for a missile defense—the search for the ever-elusive "shield"—again circulating, the Nike sites, and their ever more powerful, ever more quickly outmoded successors, are an entombed reminder of the impermanence of these dreams. It is time they came in from the cold.

Overleaf: Coastal defense bunker and suburban housing near San Pedro, California

6.
THE SECRET LANDSCAPE:
Some Cold War Traces

*Because waste is the secret history, the underhistory, the way archaeolo-
gists dig out the history of early cultures, every sort of bone heap and
broken tool, literally from under the ground.*

Don DeLillo, *Underworld*

For decades, John Ingram has worked the potash mines near Carlsbad, New
Mexico, extracting the inglorious ore—used in fertilizers and other applications—from beneath the cracked and rolling floor of this Chihauhaun
Desert basin, where oil derricks and scrub-oak tangles punctuate the undu-
lating dun-colored expanse. Potash mining has been a marginal presence in
this town of 27,000 since u.s. Borax and Chemical pulled out in 1967, but a
far more lucrative form of mining has come to Carlsbad in the last decade.
Ingram, along with the more than 1,000 other employees of the Department
of Energy's (DOE) Waste Isolation Pilot Project—known as WIPP—are now in
the business of mining space. "Space miners," as they are called, dig not for
precious raw materials but to create empty chambers, a warren of rooms
lodged some half-mile underground in a 250-million-year-old salt bed. Into
those chambers will be placed thousands of barrels—filling a maximum space
of 6.2 million cubic feet—that contain transuranic waste: a time capsule of
gloves, beakers, paperwork, hooded suits and myriad other low-level para-
phernalia used in the research and production of nuclear weapons. Over
time, it is expected, the salt beds, driven by overpressures, will "creep," as the
process is known, eventually caving in on the chambers and burying the
stacks of barrels in a sealed layer of crystalline salt.

Here, 2,150 feet underground, is the tomb of the Cold War, where the
peripheral apparatus that helped create the century's weapons of mass
destruction will be interred over the next three decades—some 38,000 shipments of defense-generated nuclear waste resting in a sepulchral darkness that
the Department of Energy has pledged will be isolated from human contact

"Space mining" at Waste Isolation Pilot Project, Carlsbad, New Mexico

for some 10,000 years. Thus will much of a weapons-building process that began with the mining of uranium end in a kind of mine in which the raw material is space itself, a real estate valued for its distance from civilization. There is a fitting irony that the agent that will protect us from the highest scientific achievements of the Cold War will be nature itself. A war whose missiles and command centers haunted the underworld is cooling down, if not actually ending, in a mass tomb of unknown soldiers, a subterranean storehouse of the national nightmare.

As we descend the three-leveled "conveyance" (the waste never travels in the same space as humans), Ingram's voice shifts downward in timbre as we leave the section of the tunnel lined with concrete, the sound absorbed into walls of salt flecked with iron pyrite. The ride is so smooth I have to watch the blurred gray walls rushing past to remember we are in motion. At the bottom, standing in one of the main tunnels of WIPP, where gusts from intake valves push dust through the uniform 80-degree warmth of the underground, Ingram wants me to know that most miners would be happy to work in such a place. "You generally don't have lights and refrigerated office buildings in a production mine," Ingram says as we speed down a corridor on an electric cart. "The only light you have in a production mine is the one on your head." Miners do wear headlamps here, and the other hallmarks of a mine are all in place. A "Rope-a-Com" communication device housed in the elevator recalls the days when miners would send signals to the top with a tug on a rope, and as Ingram pulls over to where a miner is readying a remote-control borer for digging (known down here as "hogging"), he points to a series of etchings on the wall, a dull gray slab. "The top of this cut is known as the 'back,'" Ingram explains, gesturing at the broad cross-section, "on account of miners were always hitting their back against it. They said they were always rubbing their ribs on the side, so the middle portion became the 'rib.' And the bottom is the floor." When I ask the miner about the difficulties of spending entire days underground, he shrugs. "The first few years I wasn't familiar with it, so I wasn't entirely comfortable. Now I prefer it," he says, gesturing upwards with a barely masked contempt. "People are pretty tight down here. It's dusty, but it's a mine."

We drive to an intersection near a massive airlock door, and Ingram takes a small hammer and begins to chip at a cluster of salt crystal jutting out from the corner, trying to locate a piece that will contain a small, sealed pocket of moisture dating from the bed's formation. As he does, he explains the varying strata visible on the wall. "This reddish area here, that's what used to be the bottom of a great lake." He points to another layer of salt, virtually transparent. "Anywhere you look in the entire underground you can see that salt. It's so perfectly aligned that they can line up an infrared beam along that line and mine 7 feet above, 5 feet below." He hands me a piece of what looks like rock candy, and as I rotate it, a white speck shining dimly within shifts with the movement, like the air bubble in a level. "That wall is solid for the next 300 miles," Ingram says, pointing at the glistening facade. "There's no way you're gonna *Shawshank Redemption* yourself out of here."

As we drive on, Ingram points to various rooms, dedicated to various states from which the waste originated. Each room is a uniform 300 feet long, 33 feet wide, and 13 feet high. The salt walls soften the light, bathing the room in a glow that just as well might be coming from ice. In "Room 6," the creep is already fairly advanced: The ceiling noticeably droops, and the floor has begun to arc upwards, driven by the 2,200-pounds-per-square-inch downward pressure on the walls. Inside a neighboring room, a pair of floodlights illuminates a row of silver barrels, gleaming at the end of the chamber like ancient treasure, a band of yellow "Caution" tape marked with radiation symbols stretched in

Transuranic nuclear waste housed 2,150 feet below the Earth's surface, Waste Isolation Pilot Project, Carlsbad, New Mexico

front. "Fifteen years ago we came down and built and created a city," says Ingram. "A world within a world." After a decade-long legislative and legal impasse, the chambers are gradually being stocked with the refuse of the Cold War, as trucks, each holding three massive Transuranic Package Transporters, Model II (TRU-PACT II) canisters—giant units shaped like D-cell batteries that have been designed to withstand thirty times the pressure of a typical highway accident—make their way from sites ranging from Illinois's Argonne National Laboratory to the Rocky Flats Environmental Technology Site near Boulder, Colorado. "Everybody's afraid of a little ol' piece of transuranic waste," says Ingram. "We weren't educated as a nation as we should have been—the word nuclear scares you to death. People don't realize there's a lot more dangerous stuff being transported over the nation's interstates right now. You probably drove right next to a butane transporter, but you didn't notice it because you're used to it. But if you were to look over at one of our trucks and it had a radiation insignia on it, you'd be scared to death."

WIPP is a remarkable place, the world's only deep-underground salt-bed nuclear waste storage facility. In the early stages of nuclear proliferation, scientists and policymakers had already realized the need for a place to ship the gradually mounting waste materials of defense research and production. In 1957, the year of the Sputnik launch, the National Academy of Sciences wrote, "Disposal in cavities mined in salt beds and salt domes is suggested as the possibility promising the most practical immediate solution of the problem."[1] In 1972, a site near Lyons, Kansas was chosen as the nation's most optimal site; however, the site was soon abandoned, notes the DOE, "because of concerns about the many holes that had been drilled through the site, the risk of salt dissolution, and political opposition." In Carlsbad they found a salt bed that had not seen moisture in 250 million years, and a population that was familiar with mining and economically depressed. Now, in a manner similar to the Superfund site of the former mining town of Butte, Montana, where an open-pit mine now turned to a lake of acid sits in the center of town, Carlsbad seeks salvation in its waste. "The dream that Carlsbad will become a center for nuclear waste research and development is entirely possible," the DOE's WIPP manager said. "The prospects for a bright future can be a reality. The infrastructure is in place. The educated work force is in place."[2]

What is most remarkable about WIPP is not its history, however, but its future. WIPP is a chronicle of an ancient civilization foretold, a 10,000-year stare into a future about which one can only begin to speculate. The planners of WIPP are dealing with materials whose half-life exceeds that of recorded history ("It must have been biblical," marvels Ingram, who as it turns out is also a Baptist minister), and thus face the design challenge of communicating the nature and function of WIPP to whomever might find it ten millen-

Empty TRU-PACT nuclear waste canisters, Waste Isolation Pilot Project, Carlsbad, New Mexico

nia from the present. The Department of Energy created a "Human Interference Task Force," comprised of linguists, anthropologists, science journalists, and others to study what it called "potential scenarios of human intrusion to the WIPP site." The DOE now has in place a plan for what it calls "passive institutional controls"—warning signs, in essence—that will be placed throughout the WIPP site when it is ultimately sealed. As the DOE describes it, "the objective of the design is to tell our descendents that the area at the WIPP site location is not totally in a natural state, that man has clearly marked for a good reason." DOE's final design is based on a concept it calls "defense in depth," which provides a series of layers of information. Among the defenses are a massive earthen berm that will cover the entrance of the disposal facility; some 33 feet wide and with an area of 2,858 feet by 2,354 feet, the berm will be strategically angled to reduce erosion; a series of granite "perimeter monu-

Waste Isolation Pilot Project, Carlsbad, New Mexico

ments," some 25 feet high—weighing nearly 20 tons—and engraved with warnings in seven languages; an "information center," a 40 x 32 x 15-foot structure (placed in the middle of the "repository footprint") whose interior and exterior walls will feature engraved written and pictographic warnings (the structure is without a roof, to allow natural light); and a series of small warning markers, made of granite, aluminum oxide, and fired clay (precious materials cannot be used for fear that they will be stolen, as with the tombs of the Egyptian kings) will be randomly buried, like landmines, throughout the WIPP area. Archives on the specifications and purpose of WIPP will also be maintained at various places throughout the world.

WIPP is without a doubt the most anticipatory space ever constructed, a place that is paradoxically meant to reveal its function to an unthinkable future through the means we typical associate with the prehistoric past:

stone slabs, engraved obelisks, ceremonial markers. The space cannot assume the permanence of language, of geology, or even of architecture, for it is unlikely that the WIPP site itself will communicate any obvious symbolism through its form. The specter of a visitor some 10,000 years from now encountering the nuclear hieroglyphics in the sands of WIPP recalls Walter M. Miller's post-apocalyptic fable *A Canticle for Leibowitz* (1959), in which the adept of a future religious order discovers, in the deserts of Utah, an underground chamber labeled with the ominous words "Fallout Shelter" (fallout being equated with a mythical beast). In Miller's novel, the adept's discovery of "pre-deluge" technical documents, mysterious writings known only to a few, resurrects nuclear armaments and initiates a new course toward doomsday. For the excavator of many eons hence, one has to wonder whether this waste and the weapons for whose production it was generated will bear any meaning, or whether it will all seem, when viewed next to some unfathomable new weapon, like the stone arrowheads and wood shields of a primitive society.

The underground labyrinth of nuclear waste storage, which occupies roughly 3 square miles (enclosed by a 10,000-acre "buffer") of land formerly owned, like most of the state, by the Bureau of Land Management, is a mere fragment of the sprawling subterranean landscape of southern New Mexico. As I drive back to the WIPP offices in Carlsbad with Ken Aragon, a DOE public affairs official, he points to a smokestack and a group of buildings to the left, far in the distance, and then to another similar looking facility to the right. "You can get from there to here underground," Aragon says. "They've been mining here since the mid-thirties, twenty-four hours a day, three-hundred and sixty-five days a year. There must be a hundred thousand miles of tunnels."

As with the Cold War landscape in general, however, the signs of activity are not limited to the underground, and extend into the everyday lives of the citizenry. While staying in the town of Roswell, a place where the UFO "research centers" stand out rather gaudily in a setting dominated by ecumenical churches and the appurtenances of dairy farming, I noticed that a freshly paved and marked bypass road had been built around the city, away from the town's well-preserved 1950s-era Main Street. As Aragon explains it, the bypass is just a small part of a network of new and refurbished roadways implemented to accommodate the expected volume of waste shipments headed to Carlsbad from sites as far away as Georgia. "I-285 from Roswell used to be a two-lane highway," Aragon says. "The trucks will come down I-40, all the way from Klein's Corners, and turn onto 285. That's going to be four-lane all the way to Carlsbad." The cost of building the so-called "WIPP

"Because waste is the secret history..."

route" is being underwritten by the DOE, which is paying the state $20 million a year over a fifteen-year period. Trucks carrying the TRU-PACT II will soon become as familiar as any other long-haul rig.

There is no small irony in the fact that the trucks carrying nuclear waste will otherwise be traveling standard interstate highways, given that the system of coast-to-coast roads inaugurated by Dwight D. Eisenhower was, if not a direct byproduct of Cold War military contingency, at least touted by its proponents for its importance in national defense, reflected for many years in its very name: The National System of Interstate and Defense Highways. A certain myth holds that the interstate system was designed and planned entirely for military purposes, or to aid the evacuation of large cities during atomic attack, but this is making too much of what was in reality an additional sales pitch for the largest public works program ever undertaken in America—what Phil Patton has called "the last New Deal Program and the first space program, combining the economic and social ambitions of the former with the technological and organization virtuosity, the sense of the national prestige and achievement, of the latter."[3] Still, as the diverse system of Garden City-inspired parkways gave way to the rigidly standardized interstate system, one can discern traces of military contingency. For one, the desires of the road lobby coincided with those of civil defense planners; the American Association of State Highway Officials' own civil defense committee argued that the design of streets needed to consider both evacuation needs and the expected postwar recovery work.[4] For another, there is the more obviously suggestive fact that one can find the majority of the nation's Cold War military installations located close to an interstate highway; the layout itself, it has been noted, closely resembles the 1922 plan drawn by General John J. Pershing for a network of roads vital to national defense.[5] When federal highway officials were plotting in the early 1960s the construction of interstate highway expansions in the then quite sparsely populated (and newly added) state of Alaska, the layout criteria were made quite clear: "Routes of the Interstate System should be selected to serve the highway movement to and from military and naval establishments in war industries."[6]

Another military consideration has been seen in the design of the road itself: Curves and elevations were flattened to allow faster travel and to allow, it is said, military convoys to hold their speed going uphill. That this benefit extended to trucking was ancillary. One might also consider the German *Autobahn*, the inspiration for the Pennsylvania Turnpike and other American roads. As one account notes, "When German motorways built in the 30s were strong enough to take the axle weight of today's traffic, it seems more probable that the actual design criteria was the German tank rather than any forecast of future transport tonnage."[7] Historian John Stilgoe sees another function lurking in the design of the Interstate: "By the early 1950s, planners in the Strategic Air Command knew that Soviet missiles would almost certainly destroy air force bomber bases, but that aircraft returning from first strikes might find safety, fuel, and more bombs cached alongside the Military and Interstate Highway System. So from the start, no power lines bordered the new highway, and except in a few places where federal authorities merged existing turnpikes into the new system, broad shoulders of mowed grass, not even ornamental plants, bordered the pavement."[8]

The traces of war contingency found in the highway system are not merely historical relics. In its 2001 fiscal report, the Federal Highway Administration devotes an entire chapter to "National Security," focusing on what is called the "Strategic Highway Network," or STRAHNET, for short. As the FHA describes it, "STRAHNET is a system of public highways that is a key deterrent in U.S. strategic policy. It provides defense access, continuity, and emergency capabilities for movements of equipment and personnel and equipment in war. It is about 61,000 miles, including the 45,400 Interstate and Defense Highways and 15,600 miles of other important public highways."[9] STRAHNET emphasizes such traffic flows as troops to ports of embarkation, and requires roads with sufficiently strong bridges. In certain ways, the military is more reliant on highways than ever, since the majority of troops are no longer "forward deployed," i.e., stationed at international airbases. The fast channeling of dispersed forces has gained strategic precedence over fixed, large-scale military installations. As the Department of Defense's Military Traffic Management Command Transportation Engineering Agency (an agency whose acronym needs its *own* acronym) notes, "With DOD's current emphasis on continental US-based military units, the NHS will play an increasingly important role in new deployment scenarios."[10] In Operation Desert Storm, it was estimated that the military transported the equivalent of the city of Richmond, Virginia; before this equipment could be flown or shipped to the Persian Gulf, it first had to go down some of STRAHNET's many miles.

Most travelers on the National Highway System would not pause to consider that the highway, with its uniform 12-foot-wide lanes and theoretically continual movement, is a "key deterrent in U.S. strategic policy." Yet roads have always had a military connotation; they have always served as expressions of state power, creating systems of circulation deemed most important to the national interest. In the United States today we tend to think of military operations as things that happen *elsewhere*, and national defense is envisioned as Pentagon spending figures, aircraft carriers performing maneuvers off some foreign shore, advertisements showing special forces plunging into hostile terrain. But the highways are just one element of a vast layer of military landscape that sits, like a transparent overlay, on top of the existing landscape; what functions one way in everyday life might function differently during a national emergency.

The writer Tony Hiss has noted, the number of acres under military use in the United States grew from about 3 million in 1937 to more than 30 million acres by the apex of the Cold War[11] (a further 960 million acres of aerial space were similarly reserved). This process of "military sprawl," as he terms it, occurred gradually and quietly, as parcels of land that were most likely already under some form of government control were ceded to the military, whose ever-expanding weapons programs and dictates of secrecy required the creation of enormous, covert landscapes.

What was occurring more generally during the Cold War was a militarization of space—not merely the sequestering of territory but control over the way space is conceived, depicted, and managed. The most striking example is the World Geodetic System, a program initiated by the Department of Defense in 1960. The WGS, as it is called, emerged as a necessary corollary to the strategic targeting of nuclear weapons against sites that were, literally, on the other side of the globe. As geographers John Cloud and Keith Clarke have noted, the intercontinental range of the missile rendered obsolete the various sets of conflicting national data—in essence, geographical surveys of the Earth's shape and position, mathematical models tied to a fixed point of origin (in the U.S., it was Meades Ranch, Kansas)—that had been established decades before. What was needed was a "world system" of geographic information—a standardized global map, or, if you will, "global geo-referenced remote sensing databases"—that could ensure not only the accurate targeting of missiles, but a consistent reference point for locating the enemy's strategic installations.[12] While mapping and surveying have long been crucial to the military enterprise, in the Cold War, where weaponry was expected to travel ever further to hit targets with increasing accuracy—and where much geographic information was unobtainable because of hostile airspace—the knowledge of a terrain that could not be seen (but acquired instead by the emerging science of "remote sensing") became paramount. In one peculiar instance described by Cloud and Clarke, the United States, drawing on survey data of Eurasia captured from the German army in World War II, then used satellite imagery to access the historical survey markers and track current Soviet positions: "CORONA [military intelligence satellite] photography was used to relocate the remains of survey towers from the original surveys, allowing geodetic corrections of immense strategic value for 'locking in' the positions of Soviet facilities in interior Eurasia."[13] With the emergence of the CORONA and other space-based reconnaissance and surveillance satellite programs in the 1960s, the military was able to further refine the WGS. The system that was ultimately deployed by the Defense Mapping Agency in 1972 featured inputs from a wide array of military and commercial sources, ranging from the navy's Navigational Satellite System and the army's SECOR (Sequential Collation of Range) Equatorial Network to the Smithsonian Astrophysical Observatory.

The Cold War plotting of WGS was to become the way the world imagined itself, as the data and intelligence assets of military technology were gradually and selectively transferred to civilian use. As Cloud and Clarke write, "Since the middle 1960s, USGS [the United States Geographical Survey] has been publishing maps with collar data that say 'based on aerial photography and other source data.' The 'other source data,' for a third of a century, has been the best intelligence assets of the American government."[14] This transfer was not complete, however, for the value of Cold War military intelligence is usually found in its secrecy. Military satellites, as Cloud and Clarke describe it, were "capable of much more productive applications" than their civilian counterparts: a "resolution gap" separated the two. The military, in the name of the national interest, possessed a greater knowledge of and command over the Earth itself. The implications of this became apparent with the rise in popularity of the Global Positioning System (GPS) in the 1980s. GPS units, which became prized by everyone from hikers to mariners for their ability to transmit real-time location data via signals received from the military's NAVSTAR satellites, had just one flaw: The data was never entirely correct. The reason had less to do with the technology of the units themselves than with a filter of sorts, employed by the military and termed "Selective Availability," that degraded the accuracy of the positional reading, essentially meaning that the reading it gave could never be closer than 300 feet to the actual position. There were myriad commercial applications being tested for GPS—onboard navigational devices for cars, a mobile phone device that would automatically transmit the caller's location to rescue personnel on 911 calls—but none of these were realistically plausible until the government announced, in May of 2000, that Selective Availability would be discontinued.

A month prior to the announced ending of Selective Availability, another vestigial trace of Cold War information control had been erased: A North Carolina company called Aerial Images Inc., released formerly classified aerial images of the legendary U.S. Air Force base at Groom Lake, Nevada, otherwise known as Area 51. Ironically, the images were acquired from the Soviet space-imaging service known as *Sovinformsputnik*; the commercial satellite Ikonos, meanwhile, began offering images over the Internet that far exceeded the capabilities of Cold War-era satellites, but still had only one-tenth the resolution of the military's current platform. The Area 51 disclosures followed the declassification of some 800,000 images culled from the Corona program. Landscapes that had been taken out of the public domain could now be viewed by anyone, albeit as a brief snapshot taken during the sporadic flyover of the satellite. "Transparency" was the new keyword. It meant allowing everything to be viewed at all times—the geospatial surveillance version of the glass-curtain wall. New technologies allowed for satellite imagery with resolution down to one meter. The implications seemed revolutionary. As the technofetishist *Wired* enthused, "With 1-meter imagery you can see how fast-growing suburbs are actually spreading, and what services they need. You can plan roads, power lines, water mains, ATMs, fast-food outlets. You can get a high level of detail and precision in your planning without having to do on-site surveying. In effect, you get to see the world exactly as it is, more or less whenever you want."[15]

As new as this seemed, it was a familiar refrain, sounded by those who viewed the Earth from the first balloon flights of the eighteenth century, and having evolved through the greatest episodes of mass destruction ever witnessed. The omniscient eye, democratized, would allow "objective" viewing of the planet, to "see the world exactly as it is," as if the aerial view held greater truth than the perspective from ground zero. Ironically, as satellite-based imaging systems evolved, so too did computer systems for evaluating the data obtained. Automated information was being evaluated with automated interpreters. By the end of the 1970s, writes historian William Burrows, computers "were routinely being used to correct for distortions being made by the satellites' imaging sensors; to further facilitate the interpretive process, the computers have been fed recognition data from a vast quantity of objects ranging from uranium ore to rail-road tracks to IVRM silos and are programmed to alert the interpreters when such objects appear in new imagery."[16] Still, supposedly "objective" aerial information is still an elusive commodity, as was revealed during an episode in April 2001, after the capture of a United States EP-3E surveillance plane by China. As satellites tracked the grounded plane, an early image showed an apparent disassembling of the plane—a large "shark bite" taken out of the fuselage—that was later revealed to be false. "It's either a digital transmission error or a manipulation glitch," an unnamed intelligence official told the *New York Times*.[17] Despite such distortions, there still exists a teleological fantasy that the ever-finer aerial views represent higher and higher stages of knowledge; a parallel strand in military thought sees in progressively more effective targeting the mechanization of the battlefield. In the Persian Gulf War, the Cold War constructs of aerial intelligence and automated killing were brought to their fullest expression: The aerial vision of truth was contained by the weapon itself. An image showed us with terrifying immediacy that the "smart weapon" was headed to its target, and as it struck the picture went blank— the weapon itself was the narrative, its impact the conclusion. The 1-meter view has, of course, not prevented the accidental bombing of the wrong embassy, nor does it accurately depict the collateral damage from the still oxymoronic "precision bombing." Nor has the specter of real-time global surveillance stemmed war, genocide, human rights abuses, deforestation, urban sprawl, or any other malady. As aerial photographs of the once-secret landscapes of the Cold War are made freely available by the former mechanisms of the Cold War, truth is ever more visible, yet ever more elusive.

The buildings of Survival City were never engulfed in blast waves, never saw their careful engineering exposed to the precisely calibrated overpressures. The missiles were never launched, and the men came home. The array of blast-proof building and radiological defense engineering presented here seemed the architectural equivalent of a massively expensive and wasteful arms race, the 1950s fallout shelter a quixotic relic of a naïve, terrified populace. The Cold War is literally being buried, the fires extinguished as the body is laid to rest. However, its effects and vestiges remain, sometimes in surprising guises.

When one reads today about "security architecture," the subject does not typically refer to bunkers or defense installations, but to the Internet. With an increasing amount of governmental and commercial activity occurring across data networks, the "landscape" of business and government has been reconstituted virtually—witness the recent attempts, linked to the government of Indonesia, to cripple a fledgling East Timorese "sovereign" Internet domain. Security firms such as Pilot Network Services offer "round-the-clock network-based security" and an "advanced, distributed security architecture" called the Pilot Heuristic Defense Infrastructure. This defensive architecture bristles with architectural metaphors (e.g., "firewalls") but is of course utterly invisible, and here too is a lasting legacy of the Cold War. It was the research of the Department of Defense's Advanced Research Projects Agency (operating on a principle devised by the Rand Corporation's Paul Baran) that famously led to the Internet, the attempts to design a decentralized, "packet"-based network that would ensure a retaliatory "second strike" capability from one point in the network even if other nodes had been disabled. There was no center of power in the Cold War, no infrastructural heart to render inoperable with a single bullet. The chains of command were invisible, flowing through the ether, an ongoing signal. That the "Information Superhighway" should have emerged as a metaphor is not surprising, for both the National Highway System and what became known as ARPANET shared certain expressions of Cold War logic: a massive, decentralized network that linked the country and could, in the event of a nuclear war, keep open sufficient lines of communication.

Even the Internet requires some amount of centralization, however, and in the myriad "data centers" that have begun to dot the American landscape one can see a contemporary incarnation of the Cold War architectural ethos. Data centers are the physical housings of websites, where the infrastructure required to run the network services of corporations such as Intel or MCI WorldCom are kept in facilities that provide security, redundancy, and anonymity. A typical data center is the so-called "CyberFortress" designed by the Maryland company DataCentersNow. According to the company, "a CyberFortress is a freestanding, newly constructed one or two-story hardened core and shell building designed for the requirements of infrastructure-based telecommunications firms seeking mission critical compatible facilities."[18] The CyberFortress walls are 7.25-inch-thick concrete panels designed to withstand 4,000 psi as well as 150-mile-per-hour winds, and the building is free of windows. Curiously, the CyberFortress features the appearance of glass—smoked spandrel glass—but this has merely been placed over slabs of concrete. The false windows serve two purposes. "You don't want a building that looks like a bunker," said a zoning official in Virginia, where many data centers are located.[19] The windows are not merely aesthetic, however, but a form of camouflage: The theory is that a building that resembles a bunker will draw undue attention to itself. Even with the false windows, data centers, whose locations are often not revealed, still resemble "black boxes," structures whose exterior appearance gives no hint of their interior functions. If the Cold War facilities such as Site R and Mount Weather were meant to protect the enduring survival of a network of command and control—providing a redundant "backup" if another element was destroyed—the data centers are similarly quasi-visible fortresses protecting a network that itself has no physical expression. A key difference is that the hardening of data centers—using techniques learned during the Cold War—is done less for the possibility of nuclear war than for a terrorist attack. "These are the sites the government believes terrorists will go after," a security official told the *Washington Post*.[20]

Survival City, apart from a series of test buildings in the Nevada desert, was an *idea*: That one could, through architectural and engineering ingenuity, design for survival against atomic attack. From the beginning, it was troubled by the discrepancy between the physical requirements of defensive architecture and the desire to create an architecture that was livable (a dissonance that remains). In the end, the weapons grew too powerful, while the will to survive was weakened by the mixed messages about the possibility of survival and the prospects for a post-nuclear world. Survival City was a brief moment in the history of the city, a return to the notions of violence and protection inherent in the city's historical founding. If Survival City in its most extreme manifestation has disappeared, however, a number of its symptoms persist. The city survived, but new anxieties were to arise that required the full knowledge of "bombproof" building acquired in that era. The new threat was even more localized, even more invisible, even more oriented against architecture itself: The World Trade Towers, the apotheosis of corporate modernism, were literally attacked from *within*. Terrorism created new reasons to fear the mass assembly of people in urban areas, new reasons for dispersal and concrete barriers, new orderings of space and anxieties over space.

The blast-resistant architectural specialists of the Cold War, such as Weidlinger Associates (as the firm puts it, "one of the first firms to initiate a systematic exploration of analytical, experimental and computational techniques to achieve theoretical solutions with practical applicability to the response of structures subject to nuclear weapons"), did not go out of business. Instead, the techniques honed during that period were transferred to defense against individual attacks—an architectural peace dividend of sorts. As the company's own history notes, "the knowledge gained in the area of nuclear weapons effects was later applied to conventional weapons and explosives"; the firm's most recent projects range from "vulnerability assessment" and "blast design" of a new federal complex in Oklahoma City to a Defense Threat Reduction Agency-sponsored "Computational Weapon Target Interaction," meaning, the "calculation of response of weak above ground structures and above and below ground hardened facilities, blast doors and internal equipment to conventional weapons effects."[21]

In the Cold War, the specter of violence was abstract in an everyday sense, but could ultimately be understood in terms of geopolitical dynamics, national myths, and weapons bearing mythological names. As that framework disintegrates, notes historian Richard Slotkin, "we are in the process of giving up a myth/ideology that no longer helps us see our way through the modern world, but lack a comparably authoritative system of beliefs to replace what we have lost."[22] When the aforementioned downing of the U.S. surveillance plane by China seemed to augur a resuscitation of Cold War hostilities, the United States found that its presumptive enemy was an important trading partner. In the *Wall Street Journal* and other publications, one could find articles full of stern warnings from U.S. officials, and a few pages later advertisements from Federal Express boasting about their service to countries such as China. As Christopher Hitchens has noted, the United States forges ahead with its "missile shield" against a country that it has always anticipated as one massive looming market: "So it is an arms race at one end and a Starbucks deal at the other."[23]

In the post-Cold War world, the specter of violence has become less cataclysmic, but the loss of a primary enemy has seemingly been accompanied by an expansion in the sources and methods of violence, a bewildering inventory of "rogue states," lone gunmen, truck bombers, urban nerve gas attacks, and computer hackers. In the bombing of the Alfred P. Murrah Building in Oklahoma City, which reinvigorated the idea of protective construction for government facilities, the culprit himself seized on the perceived desire to see some larger force at work: "Because the truth is, I blew up the Murrah Building, and isn't it kind of scary that one man could wreak this kind of hell?"[24]

The Cold War required a reformulation of space; Paul Virilio writes that "fortification, which was geophysical in the ancient times of the Great Wall of China or the Roman *limes*, has suddenly become physical and even 'micro-physical,' no longer located *in the space* of a border to defend, or in the covering or armor of a casemate or tank, but *in the time* of instantaneous electromagnetic countermeasures."[25] The transition to a post-Cold War world also required a new space—the "doomtowns" of the nuclear age replaced by mock "terror towns" in which low-intensity urban combat and counterterrorist scenarios could be reenacted. Even the Dugway Proving Ground was reinventing itself for the new regime, with Utah Senator Orrin Hatch proposing in 1996 (a year after the nerve gas attack on the Tokyo subway system) a facility at Dugway that would have "the capacity to produce controllable releases of chemical and biological agents from a variety of urban and suburban structures, including laboratories, small buildings and homes."[26]

Architecture, which in other eras relied on overt symbolism to connote state power and themes of defense and security, finds itself in a crisis of representation: How does one design for security without simultaneously heightening feelings of insecurity? This intersects a larger question about how one copes with the potential for militaristic violence in a time of supposed peace. In the construction of a new United States Embassy in Berlin, the entrants in the architectural competition attempted to move away from the precepts of the "Inman Standard" (the design specifications enacted by law after the Lebanon u.s. Marine barracks bombing), as State Department personnel had complained of "living behind walls" and a procession of bunkerlike structures; still, stringent security codes needed to be met. As *Architectural Record* observed, "Protecting personnel had to be reconciled with State's desire to offer a facility that is inviting to the public, a good civic neighbor, and a register of American values. Writ large, this is the same—often contradictory—charge architects face more and more as fear of crime and terrorism rises."[27] This, in essence, is the same conundrum faced by the civil defense planners of the Cold War: How can one build a bunker that does not look like a bunker? Physically, it can be done, but how is this conflict between the symbolic virtues of a building (e.g., openness, democracy, public spaces, access) and its underlying character (sensors, surveillance, setbacks, hardening, "mantraps," and closed access points) to be resolved?

Ultimately, whether in the Cold War or in an age of terrorism, the question is about the way violence is built into the landscape. The Cold War put the nation on a survival footing, brought the tremors of an unrealized war into the textures of everyday life, and fractured the national consciousness in two. On the surface was an ostensible stability marked by progress and the spreading of the "American way," but underneath, a repressed subconscious of murky chambers, false fronts, and assassination plots. That the Cold War has presumably ended, that fallout shelters are now the stuff of jokes, that civil defense sirens no longer wail—none of these conditions offers assurance that the specter of violence and the questions of survival and security that so haunted the nation during that period have ended. Surveying contemporary architecture and design, one might expect to see a language of openness and optimism replacing the coding of the Cold War, marked by defensiveness and doom. But paradoxically, the vernacular design of the Cold War was all about optimism—the Satellite motels, the soaring tailfins of cars, giant picture windows gazing onto serene blocks—and in the contemporary scene, there is an obsession with defense. The sport-utility vehicle promises "four wheels to survival" in the suburban jungle, while houses marked by an ostensible sense of openness sit behind invisible security sensors, the signs of security companies dotting their lawns like the familiar warnings of the military's protected space. We cannot safely laugh at the naïve fears expressed by the Cold War environment without acknowledging our own.

A shooting spree by a student at a school in Santee, California in March 2001—one of a spate of what have become familiar episodes—demonstrates how the echoes of Cold War culture can sound in unexpected places. Santee, a mostly white, middle-class suburb of San Diego, was perceived by residents as a place where precisely such a thing as a school shooting would not occur. "I searched and searched all over the country for a place were my kids would be safe and I chose Santee," one resident said after the shootings. Residents lived in places such as the "New Frontier" gated community, and the town had the county's second-lowest crime rate. It was, as the mayor said, a place of "Little League and doctors—it is America."[28] But the idea that "it can't happen here" resonates with Cold War meaning.

As John Stilgoe noted in *Borderlands* (1988), his study of the rise of suburbia, places like Santee grew as returning veterans from World War II sought refuge in communities unlike those centralized historic cities they had seen destroyed in Europe and Japan. "In California," writes Stilgoe, "the warm, sunny land settled by so many discharged veterans educated by firebombed cities and by Hiroshima and Nagasaki, the flight from ground zero was fastest."[29] America had barely begun enjoying the fruits of postwar prosperity when the Soviet explosion of an atomic bomb plunged it into another conflict. The idea of Soviet nuclear attack would gradually become part of everyday life through training films, pamphlets, and, at the height of the Berlin blockade, a brief flurry of fallout shelter building. But the emerging civil defense culture, in its refusal to allot money for public fallout shelter building, placed the emphasis of survival on the homefront, which by the late 1950s, was already emphatically shifting toward the suburbs—between 1948 and 1958, more than 80 percent of new housing was suburban. Cities, whose densities made them ideal nuclear targets, were written off in terms of defense, just one more symbolic gesture in a series of postwar governmental edicts in favor of suburbia.

The civil defense films of the 1950s usually depicted idealized small towns and suburbs on the order of Santee, with their white picket fences, orderly streets, perfect lawns, and strong family units. They were, to paraphrase the mayor of Santee, "America." With titles like "Alert Today, Alive Tomorrow," the films stressed neighborliness and volunteerism, positing the single-family detached home as the last line of atomic defense. "This country was practically built by this neighborly feeling," one narrator intones. Yet within a decade, on the cusp of Kennedy's "New Frontier," civil defense had taken a rather different turn, as a number of Americans began building private shelters and the full ramifications of a nuclear attack were coming to light. Suddenly, civic bonhomie was replaced by a creeping distrust, exemplified in the comments of one Chicago man who threatened to mount a machine gun atop his shelter to keep people out. Neighborliness, it turned out, extended only so far in the context of nuclear holocaust. The anthropologist Margaret Mead, in a 1961 article for the *New York Times*, wondered if the crisis of civil defense had not exposed something of what the novelist John Keats called "the crack in the picture window," the social flaws behind the new American utopia: "Drawn back in space and in time, hiding from the future and the rest of the world, they turned to the green suburbs, protected by zoning laws against members of other classes or races or religions, and concentrated on the tight, little family. They idealized the life of each such family living alone in self-sufficient togetherness, protecting its members against the contamination of different ways or others needs . . . t he armed, individual shelter is the logical end of this retreat from trust in and responsibility for others."[30]

In Santee, home of the new "New Frontier"—and one can see in the gated community a faint trace of the fallout shelter, an enclave of defensible space built to ward off a perceived yet invisible threat—residents thought they had found safety from violence. But where children of the Cold War were taught "duck, and cover" drills, the children of towns like Santee learn new exercises, like "Code Red" security drills, and fear a new invisible threat—one that would not come from above, but from within. The Cold War idea that peace could be maintained even as the landscape was militarized is like the current thinking that Americans can be "protected" by the ubiquitous presence of guns— our own internal, ongoing arms race. The missiles were never fired, but the bullets continue to fly. As the Cold War and its relics are buried, we should remember one of its enduring architectural lessons: There is no safety in walls.

SEPTEMBER 11, 2001

Unflinchingly stalwart, this pair of foursquare, sheer towers has changed—probably forever—the madcap profile of lower Manhattan.

G. E. Kidder Smith, *Source Book of American Architecture*

It was a day on which every detail, when later examined, loomed impossibly large. My wife and I were eating breakfast near the window in our bedroom, which faces what was on that last morning a skyline dominated by the World Trade Center. It was not a direct view—I usually had to step to the window itself and peer to the right, across the rows of brownstones and backyards criss-crossed with hanging laundry that mark my neighborhood of Carroll Gardens. We normally would have been eating in the living room, but as we were under-going some home renovations, we had moved into the bedroom to avoid the noise and dust. From there, we were able to hear a low but distinct boom of some sort, somewhere south, perhaps on the water, not loud enough to startle but enough to cause us to turn to each other and ask: "What was that?" Out of some nervous reflex I said: "Sounds like a plane crash."

But this is a city, I thought. *Things happen.* Heavy trucks rumble down the street. Massive freighters dock a dozen blocks away, in the few remaining docks of South Brooklyn, and dispense their loads. Airplanes soar overhead every few minutes, sometimes loudly enough to lightly vibrate the window panes in our apartment. As we got ready to begin the day, pulled by the inex-orable current of routine, I was told by one of the workmen, in Spanish that I could falteringly comprehend, that a plane had hit *los torres*, and it was not until he pointed in the general direction of lower Manhattan that I under-stood what he meant. Racing to the window, craning my neck to see that the scene normally shimmering so reliably on the horizon had been transformed, and with an immediate and clenching chill I saw a fireball, churning orange and black, spiraling furiously from the building's side. Turning on CNN, I

September 11, 2001: View from the author's window, Brooklyn, New York learned the spare initial facts: that a jet had hit one of the towers, and that it seemed to be intentional.

Somehow, the morning routine still prevailed, as we were both running late for what seemed at the time important meetings. I turned off the television and we left the house, but not before I paused to finish off a roll of film from my window; as I hastily pointed the camera toward the smoke, I incredibly did not even notice—as I later would, looking at the printed photographs—that the second tower had already been hit. Craning for a better angle, I had not even seen the thing at which I was looking. As we boarded the subway, with the morning crowds massing as always, the news was being filtered and dissected among small groups of passengers sitting across from each other, and there was a palpable sense of subdued unease rather than discernible fear.

I emerged at Broadway and Houston Street to a scene that seemed latently orderly, even though a steady tide of people were walking north, away from the smoke, some in the street. As I rounded Houston onto Greene Street, hoping to get a cup of coffee, I heard a chorus of screams, with one man's repeated "Oh my God" rising memorably above, and as I looked down Greene I saw one of the towers in its last stages of collapse, a cascade of dust spilling into the surrounding airspace, a kind of billowing mushroom cloud in reverse. The mood discernably shifted, as if the collective faith on that street had been shattered; crashing a plane into the building was one thing, but bringing it down altogether had altered the equation: A building on fire was still a building, some kind of symbol, a standing embodiment of faith in engineering. Now people who turned around briefly to watch stepped up their pace, cell phones to their ears but only a few mouths moving, the others searching in vain for a signal. I stood fixed on the sidewalk, piecing together information from those who stopped to mill in stunned circles, learning only then that a second jet had hit the other tower, that a plane had hit the Pentagon, that other planes might be headed for still more targets. It felt as though the world was slipping away, and strangers turned to each other to try and put the contours of reality on something that in the individual mind had nowhere to turn save for incomprehension or hysteria. A man told me he had been on Greene Street an hour before and had seen the first plane fly overhead, had felt the buildings rumbling, had remembered it flying somewhat erratically, tilting a bit, and then just simply melting into the side of the building like a swan breaking the serene surface of a pond. He was waiting for his girlfriend, who worked on West Street, and he was shaking. As we talked with another man, there was another series of cries, and as we turned, the second building was already collapsing, and what I remember most vividly was a chunk of facade, it must have been several stories, simply plunging against the bright blue morning sky.

I began to walk the streets with the rest of the city, unsure of what to do, my phone not connecting, already hearing rumors that the subways were not working. I stood for a while with a subdued group of construction workers on the back steps of the future Prada store on Broadway, listening to the radio, and heard the AM news announcer declare that "the only words I can think to describe it are 'nuclear holocaust.'" The phrase suddenly reminded me of why I had in fact come into Manhattan that morning, to go over the final design concept for this book, this book filled with all its historically detached ruminations on nuclear war and its aftermaths, this book with its tentative conclusions about the ultimate frailty of architecture, this book which begins with a more hopeful kind of explosion and now concludes with an ominous one. Now, I and the entire city of New York seemed to have become characters in one of the nuclear war pulp novels from the 1950s I had so assiduously researched, walking *en masse* across the bridges to Queens and Brooklyn to safety, unable to reach family and friends, unsure of what to do next. Walking in parts of Brooklyn where I had never been, the road bristled with eerie markers: a rooster crowing from some house below the Williamsburg Bridge, the roof of the Brink's headquarters ringed with sunglassed and shotgun-toting guards. There was a mood of Biblical portentousness, and I later thought of an Old Testament passage that had appeared in a story by W. G. Sebald, whose words from an earlier source begin this book, in that week's *New Yorker*, the thundering admonitions from Zephaniah III, 6: "I have cut off the nations: their towers are desolate; I made their streets waste, that none passeth by."

This was not, of course, the atomic attack that had always been feared and against which we had become gradually inured. There were no massive retaliations against carefully calibrated targets; there was no radioactive fallout (notwithstanding the low cloud that would hang over the city for weeks after the attack). The damage, however horrific and vast, was but a sample of what would have been played out across an entire landscape. Still, there was an eerie similarity between what was happening before my eyes and the whole tenor of the period I had been describing. The World Trade Center ruins became instantly known as "Ground Zero," a term born of nuclear testing in the deserts of New Mexico. On NBC Tom Brokaw compared the atmosphere of Lower Manhattan to a "nuclear winter." People "downwind" walked in an acrid fog of particulates and wondered about the health implications. The President was diverted to Strategic Air Command headquarters in Omaha, while the vice president repaired to the Presidential Emergency Operations Center stronghold. For a brief time, the Internet, that Cold War-era DARPA-created device intended as a backup communications system in the event of nuclear war, indeed provided the surest means of communication. As the Cold War had portended, the attack was spontaneous, without warning, but in the post-Cold War world the enemy was not immediately recognizable, save in the speculative fashion of a "prime suspect" whose visage, firing a machine gun on some dusty steppe, came across in grainy slow-motion stock footage.

There was talk of keeping the economy running (and I remembered a 1960s *Fortune* story headlined "The Economy Can Survive Nuclear Attack"), of the renewed necessity for a missile defense system (even though this relic of Cold War thinking now looked already utterly obsolete), news of corporations that had parallel operations running in secure "bunkers," and, inevitably, discussions of New Yorkers' leaving the city altogether; that the city, which not so long before, as the New Economy began to accelerate had been praised for its density, was no longer safe, that it was in some fashion obsolete, which instantly revived a discussion that been revived at various times during the Cold War, after the bombing of Hiroshima, after the news that the Soviets had successfully tested a hydrogen bomb. A friend whose residence had been within blocks of the center (and whose daughter's baptism we had, a few months before, attended at the small Greek Orthodox church, St. Nicolas, which once stood beatifically in the shadows of the twin towers but had now been utterly destroyed by the collapsing rubble) was two days later looking for real estate in Westchester County. The city, as more than one observer noted, was now a "target."

Attention shifted to the World Trade Center itself. In 1993, when the complex was bombed, an engineer had ruminated that it had been designed to withstand the impact of a 707 jet—a plane, we are now told, that is dwarfed by the 767. The building, designed by Minoru Yamasaki, was now a "symbol," variously, of "American financial power," "democratic capitalism"—or any number of permutations on these phrases, cobbled together by news anchors—and a much different symbol than one of Yamasaki's previous buildings, the Pruitt-Igoe housing complex in St. Louis, whose own collapsing implosion had marked the putative end of large-scale modernist housing projects. Architecturally the truth was, the Trade Center was a building toward which some ambivalence had always been felt. But it was no longer a building. It was beyond architecture; it was an icon of a way of life and a site where thousands had died, a place where something had imprecisibly changed about the country. In the span of an hour, the Trade Center had been elided from the skyline, and as I write, the city is still going through the process of reconfiguring its "image of the city," of acquiring a new view, of reconciling memories that no longer correspond to a physical place, of creating a new method of wayfinding when one can no longer orient oneself by the squared spires (which had admittedly seemed to glower rather than soar) to the south, and suddenly all previous and innocent depictions of the Trade Center itself come under scrutiny, as if the very image of the building in its previous life is now an indecent act of gratuitous exploitation.

As I watched the endless replays of the plane hitting the towers, I could not help but think back to the historical footage from Survival City, where the repeated images of an atomic blast wave sweeping away a house, however distant they seem, were as emblematic of their time as the Trade Center images will now seem to ours. In the era of atomic anxiety, the city was presumed untenable, people worried about going to work in tall buildings, and architects worked in vain to fashion a bombproof architecture; in the end, neither precept proved viable, nor desirable—and after all, what life was worth living underground, or among the radioactive rubble? Now, as I write, there are military jets roaring overhead, and a cloud hangs over the tip of Manhattan like a stalled weather system. The city has been shaken again, and architecture has provided an uncertain shelter, and those same impulses, reborn—to leave the city, to construct buildings capable of withstanding attacks—are ultimately just as untenable now as they were fifty years ago, for what would life be without cities and without architecture that promoted the positive values of civic life? The riches—material, intellectual, cultural, and spiritual—of the city, as Lewis Mumford once observed, have always made it a "visible object" for "collective aggression"; to abandon it would be the first surrender of a civilization whose own survival depends on the city. If we cannot build against the worst acts of humankind, then we must continue to build in hopeful emulation of the best.

—Brooklyn, September 17, 2001

NOTES:

INTRODUCTION

1. Stephen L. Schwartz, ed., *Atomic Audit: The Costs and Consequences of U.S. Nuclear Weapons Since* 1940 (Washington, D.C.: Brookings Institution Press, 1998), 3.
2. Don Delillo, *Underworld* (New York: Scribner, 1998), 76.
3. Federal Civil Defense Administration, *Four Wheels to Survival* (Washington, D.C.: Government Printing Office, 1955), n.p.
4. John Le Carré, *The Spy who Came in from the Cold* (New York: Coward McCann, 1954), 3.
5. Lewis Mumford, *From the Ground Up* (New York: Harcourt, Brace and World, 1956), 164.
6. Stephen Whitfield, *The Culture of the Cold War* (Baltimore: Johns Hopkins University Press, 1996), 220.
7. Edgar Bottome, *Balance of Terror* (Boston: Beacon Press, 1986), 22.
8. Quoted in Richard Rodgers, *Technological Landscapes* (London: Royal College of Art, 1999), 49.
9. Mumford, 164.
10. John Ely Burchard, "Architecture in the Atomic Age," *Architectural Record* (December 1954): 120.
11. Paul Tibbets, *The Tibbets Story* (New York: Stein and Day, 1978), 58.
12. Wallace Stegner, *Mormon Country* (New York: Duell, Sloane & Pearle, 1944), 52.
13. Tom Englehardt, *The End of Victory Culture* (New York: Basic Books, 1995), 77.
14. "Utah Escapes Missiles," *High Country News,* 3 April 1995.
15. Capt. Napolean B. Byers, "EMP," *Air Force* (September 1985): 117.
16. F. T. Marinetti, *Let's Murder the Moonshine* (Los Angeles: Sun and Moon Press, 1991), 81.
17. William J. R. Curtis, *Modern Architecture Since* 1900 (New York: Phaidon, 1996), 400.

18. Quoted in Fred Kaplan, *The Wizards of Armageddon* (New York: Simon and Schuster, 1983), 225.

19. J. G. Ballard, *The Terminal Beach* (London: Gollancz, 1974), 183.

CHAPTER 1

1. J. B. Jackson, *Discovering the Vernacular Landscape* (New Haven: Yale University Press, 1984), 136.

2. Quoted in Beumont Newhall, *Airborne Camera: The World from the Air and Outer Space* (New York: Hastings House Publishers, 1969), 9.

3. Newhall, 13.

4. Philip Gilbert Hamerton, *Landscape* (Boston: Roberts Brothers, 1885), 12.

5. Hamerton, 12.

6. Robert Hughes, *The Shock of the New* (London: British Broadcast Corporation, 1980), 14.

7. Newhall, 53.

8. Quoted in Geoffrey Batchen, *Each Wild Idea: Writing Photography History* (Cambridge, Mass.: MIT Press, 2001), 11.

9. Grove Heiman, *Aerial Photography: The Story of Aerial Mapping and Reconnaissance* (New York: MacMillan, 1972), 38.

10. Lee Kennet, *A History of Strategic Bombing* (New York: Charles Scribner's Sons, 1982), 2.

11. Giulio Duohet, *The Command of the Air* (New York: Coward McCann, 1942), 3.

12. Kennet, 7.

13. Kennet, 32.

14. Kennet, 9.

15. Raymond Fredette, *The Sky on Fire: The First Battle of Britain* 1917–1918 *and the Birth of the Royal Air Force* (New York: Holt, Rinehart, and Winston, 1966), 4.

16. Fredette, 25.

17. Kennet, 33.

18. Newhall, 51.

19. Dache M. Reeves, *Aerial Photographs: Characteristics and Military Applications* (New York: Ronald Press Company, 1927), 118.

20. Royal Air Force, Branch Intelligence Section, *Characteristics of the Ground and Landmarks in the Enemy Lines Opposite the British Front from the Sea to San Quentin*, no. 36 (London: Royal Air Force F.S. Publications, 1918), 12.

21. Royal Air Force, Branch Intelligence Section, 7.

22. Sarah Ganz, *Modern Starts: People, Places, Things* (New York: Harry N. Abrams, 1999), 259.

23. Quoted in Michael Sherry, *The Rise of American Air Power* (New Haven: Yale University Press, 1987), 181.

24. Reeves, 242.

25. Reeves, 39.

26. Roy M. Stanley II, *To Fool a Glass Eye* (Washington, D.C.: Smithsonian Institution Press, 1998), 23.

27. Royal Air Force, Branch Intelligence Section, 17.

28. Kennett, 33.

29. Fredette, 24.

30. Fredette, 68.

31. Duohet, 288.

32. Quoted in Kennet, 18.

33. *The New Yorker* (December 11, 1943): 25.

34. Kennet, 130.

35. Sherry, 323.

36. David MacIsaac, *Strategic Bombing in World War Two: The Story of the United States Strategic Bombing Survey* (New York: Garland Publishing Company, 1976), 88.

37. David Irving, *The Destruction of Dresden* (London: W. Kimber, 1963), 163.

38. United States Strategic Bombing Survey, Physical Damaged Division, *Fire Raids on German Cities*, no. 61 (Washington, D.C.: U.S. Strategic Bombing Survey, 1945): 41.

39. Horatio Bond, ed., *Fire and the Air War: A Compilation of Expert Observations on Fires of the War Set by Incendiaries and the Atomic Bombs, Wartime Fire Fighting, and the Work of the Fire Protection Engineers Who Helped Plan and the Destruction of Enemy Cities and Industrial Plants* (Boston: National Fire Protection Association International, 1946), 21.

40. Sherry, 58.

41. Sherry, 275.

42. Fairchild Camera and Instrument Corporation, *Focusing on Victory: The Story of Aerial Photography at War* (Jamaica, New York: Fairchild, 1944), 2.

43. United States Strategic Bombing Survey, Morale Division, *The Effect of Bombing on Health and Medical Care in Germany* (Washington, D.C.: War Department, 1945), 22.

44. MacIssac, 57.

45. U.S. Strategic Bombing Survey, Physical Damaged Division, exhibit h–14.

46. U.S. Strategic Bombing Survey, Physical Damaged Division, 310.

47. Martin Pawley, *Architecture Versus Housing* (New York: Praeger Publishers, 1971), 46.

48. Eric Bird, "Town Planning Lessons of the Fire Blitz," quoted in Bond, ed., 12.

49. G. and E. G. McAllister, *Town and Country Planning* (London: Faber and Faber, 1941), 12.

50. Konrad F. Wittmann, ed., *Industrial Camouflage Manual* (New York: Reinhold Publishing Corporation, 1942), 7.
51. Le Corbusier, *The Aircraft* (1935, reprinted New York: Universe, 1988), 11.
52. Adolf Max Vogt, *Le Corbusier, the Noble Savage: Toward an Archaeology of Modernism* (Cambridge, Mass.: MIT Press, 1998), 110.
53. Le Corbusier, *Towards a New Architecture* (New York: Payson and Clarke Ltd., 1927), 127.
54. Le Corbusier, *Towards a New Architecture*, 127.
55. Jose Luis Sert, *Can Our Cities Survive?* (Cambridge, Mass.: Harvard University Press, 1942), 66.
56. Eric Mumford, *The CIAM Discourse on Urbanism* (Cambridge, Mass.: MIT Press, 2000), 90.
57. Mumford, 90.
58. Fairchild Camera and Instrument Corporation, 33.
59. Melville C. Branch, *City Planning and Aerial Information* (Cambridge, Mass.: Harvard University Press, 1971), 39.
60. J. K. S. St. Joseph, ed., *The Uses of Air Photography: Nature and Man in a New Environment* (London: John Baker Publishers, 1966), 30.
61. Branch, 31.
62. E. A. Gutkind, *Our World from the Air* (New York: Doubleday, 1952), 7.
63. Kevin Lynch, *The Image of the City* (Cambridge, Mass.: MIT Press, 1960), 13.
64. St. Joseph, ed., 163.
65. Newhall, 115.

CHAPTER 2

1. Eric Mumford, *The CIAM Discourse on Urbanism* (Cambridge, Mass.: MIT Press, 2000), 90.
2. Office of Scientific Research and Development, National Defense Research Committee, "Fire Warfare: Incendiaries and Flamethrowers," *Summary Technical Report of Division* 11, vol. 3 (Washington, D.C.: GPO, 1946), 70.
3. Office of Scientific Research and Development, National Defense Research Committee, 70.
4. Office of Scientific Research and Development, National Defense Research Committee, 75.
5. Standard Oil Company, *Design and Construction of Typical German and Japanese Test Structures at Dugway Proving Grounds, Utah* (Maryland: Technical Library, Edgewood Arsenal, n.d.), 6.
6. Standard Oil Company, 8.
7. Horatio Bond, ed., *Fire and the Air War: A Compilation of Expert Observations on Fires of the War Set by Incendiaries and the Atomic Bombs, Wartime Fire*

Fighting, and the Work of the Fire Protection Engineers Who Helped Plan and the Destruction of Enemy Cities and Industrial Plants (Boston: National Fire Protection Association International, 1946), 187.

8. Kathleen James, *Erich Mendelsohn and the Architecture of German Modernism* (Cambridge and New York: Cambridge University Press, 1997), 235.

9. James, 235.

10. Erich Mendelsohn to William Bruck, Stalick and Schiller, 7 December 1941, Erich Mendelsohn Archives, J. Paul Getty Center, Los Angeles, Calif.

11. William J. R. Curtis, *Modern Architecture Since 1900* (New York: Phaidon, 2000), 398.

12. Sherry, 255.

13. Bond, ed., 234.

14. *Time* (October 2, 1950): 12.

15. Department of Civil and Sanitary Engineering, Massachusetts Institute of Technology, *Proceedings of the Conference on Building in the Atomic Age* (Cambridge, Mass.: MIT, 1952), 108.

16. Lewis Mumford, *The City in History* (New York: Harcourt, Brace and World, 1961), 45.

17. Tracy B. Augur, "Security Factors in the Planning of Urban Regions," *Bulletin of the American Institute of Architects* (May–June 1952): 9.

18. Fred Kaplan, *The Wizards of Armageddon* (New York: Simon and Schuster, 1983), 243.

19. Hudson Institute, *Nonmilitary Defense Policies: A Context, Reappraisal, and Commentary*, vol. 1 (Harmon-on-Hudson: Hudson Institute, 1964), 5-2.

20. *Life* (August 8, 1950), 41.

21. Anthony Vidler, *Warped Space* (Cambridge, Mass.: MIT Press, 2000), 51.

22. Quoted in Nicholas Fyfe, *Images of the Street* (London and New York: Routledge, 1998), 48.

23. "The Atomic Bomb and Our Cities," *Bulletin of the Atomic Scientists* (August–September 1950): 36.

24. "The Atomic Bomb and Our Cities," 30.

25. "The Atomic Bomb and Our Cities," 244.

26. Augur, 10.

27. Augur, 262.

28. *Progressive Architecture* (September 1951): 77.

29. *U.S. News and World Report* (October 7, 1949): 18.

30. "The Atomic Bomb and Our Cities," 247.

31. Quoted in *The New Republic* (September 21, 1953): 24.

32. Department of Civil and Sanitary Engineering, MIT, 109.

33. Peter Hall, "The City of Theory," in *The City Reader*, ed. Richard T. LeGates and Frederic Stout (London and New York: Routledge, 1996), 386.

34. Quoted in Joan Ockman, ed., *Architecture Culture, 1943–1968: A Documentary Anthology* (New York: Columbia University Graduate School of Architecture, Planning, and Preservation and Rizzoli, 1993), 406.

35. Lewis Mumford, *The Urban Prospect* (New York: Harcourt, Brace & World, 1968), 77.

36. *Bulletin of the Atomic Scientists* (August–September 1950): 265.

37. "The Atomic Bomb and Our Cities," 244.

38. *The American City* (January 1951): 107.

39. Ockman, 196.

40. Vincent Scully, *American Architecture and Urbanism* (New York: Praeger Publishers, 1969), 245.

41. Federal Civil Defense Administration, *Four Wheels to Survival* (Washington, D.C.: GPO, 1955).

42. H. G. Welles, *The War in the Air* (London: George Dell and Sons, 1908), 14.

43. Quoted in Spencer Weart, *Nuclear Fear: A History of Images* (Cambridge, Mass.: Harvard University Press, 1988), 221.

44. Quoted in Weart, 221.

45. Quoted in Kermit Carlyle Parsons, "Shaping the Regional City: 1950–1990," *Address to the Third National Conference on American Planning History* (Washington, D.C.: Society for American City and Regional Planning History, 1989), 662.

46. Quoted in Parsons, 665.

47. Quoted in Parsons, 665.

48. *Effects of the Air Attack on the City of Hiroshima* (Washington, D.C.: United States Strategic Bombing Survey, Urban Areas Division, 1947), 3.

49. *Las Vegas Review Journal* (February 28, 1955).

50. Department of Civil and Sanitary Engineering, MIT, 4.

51. Department of Civil and Sanitary Engineering, MIT, 8.

52. Department of Civil and Sanitary Engineering, MIT, 12.

53. News release, Nevada Test Organization, 10 July 1957.

54. U.S. Bureau of Yards and Docks, *Studies in Atomic Defense Engineering, NAV-DOCKS P-290.2* (Washington, D.C.: Department of the Navy, Bureau of Yards and Docks, 1962).

55. News release, Nevada Test Organization, May 1957.

56. *Architectural Forum* (July 1954): 79.

57. "Atomic Ruins Reveal Survival Secrets," *Popular Science* (July 1955): 218.

58. Carol Ahlgren and Frank Edgerton Martin, "From Dante to Doomsday: How a City without People Survived a Nuclear Blast," *Design Book Review* 17 (Winter 1989): 27.

59. News release, Nevada Test Organization, May 1957.

60. News release, Nevada Test Organization, May 1957.

61. News release, Nevada Test Organization, May 1957.

62. *Las Vegas Review Journal,* 18 March 1953.

63. *The New Mexican,* 19 March 1953.

64. *Washington Post,* 18 March 1953.

65. *The Albuquerque Journal,* 15 March 1953.

66. *New Mexican,* 15 March 1953.

67. *Operation Doorstep* (Washington, D.C.: Federal Civil Defense Administration, 1954).

68. *New York Times,* 16 March 1953.

69. William Gray Johnson, Nancy S. Goldenberg, and Susan R. Edwards, "The Japanese Village at the Nevada Test Site: A Relic of Nuclear War," *Cultural Resource Management* 14 (1997): 21.

70. Alan Hess, *Viva Las Vegas: After-Hours Architecture* (San Francisco: Chronicle Books, 1993), 53.

71. Johnson, et al., 70.

CHAPTER 3

1. *Science* (November 17, 1967): 57.

2. *New Buildings With Fallout Protection* (Washington, D.C.: Department of Defense, Office of Civil Defense, January 1965), 2.

3. *The New Yorker* (March 5, 1963): 22.

4. "Problems of Passive Defense," *Journal of the American Institute of Architects* (May 1949): 207–10.

5. Quoted in Department of Civil and Sanitary Engineering, MIT, *Proceedings of the Conference on Building in the Atomic Age* (Cambridge, Mass.: MIT, 1952), 115.

6. *Architectural Forum* (April 1958): 57.

7. *Shelter Design in New Buildings* (Washington, D.C.: Office of Civil Defense, 1965), 7.

8. *Architectural Forum* (April 1958): 58.

9. *Architectural Record* (March 1964): 41.

10. Quoted in Allan M. Winkler, *Life Under a Cloud: American Anxiety About the Atom* (New York: Oxford University Press, 1993), 121.

11. *Reducing the Vulnerability of Houses* (Washington, D.C.: Office of Civil Defense, 1963), 16.

12. Fred N. Severud and Anthony F. Merrill, *The Bomb, Survival, and You: Protection for People, Buildings, Equipment* (New York: Reinhold Publishing Corporation, 1954), 13.

13. Guy Oakes, *The Imaginary War* (New York: Oxford University Press, 1994), 146.

14. Severud and Merrill, 232.
15. Office of Civil Defense, *Reducing the Vulnerability of Houses*, 13.
16. Defense Civil Preparedness Agency, Department of Defense, and the Department of Architectural Engineering, Pennsylvania State University "Cost Benefits in Shelters" (Washington, D.C.: GPO, 1972), 9.
17. *Incorporation of Shelter into Apartments and Office Buildings* (Washington, D.C.: Office of Civil Defense, 1962), 1.
18. Thomas Hine, *Populuxe* (New York: Alfred A. Knopf, 1986), 53.
19. "Can a House Be Blast Resistant?" *Architectural Record* (September 1955): 23.
20. "A-bomb Resistant Buildings," *Architectural Forum* (July 1954): 56.
21. *Progressive Architecture* (September 1951): 24.
22. *Civil Defense Shelters: A State-of-the-Art Assessment* (Washington, D.C.: Federal Emergency Management Association, 1986), 14.
23. "Architecture Versus Violence," *Domus* (April 1981): 37.
24. Gifford H. Albright, ed., *Planning Atomic Shelters: A Guidebook for Architects and Engineers* (University Park, Pa.: University of Pennsylvania Press, 1961), 3.
25. *Architectural Record* (December 1963): 29.
26. *Architectural Record* (December 1963): 29.
27. *Architectural Record* (December 1963): 29.
28. 1969 *Architectural Awards Buildings with Fallout Shelters* (Washington, D.C.: American Institute of Architects and the Office of Civil Defense, 1970), 5.
29. Vincent Scully, *American Architecture and Urbanism* (New York: Praeger Publishers, 1969), 200.
30. *Architectural Design* (July 1967): 374.
31. Keith Mallory and Arvid Ottar, *The Architecture of War* (New York: Pantheon, 1973), 280.
32. Mallory and Ottar, 48.
33. "The Family Room of Tomorrow," *Interior Design* (1960).
34. *Newsweek* (October 23, 1961): 51.
35. Quoted in Alison M. Scott and Christopher D. Geist, eds., *The Writing on the Cloud:* American Culture Confronts the Atomic Bomb (Lanham, Md.: University Press of America, 1997), 48.
36. *Newsweek* (July 22, 1963): 45.
37. Quoted in Laura McEnaney, *Civil Defense Begins at Home* (Princeton, N.J.: Princeton University Press, 2000), 71.
38. McEnaney, 110.
39. McEnaney, 71.
40. *Good Housekeeping* (November 1958): 61.
41. *Boston Globe*, 12 December 1999.
42. *Interiors* (December 1950): 41.
43. *Time* (September 1, 1961): 32.

44. Advertisement. Collection of the Author.

45. *Look* (December 1961): 71.

46. Hine, 135.

47. "The Geopolitics of Hibernation," *Internationale Situationiste* 7 (April 1962): 7.

48. *Newsweek* (April 26, 1982): 63.

49. Federal Emergency Management Association, 87.

50. Federal Emergency Management Association, 4.

51. Terry Isaacs, "Silos and Shelters in the Pecos Valley: The Atlas ICBM in Chaves County, New Mexico, 1960–1965," *New Mexico Historical Review* (October 1993): 355.

52. "Nuclear-Age School," *The Saturday Evening Post* (January 26, 1963): 64.

53. "A School That's Ready for the Atomic Age," *San Francisco Chronicle*, 20 March 1989.

54. *Time* (February 5, 1965): 62.

55. "Design for Survival?" *Time* (September 6, 1954): 17.

56. Elliot Willensky and Norval White, eds., *AIA Guide to New York City* (New York: Harcourt, Brace, Jovanovich, 1988), 70.

57. Joan Ockman, ed., *Architecture Culture, 1943–1968* (New York: Columbia University Graduate School of Architecture, Planning, and Preservation and Rizzoli, 1993), 18.

58. "Building Against the Atom," *Newsweek* (November 20, 1950): 96.

59. Margot Henriksen, *Dr. Strangelove's America* (Berkeley: University of California Press, 1997), 85.

60. John Burchard and Albert Bush-Brown, *The Architecture of America: A Social and Cultural History* (Boston: Little, Brown and Company, 1961), 403.

61. Mitchell Schwartzer, "Modern Architectural Ideology in Cold War America," in *The Education of the Architect: Historiography, Urbanism and the Growth of Architectural Knowledge*, ed. Martha Pollak (Cambridge, Mass.: MIT Press, 1997), 96.

62. Burchard and Bush-Brown, 403.

63. Quoted in Schwartzer, 96.

64. Lewis Mumford, *From the Ground Up* (New York: Harcourt Brace Jovanovich, 1956), 59.

65. Mumford, 60.

66. Mumford, 60.

67. Information taken from the NASA government website.

68. Quoted in Richard Gid Powers, "The Cold War in the Rockies: American Ideology and the Air Force Academy Design" *Art Journal* (Summer 1974): 304.

69. Powers: 304.

70. Powers: 304.

71. Quoted in Robert Bruegmann, ed., *Modernism at Midcentury: The Architecture*

of the United States Air Force Academy (Chicago: University of Chicago Press, 1994), 89.

72. Bruegmann, 307.

73. Bruegmann, 89.

74. John Ely Burchard, "Architecture in the Atomic Age," *Architectural Record* (December 1954): 120.

75. Mark Dery, quoted in *Prefiguring Cyberculture: Informatics from Plato to Haraway*, ed. Darren Tofts, Annemarie Jonson, and Alessio Cavallaro (Sydney: Power Publications, 2001).

76. *How Modern Was My Valley* (Los Angeles: Los Angeles Conservancy, 2001).

77. *Los Angeles Examiner,* 26 June 1961.

78. Vincent Scully, *Modern Architecture: The Architecture of Democracy* (New York: George Braziller, 1961), 1.

79. Peter Cook, et al., eds., *Archigram* (New York: Praeger Publishers, 1973), 48.

80. Cook, et al., eds., 48.

81. George Collins, *Visionary Drawings of Planning and Architecture* (Cambridge, Mass.: MIT Press, 1979), 38.

82. Lesley Jackson, *The Sixties: Decade of Design Revolution* (London: Phaidon, 1998) 99.

83. Jackson, 99.

84. *New York Times Magazine* (July 26, 1970): 27.

85. *Newsweek* (August 16, 1976): 79.

86. Collins, 45.

87. Collins, 51.

88. Peter Reyner Banham, *Scenes in America Deserta* (Salt Lake City: Gibbs M. Smith, 1982), 211.

89. *The Schoharie Valley Townsite: A Protected Community for the Nuclear Age* (Ithaca, N.Y.: Cornell University, College of Architecture, 1961), 1.

90. *The Schoharie Valley Townsite*, iii.

91. *The Schoharie Valley Townsite*, iii.

92. *The Schoharie Valley Townsite,* iii.

93. Telephone interview with author, 12 March 2001.

94. James Bamford, *The Puzzle Palace: A Report on America's Most Secret Agency* (New York: Houghton Mifflin, 1982), 87.

95. Bamford, 87.

96. Quoted in K. Michael Hays, "Introduction," in Ezra Stoller, *Whitney Museum of Art* (New York: Princeton Architectural Press, 2001), 4.

97. John M. Findlay, "The Off-Center Seattle Center: Dowtown Seattle and the 1962 World's Fair," *Pacific Northwest Quarterly* 80 (January 1989): 131.

98. *New York Times,* 22 January 2001.

99. Rosemarie Haag Bletter, et al., *Remembering the Future: The New York World's*

Fair from 1939 *to* 1964 (New York: Rizzoli, 1989), 17.

100. Haag Bletter, et al., 126.

101. Quoted in Haag Bletter, et al., 126.

102. *Houston Chronicle,* 12 May 1996.

103. *Houston Chronicle,* 12 May 1996.

CHAPTER 4

1. *The New Yorker* (December 3, 1947): 41.

2. Quoted in Department of Civil and Sanitary Engineering, MIT, *Proceedings of the Conference on Building in the Atomic Age* (Cambridge, Mass.: MIT, 1952), 86.

3. Guy B. Panero, "Mines and Other Concepts," in *Protective Construction in a Nuclear Age*, vol. 1, *Proceedings of the Second Protective Construction Symposium, 24–26 March,* 1959 (New York: MacMillan Company, 1961), 85.

4. William M. Brown and Herman Kahn, *Nonmilitary Defense Policies: A Context, Reappraisal, and Commentary*, vol. 1 (Harmon-on-Hudson, N.Y.: Hudson Institute, 1964), 2.

5. *Las Vegas Sun,* 11 August 1957.

6. "Operation Granite: Sweden Goes Underground," *The New York Times Magazine,* (May 22, 1964): 24.

7. Lewis Mumford, *The City in History: Its Origins, its Transformations, and its Prospects* (New York: Harcourt, Brace and World, 1961), 479.

8. Quoted in Rosalind Williams, *Notes On the Underground: An Essay on Technology, Society, and the Imagination* (Cambridge, Mass.: MIT Press, 1990), 17.

9. Williams, 191.

10. Keith Mallory and Arvid Ottar, *The Architecture of War* (New York: Pantheon, 1973), 243.

11. Sir Arthur Harris, *Bomber Offensive* (London: Greenhill Books, 1990), 251.

12. Vivian R. Row, *The Great Wall of France: The Triumph of the Maginot Line* (London: Putnam, 1959), 77.

13. Mallory and Ottar, 103.

14. Row, 295.

15. Herman Kahn, "Why Go Deep Underground?" in *Protective Construction in a Nuclear Age,* 5.

16. Quoted in Brown and Kahn, 4.

17. Paul Boyer, *By the Bomb's Early Light* (New York: Pantheon, 1985), 110.

18. Boyer, 10.

19. "Fallout Shelters," *Architectural Forum* (April 1958): 133.

20. "Subterranean Atomic Suburbia," *Interiors* (February 1953): 70.

21. Mumford, 481.

22. *Newsweek* (November 20, 1961): 48.

23. *Newsweek*: 48.

24. Robert S. Conte, *The History of the Greenbrier: America's Resort* (Charleston: The Greenbrier, 1998), 201.

25. Richard Sauder, *Underground Bases and Tunnels* (Kempton, Ill.: Adventures Unlimited Press, 1906), 70.

26. *Life* (September 15, 1961): 95.

27. Richard Ned Lebow and Janice Gross Stein, *We All Lost the Cold War* (Princeton, N.J.: Princeton University Press, 1994), 23.

28. *Miami News*, 22 October 1962.

29. C. V. Chester, "Incorporating Civil Defense Shelter Space in New Underground Construction," excerpted in *The Potential of Earth-Sheltered and Underground Space*, ed. T. Lance Holthusen (New York: Pergamon Press, 1982), 39.

30. *Time* (October 20, 1961): 24.

31. Edward Zuckerman, *The Day After World War* III (New York: Viking, 1984), 223.

32. Fletcher Knebel, *Seven Days in May* (New York: Harper and Row, 1962), 31.

33. *The Houston Chronicle*, 20 April 1992.

34. *Newsweek* (April 26, 1982): 33.

35. *The Village Voice*, 15 February 1973.

36. *Los Angeles Times*, 19 April 1992.

37. *The Nation* (December 6, 1965): 59.

38. *The Wall Street Journal* (August 5, 1987).

39. *Business Week* (December 27, 1969): 72.

40. Telephone interview with author, 19 May 2001.

41. Information taken from Boeing's corporate website, www.boeing.com.

42. William Arkin, "The Praetorian Guards," *Bulletin of the Atomic Scientists* (March–April 2001): 80.

43. *Legacy of Peace: Mountain with a Mission. NORAD's Cheyenne Mountain Combat Operations Center* (Albuquerque: New Mexico Engineering Research Institute, 1996), iii.

44. NORAD press release from 1966 (no date available).

45. *U.S. News and World Report* (January 24, 1966): 54.

46. Paul Bracken, *The Command and Control of Nuclear Forces* (New Haven: Yale University Press, 1983), 187.

47. Jon Elliston, "Big Hole, Deep Secret," *The Independent Weekly* (December 13, 2000).

CHAPTER 5

1. Quoted in *Minuteman Missile Sites: Management Alternatives, Environmental Assessment* (Denver, Col.: National Park Service, 1995), 29.

2. Ernest Schwiebert, *A History of the U.S. Air Force Ballistic Missiles* (New York: Praeger Publishing, 1965), 189.

3. *Time* (January 25, 1960): 126.

4. *Fortune* (August 1963): 125.

5. *Time* (January 25, 1960): 48–49.

6. *Minuteman Missile Sites*, 34.

7. "Buildings for the Space Age," *Architectural Forum* (September 1960): 117.

8. "Buildings for the Space Age": 117.

9. "Buildings for the Space Age": 118.

10. John C. Lonnquest and David F. Winkler, *To Defend and Deter: The Legacy of the United States Cold War Missile Program* (Champaign, Ill.: U.S. Army Construction Engineering Research Laboratories, 1996), 79.

11. Loonquest and Winkler, 84.

12. *The Topeka Capital-Journal*, 22 November 2000.

13. See Phil Patton, *Dreamland* (New York: Villard, 1998).

14. Joseph Gies, *Wonders of the Modern World* (New York: Thomas Y. Crowell Company, 1966), 199.

15. Quentin Hughes, *The Art of Defence from the Earliest Times to the Atlantic Wall* (London: Beaufort, 1991), 2.

16. Tom Englehardt, *The End of Victory Culture* (New York: Basic Books, 1995).

17. Nels Parson, *Missiles and the Revolution in Warfare* (Cambridge, Mass.: Harvard University Press, 1962), 38.

18. *New York Times*, 17 May 1956.

19. *Business Week* (May 8, 1954): 108.

20. *Time* (April 6, 1953): 46.

21. *Chicago Sun-Times*, 20 November 1955.

22. Max Shulman, *Rally Round the Flag, Boys!* (New York: Doubleday, 1956), 66.

23. *New York Times*, 1 September 1953.

24. Egon Eis, *The Forts of Folly: The History of an Illusion* (London: Oswald Wolff, 1959), 88.

25. *Business Week* (September 23, 1967): 81.

26. J. B. Jackson, "Landscape as Seen by the Military," in *Discovering the Vernacular Landscape* (New Haven: Yale University Press, 1984), 133.

27. *Last Line of Defense: Nike Missile Sites in Illinois* (Denver, Col.: National Park Service, 1996), 11.

28. *Chicago Tribune*, 8 May 1990.

CHAPTER 6

1. U.S. Department of Energy, Carlsbad Area Office, *Pioneering Nuclear Waste Disposal* (Washington, D.C.: Department of Energy, 2000), 5.

2. *Los Angeles Times,* 8 June 1998.

3. Phil Patton, *Open Road: A Celebration of the American Highway* (New York: Simon and Schuster, 1986), 85–86.

4. Chester E. Chellman, "Street Design: Design Intent, History, and Emerging Concepts," in *Land Development* (National Association of Homebuilders, Spring/Summer 1995), 14.

5. Henry Moon, *The Interstate Highway System* (Washington, D.C.: Association of American Geographers, 1994), 12.

6. Committee on Public Works, House of Representatives, *Report on Extension of National System of Interstate and Defense Highways Within Alaska and Hawaii* (Washington, D.C.: GPO, 1960), 21.

7. Keith Mallory and Orvan Ottar, *The Architecture of War* (New York: Pantheon, 1973), 111.

8. John Stilgoe, *Outside Lies Magic: Regaining History and Awareness in Everyday Places* (New York: Walker and Co., 1998), 94.

9. Federal Highway Administration, *Fiscal Year* 2001 *Performance Plan.* See www.fhwa.dot.gov.

10. Information taken from the Military Traffic Management Command website, www.tea.army.mil.

11. Terry Evans, *Disarming the Prairie* (Baltimore: Johns Hopkins University Press, 1998), 1.

12. John G. Cloud and Keith C. Clarke, "Through a Shutter Darkly: The Tangled Relationships Between Civilian, Military, and Intelligence Remote Sensing in the Early U.S. Space Program," in *Secrecy and Knowledge Production*, ed. Judith Reppy, *Cornell University Peace Studies Program Occasional Papers* 23 (Ithaca: Peace Studies Program, 1999), 7.

13. Cloud and Clarke, 12.

14. John Cloud and Keith C. Clarke, "The Fubini Hypothesis: The Other History of Geographic Information Science," paper delivered at the International Conference on Geographic Information and Society, University of Minnesota, Minneapolis, 1999.

15. "Private Spy," *Wired* (August 1997): 33.

16. William Burrows, *Deep Black* (New York: Berkeley Books, 1986), 21.

17. *New York Times* (11 April 2001).

18. Information taken from the Data Centers Now website, www.datacentersnow.com.

19. *Washington Post*, 9 November 1999.

20. *Washington Post*, 9 November 1999.

21. Information taken from the Weidlinger Associates website, www.weidlinger.com.

22. Richard Slotkin, *Gunfighter Nation: The Myth of the Frontier in Twentieth Century America* (New York: Athaneum, 1992), 654.

23. Christopher Hitchens, *The London Review of Books* (5 April 2001): 9.

24. *New York Times* (29 March 2001).

25. Paul Virilio, *Bunker Archaeology* (New York: Princeton Architctural Press, 1994), 205.

26. *The Deseret News*, 18 March 1996.

27. "Berlin's New U.S. Embassy: Safeguarding a Symbol," *Architectural Record* (March 1996): 36.

28. *New York Times* (9 March 2001).

29. John Stilgoe, *Borderland: Origins of the American Suburb,* 1820–1939 (New Haven: Yale University Press, 1988), 303.

30. *New York Times Magazine* (26 November 1961): 124.

ACKNOWLEDGMENTS

Many people shared their time, expertise, and defunct missile silos with me, or otherwise gave me literal and/or intellectual shelter as I traveled the roads of atomic America writing this book. Eugenia Bell helped to initiate and conceptualize the book at Princeton Architectural Press before heading west of the Mississippi; Nancy Eklund Later admirably and graciously picked up the project in midstream and winningly helped to bring legibility to its sprawling geography. Photographer Walter Cotten helped me to see the military landscape, both in person and in his eerily evocative images, in which I found a kindred, visual "voice." Christopher Wilcha, a friend and frequent fellow traveler, accompanied me on any number of expeditions, sharing his Honda and his sardonic wit. Matthew Coolidge at the Center for Land Use Interpretation provided inspiration, ideas, and images. The support of a number of editors allowed me to make initial explorations of the Cold War landscape: Julie Lasky at the late, lamented *Interiors*; Joseph Holtzman at *nest*; Tim Griffin (during his all-too-brief stint) and then Mary Dery at *Artbyte*; Karen Steen at *Metropolis*; Andrew Hultkrens at *Bookforum*; Connie Rosenblum at The *New York Times*; and Chris Lehman at The *Washington Post*. Joan Ockman and Phil Patton gave me invaluable insight into the period and its peculiar heirlooms. The funds of no institutions, it should be noted, were depleted in the writing of this book.

Along the route of atomic America, many people opened their doors (blast and otherwise): Capt. Jeffrey Dean and Ben Borth gave me a Baedeker-worthy tour of the North American Aerospace Defense Command; Tim Pavek, of Ellsworth Air Force Base, South Dakota, gave me a daylong tour of the region's missile installations; Bill Johnson of the Desert Research Institute and the Department of Energy's LaTomya Glass endured the over-100 degree heat to show me the Nevada Test Site; Don Speulda of the u.s. Army Corps of Engineers helped me to play my part in the dismantling of North Dakota's nuclear arsenal; Rich Garcia of the u.s. Air Force Special Weapons Laboratory was my able escort at Kirtland Air Force Base; John Grant and Bill Rose of the Palm Beach Maritime Museum opened up John F. Kennedy's fallout shelter for me; Fritz Bugas took me through the doomsday rooms of the Greenbrier Hotel's congressional fallout shelter; John Pike of Globalsecurity.org, who knows where a lot of Cold War bodies are buried, helped me understand the Continuity of Government Program; Bruce

Francisco laid out the welcome mat in front of his newly domesticated Atlas F missile silo in Plattsburgh, New York; Nike missile historian Don Bender and Capt. Eugene Ruppert of the New York City Police Department accompanied me to the potter's field (and former missile base) of Hart Island on a preternaturally frigid December day; Joseph Juhasz of the University of Colorado gave me Hungarian food and directions to the Rocky Flats Arsenal; Mark Allen helped me unearth the Pioneer Deep Space Probe at the Fort Irwin National Training Center; Jim Eckles led the safari into the wilds of the White Sands Missile Range; Milton "Bud" Halsey showed me the workings of the only fully restored Nike missile base in the country, across the Golden Gate Bridge from San Francisco; John Ingram took me into the subterranean depths of our nation's nuclear-waste storage program; while Perry Chapman plumbed the depths of his own memory to recall the days in which planning for nuclear attack was not science fiction. My thanks to them all.

Lastly and most importantly, I am indebted to Jancee L. Dunn, the shining constellation guiding me at night and the brilliant sun greeting my waking day, for everything imaginable.

FIGURE CREDITS

Community Shelters: Planning Community Protection with Behlen (Columbus, Neb.: Behlen Manufacturing Co., n.d.): 101 bottom, 104 top, 109.

Courtesy of Columbia Pictures: 140.

Courtesy of the Center for Land Use Interpretation: 68.

Courtesy of the Department of Energy: 88, 90–91.

Courtesy of Walter Cotten and the United States Air Force: 23 top and bottom.

Courtesy of White Sands Missile Range: 40 bottom, 46.

Facts about Fallout Protection (Washington, D.C.: Office of Civil and Defense Mobilization, 1958): 99.

Peter Barreras: 96.

Protection in the Nuclear Age (Washington, D.C.: Defense Civil Preparedness Agency, Department of Defense, 1977): 157.

Shelter Designs for Protection against Radioactive Fallout (New York: Institute of Public Administration, n.d.): 101 top left and right, 104 middle left and right, bottom.

Survival in a Nuclear Attack: Plan for Protection from Radioactive Fallout (New York: State of New York, c. 1960): 3, 69, 97, 129.

Tom Vanderbilt: 9, 13 top, 13 bottom, 15, 18, 26, 28, 32, 83 top, 83 bottom, 92, 94, 134, 136, 142, 143, 158, 162, 163, 170–71, 173 top, 173 bottom, 192–93, 174 top, 192, 204.

Walter Cotton: 6, 21, 31, 35, 37 bottom, 37 top, 38, 39, 40 top, 41, 44–45, 47, 49, 121, 165, 184, 187, 189, 190.

Your Family Survival Plan (Washington, D.C.: U.S. Department of Agriculture and the Office of Civil Defense, Department of Defense, 1963): 98.

United States Air Force: 128, 151, 152 top, 152 bottom, 156.

United States Army: 174 bottom.

United States Strategic Bombing Survey: 60, 63, 66, 71.

This book was designed by Josh Hooten
and printed and bound by Thomson-Shore, Inc.,
Dexter, Michigan

The text face is Adobe Garamond
supplemented with Trade Gothic.

The paper is Williamsburg, made by
International Paper Company,
and is acid-free.

EATING UTENSILS AND FOOD

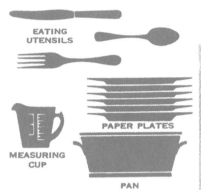

EATING UTENSILS

MEASURING CUP

PAPER PLATES

PAN

CUPS

NAPKINS

BOTTLE OPENER

CAN OPENER

POCKET KNIFE

WATER

FOOD AND CONTAINERS

CLOTHING AND BEDDING

SEWING KIT

SLEEPING BAGS

BLANKETS

EXTRA CLOTHING

SANITATION AND MEDICAL SUPPLIES

PAPER TOWELS

DISINFECTANT

GARBAGE CAN

SANITARY NAPKINS

FIRST AID KIT

HUMAN WASTE

SOAP

EMERGENCY TOILET

TOILET PAPER

NEWSPAPERS

PLASTIC AND PAPER BAGS